CHARLES WESLEY AND THE STRUGGLE FOR
METHODIST IDENTITY

Charles Wesley and the Struggle for Methodist Identity

GARETH LLOYD

OXFORD
UNIVERSITY PRESS

Great Clarendon Street, Oxford OX2 6DP

Oxford University Press is a department of the University of Oxford.
It furthers the University's objective of excellence in research, scholarship,
and education by publishing worldwide in

Oxford New York

Auckland Cape Town Dar es Salaam Hong Kong Karachi
Kuala Lumpur Madrid Melbourne Mexico City Nairobi
New Delhi Shanghai Taipei Toronto

With offices in

Argentina Austria Brazil Chile Czech Republic France Greece
Guatemala Hungary Italy Japan Poland Portugal Singapore
South Korea Switzerland Thailand Turkey Ukraine Vietnam

Oxford is a registered trade mark of Oxford University Press
in the UK and in certain other countries

Published in the United States
by Oxford University Press Inc., New York

© Gareth Lloyd 2007

The moral rights of the author have been asserted
Database right Oxford University Press (maker)

First published 2007

All rights reserved. No part of this publication may be reproduced,
stored in a retrieval system, or transmitted, in any form or by any means,
without the prior permission in writing of Oxford University Press,
or as expressly permitted by law, or under terms agreed with the appropriate
reprographics rights organization. Enquiries concerning reproduction
outside the scope of the above should be sent to the Rights Department,
Oxford University Press, at the address above

You must not circulate this book in any other binding or cover
and you must impose the same condition on any acquirer

British Library Cataloguing in Publication Data
Data available

Library of Congress Cataloging in Publication Data
Data available

Typeset by SPI Publisher Services, Pondicherry, India
Printed in Great Britain
on acid-free paper by
Biddles Ltd., King's Lynn, Norfolk

ISBN 978–0–19–929574–6

*To my parents David and Jean Lloyd
and grandparents Peter and Gladwys Boyers.
With love and gratitude*

Preface

Charles Wesley was one of the most important leaders of the eighteenth-century Evangelical Revival, an event that saw the birth of Methodism and related movements that continue to occupy a prominent place in the twenty-first-century Church. Regarded by his contemporaries as an outstanding preacher, insightful pastor, and organizer of rare ability, Charles played an invaluable part in promoting and consolidating Methodism during its difficult formative years. There was also, of course, Charles Wesley's literary genius; he is regarded as one of the greatest hymn-writers that the Christian Church has produced and at a time when few people read the sermons of John Wesley or George Whitefield, even non-churchgoers are familiar with such timeless and inspiring works as 'Love Divine' and 'Hark the Herald Angels Sing'. When George W. Bush used a line from a Charles Wesley hymn as the title of his presidential campaign biography, he had reason to expect that most people would be at least familiar with the name of its author.[1]

Charles Wesley is clearly a significant figure whose ministry has a resonance that is arguably greater than any of his Evangelical contemporaries. One would expect his story to have been well told by popular biographer and historian alike, but this is not the case; with the exception of his poetry, Charles Wesley's life and work have in fact been neglected.[2] This surprising treatment of one of the co-founders of the Methodist movement was rooted in the insecurity felt by some important figures within the nineteenth-century Wesleyan Church concerning aspects of the early history of their denomination and Charles Wesley's role in particular; their ambivalence towards Charles continues to cast a shadow over his reputation.

The major influence on the evolution of Charles Wesley biographical scholarship has been the Wesleyan minister Thomas Jackson, the

---

[1] George W. Bush, *A Charge to Keep* (New York: William Morrow, 1999).
[2] 'Unlike John Wesley, he has had few biographers, and their work is mostly out of date.' Frederick Gill, *Charles Wesley the First Methodist* (London: Lutterworth, 1964), 11.

author of a two-volume life published in 1841³ and the editor, eight years later, of Charles's journal and appended selection of letters.⁴ The conclusions that Jackson reached had an impact that still influences the way that Charles Wesley is viewed. This is regrettable as his portrayal of the co-founder of the Methodist movement was highly distorted.

Jackson was concerned with a number of themes that were ancillary to a balanced narrative of his subject's life and presentation of relevant texts. He made this clear in the introduction to the biography where he declared his intention of correcting criticism of John Wesley and offering a Methodist opinion on the development of the relationship with the Church of England.⁵ In pursuit of these objectives, Jackson was careful not to publish passages from the manuscript letters⁶ or journal⁷ that criticized John Wesley or put Methodism and its preachers in a poor light. One example of many occurs in the published journal where this comment by Charles Wesley concerning one of the preachers is omitted: 'I wish he were the only worthless, senseless, graceless man, to whom my brother had given the same encouragement [to preach]';⁸ while in Jackson's biography of Charles, the transcription of the manuscript journal entry for 26 October 1756 changes one preacher's description of the Church of England as 'Old Peg' to the more innocuous 'church'.⁹ There are other glaring omissions in Jackson's work; for example, Charles frequently used shorthand to record his most intimate and controversial views, yet his biographer misses these entirely.

---

³ Thomas Jackson, *The Life of the Rev. Charles Wesley, sometime Student of Christ-Church Oxford: comprising a review of his poetry; sketches of the rise and progress of Methodism; with notices of contemporary events and characters*, 2 vols. (London: Wesleyan Methodist Conference Office, 1841).
⁴ Charles Wesley, *The Journal of the Rev. Charles Wesley, M.A., sometime Student of Christ-Church, Oxford. To which are appended selections from his correspondence and poetry, with an introduction and occasional notes*, ed. Thomas Jackson, 2 vols. (London: Wesleyan Methodist Book Room, 1849).
⁵ Jackson, *Charles Wesley*, i. p. vi.
⁶ There are more than 800 manuscript letters by Charles Wesley in archive institutions and libraries, of which approximately two-thirds form a discrete collection in the MCA.
⁷ Principally the bound manuscript journal catalogued as DDCW 10/2, MCA (henceforth CWJ).
⁸ CWJ, 12 June 1751.   ⁹ Jackson, *Charles Wesley*, ii. 124.

Taken in isolation, such examples of Victorian sensitivity would be relatively harmless were it not for the fact they have never been corrected. After more than two hundred years, scholarship remains heavily reliant on Jackson's incomplete transcripts of the manuscript material.[10] As late as 1989, a major published collection of edited transcripts and extracts from Charles Wesley's works included thirty-three letters of which only seven were based on original manuscripts.[11] The rest were taken from Jackson's biography of Charles or his edition of the journal.[12] It should come as no surprise therefore that modern scholarship is still influenced by conclusions concerning Charles Wesley's contribution to Methodism that are more than one hundred and fifty years old.

The principal effect of Jackson's work was to fix the image of Charles Wesley in the Methodist mind as a man who should be remembered chiefly for his hymns. This view of Charles was certainly in broad agreement with that of Methodist historians writing in the generation after Jackson. Like their predecessor, they were disturbed by Charles Wesley's bitter struggle to ensure that Methodism remain a revival movement within the Church of England. Abel Stevens was representative of the views of many when he wrote the following in 1878: 'Charles Wesley whose mind, less noble than his heart, was perpetually fettered by his High-Church sentiments...His influence over his brother on any disputed question was feeble, and deservedly so...he seemed incapable of progress, only because, through his strong prejudices, he was incapable of logic.'[13]

In the twentieth century there were a few attempts to revise such dismissive opinions, but these have been hampered by a continuing

---

[10] This situation will hopefully be rectified in the near future, as a full-text edition of Charles Wesley's journal, edited by Kenneth Newport and S. T. Kimbrough, is due to be published in 2007 by Abingdon Press. A comprehensive edition of Wesley's correspondence is also being prepared by Kenneth Newport and Gareth Lloyd for publication by Oxford University Press. It is anticipated that the first of two volumes will be published in 2008.

[11] Charles Wesley, *Charles Wesley: A Reader*, ed. John Tyson (Oxford: Oxford University Press, 1989).

[12] Two letters are based on transcripts found in Jackson's biography of Charles and the rest, twenty-four in number, are from Jackson's edition of the journal.

[13] Abel Stevens, *History of the Religious Movement of the Eighteenth Century called Methodism*, new edn., 3 vols. (London: Wesleyan Methodist Book Room, 1878), i. 311–12.

dependence on the work of earlier scholars. Mabel Brailsford for example,[14] who in 1954 went further than any other historian in attempting to disentangle the strange relationship between the Wesley brothers, described Jackson's depiction of early Methodism as 'clear and faithful, and I have followed it without question'.[15] In deferring to Jackson's primacy, Brailsford was following in the footsteps of John Telford, the author in 1900 of what has been described as the standard life of Charles Wesley. He referred to 'Thomas Jackson's painstaking and judicious biography, which has been called the best history of Methodism'.[16]

In 1948 Frank Baker published a volume containing extracts from Charles's correspondence, much of which was previously unpublished.[17] Baker was the first scholar to concentrate exclusively on this material as a preliminary to a full edition of the letters, a project that was never completed. Baker's use of original sources opened up a range of material, although the book is limited in length and his commentary did not contain much in the way of new insight. Other recent biographies, such as those by Arnold Dallimore[18] and Frederick Gill,[19] offer a sound introduction to the basic facts of Charles Wesley's life, but do not substantially revise the traditional view of the man and his ministry.

There has been an occasional acknowledgement of the problem that Charles Wesley has posed for Methodist scholarship and this insightful comment by Frederick Gill in 1964 stands as a neat summary of the first two centuries of Charles Wesley studies: 'Charles' attempts to preserve its [Methodism's] original aim had failed. As a result, his memory has suffered; with some there remains a lingering

---

[14] Mabel Brailsford, *A Tale of Two Brothers: John & Charles Wesley* (London: Rupert Hart-Davis, 1954).
[15] Ibid. 12.
[16] John Telford, *The Life of the Rev. Charles Wesley, M.A., sometime student of Christ Church, Oxford*, revised and enlarged edn. (London: Wesleyan Methodist Book Room, 1900), p. xiv.
[17] Frank Baker, *Charles Wesley as Revealed by his Letters* (London: Epworth, 1948).
[18] Arnold Dallimore, *A Heart Set Free: The Life of Charles Wesley, Pre-eminent Hymn-Writer, Fearless Evangelist, Powerful Preacher* (Welwyn: Evangelical Press, 1988).
[19] Gill, *Charles Wesley*.

coolness, while to others his logical emphasis has been unwelcome, and in general no popular or clear-cut image has survived.'[20]

The aim of this book is to present a new assessment of Charles Wesley's place in church history, and also his legacy, which was very different from that of his brother. Tension and internal conflict were ever-present aspects of the early Evangelical movement and few people were more closely involved in such strife than John Wesley's aggressive and principled sibling. The troubled partnership between the Wesley brothers will represent one of the central themes of this work: founded on blood kinship and mutual faith, their special bond was one of the driving forces of the Revival for nearly twenty years, yet towards the end of their lives, their relationship was characterized by disillusion and mistrust. They came to stand for different ideals and Charles's reputation and achievements fell victim to the hero worship accorded his brother. This will also be a study of the early Methodist people: the men and women who responded in thousands to the Wesleys' ministry have tended to be overlooked by historians, yet when the opinions and concerns of the brothers' followers are examined regarding the place of their movement in relation to the Church of England, a picture begins to emerge that is very different from the paradigm.

This book is not a conventional biography, but rather an examination of the evolution of Methodism against the background of the life and ministry of one of its principal exponents. The primary theme is one of relationships, principally between John and Charles Wesley, Methodism and the Church of England, and the discordant elements within the wider Evangelical movement. It was from this volatile mix that Methodist identity emerged and the foundation was laid for the expansion of the movement at home and overseas. As the three-hundredth anniversary of Charles Wesley's birth approaches, it is time that his personal contribution to this process was given the attention that it deserves.

[20] Gill, *Charles Wesley*, 234.

Acknowledgements

Many individuals and organizations have assisted in the completion of this project. I owe a particular debt of gratitude to Liverpool Hope University for providing me with the full studentship that allowed me to write the doctoral thesis on which the book is based. Professor Kenneth Newport of the Liverpool Hope Department of Theology and Religious Studies, who supervised my postgraduate work, has been a particular source of encouragement and inspiration. I have profited enormously from his kindness and generosity.

It has been my privilege to work for the last fifteen years as the Archivist in charge of the Methodist manuscript collections at the John Rylands University Library, The University of Manchester. It is this collection, unrivalled in its coverage of the Wesleyan wing of the Evangelical Revival that provided much of the research material used in the book. I would like to thank the Archives and History Committee of the Methodist Church of Great Britain and the University Librarian and Director, the John Rylands University Library, The University of Manchester for permission to quote from material in the Archives and also for the reproduction and publication of the illustration of Charles Wesley used as the frontispiece.

The discussion in the preface of previous biographical studies of Charles Wesley is based on my article 'Charles Wesley and his Biographers: An Exercise in Methodist Hagiography', *Bulletin of the John Rylands University Library of Manchester*, 82:1 (Spring 2000), 81–99. Permission to include extracts from the article was kindly granted by Dr Dorothy Clayton, editor of the *Bulletin*. Parts of Chs. 9 and 10 have also been previously published under my authorship as '"Croakers and Busybodies": The Extent and Influence of Church Methodism in the Late 18th and Early 19th Centuries', *Methodist History*, 42:1 (October 2003), 20–32. I would like to express my thanks to the editor of *Methodist History* for permission to incorporate parts of that article into this book.

I am also grateful to my colleagues at the John Rylands Library of Manchester, who have been helpful and tolerant of my preoccupation, and especially to Dr Peter Nockles, who read through individual chapters and provided valuable criticism. Needless to say, any imperfections that remain are my own responsibility. I would also like to express my appreciation of Dr Jeremy Gregory and his colleagues in the University of Manchester School of Arts, Histories, and Cultures for their support of my attendance at academic conferences during which the ideas contained in this book were tested and refined.

Finally, I am especially thankful for the support and encouragement of my wife Yvonne, daughter Madeline, and other members of my family. They have supported and encouraged me throughout this long and sometimes tortuous project and I could not have done this without them.

Contents

List of Abbreviations	xiv
1. The Epworth Experience	1
2. Brothers in Arms: The Early Relationship and Shared Ministry of John and Charles Wesley	21
3. Cooperation, Conflict, and Controversy During the Early Years of the Revival	43
4. Charles Wesley the Paradoxical Anglican	64
5. Engagements and Marriages	88
6. Methodism in the Early 1750s	110
7. Continuing Family Quarrels and the Methodist Opinion of Charles Wesley	134
8. A New Phase of Charles Wesley's Ministry	162
9. Methodism at the Crossroads	180
10. Charles Wesley—His Final Years and Legacy	213
Concluding Remarks	234
Bibliography	243
Index	254

List of Abbreviations

CW	Charles Wesley
CWJ	Charles Wesley's manuscript journal
JW	John Wesley
JWJ	John Wesley's published journals and diaries
MCA	Methodist Church Archives (John Rylands University Library, University of Manchester)
MS	Manuscript

1

The Epworth Experience

During his long life, Charles Wesley presented a series of seemingly contradictory faces to the world. At the start of his public ministry during the middle of the 1730s, he was an insecure conservative Oxford graduate, unsure in his ministerial vocation and even his faith. Five years later, he was a fervent Evangelical confidently facing down hostile crowds and critical archbishops, riding a tidal wave of revival. By middle age he had settled back into an apparently reactionary stance with regard to Methodism and the Church of England, fearful of developments in the movement that he had helped to create and yet unwilling or unable to turn his back completely on his brother and their followers.

Charles Wesley, Methodist leader and Church of England minister, defies easy categorization and this has bedevilled commentators since his own day. On the one hand, he always exhibited certain of the characteristics of a conservative High Church Anglican and on the other he was a charismatic Evangelical who to the end of his life thought little of contravening church discipline. Charles came to personify some of the ambiguities of the Methodist movement itself. Were the Wesley brothers and their followers Anglicans or Dissenters, or did they occupy a middle ground? Answers to these questions took many decades to emerge and well into the twentieth century unresolved areas were left behind. Charles represents a continuing puzzle, one that has implications for our understanding of the influences that shaped the Wesleyan branch of the Evangelical movement. The underlying factors that determined the peculiar twists and turns of Charles Wesley's ministry can best be understood by first examining his childhood, for it is in his earliest years that some of the keys to understanding the personality and denominational identity of this complicated man can be found.

HOME AND FAMILY

Charles Wesley was born on 18 December 1707, the third surviving son and nineteenth child of the Anglican clergyman Samuel Wesley and his wife Susanna. His birthplace was the remote Lincolnshire market town of Epworth where Charles's father was the parish priest from 1695 until his death forty years later.[1] At the time of Charles Wesley's birth, Epworth had a population of about fifteen hundred and was the largest settlement for miles around.[2] The fenlands surrounding the town had been drained early in the seventeenth century but were still subject to seasonal floods, adding to the isolation of what had long been regarded as one of England's most backward regions.

The domestic environment in which the Wesley children were raised was turbulent and at times deeply unhappy. Their father Samuel was a dogmatic if well-meaning man who attempted to rule his family as well as his parish with a rod of iron.[3] In this, he was a typical eighteenth-century patriarch, but where his situation was different from many of his contemporaries was in the character of his wife and the acute intelligence and sensitivity of their children. Susanna Wesley was a remarkable woman, educated to a level far beyond what was customary for her sex and time. She was also strong-willed and conformed only so far to the subservient role expected of an eighteenth-century wife. Her serene and rather deferential exterior hid an iron resolve and while there was mutual affection between Charles's parents there were also frequent clashes; Susanna herself remarked on one occasion 'It is a misfortune peculiar to our family that he and I seldom think alike!'[4]

[1] H. A. Beecham, 'Samuel Wesley Senior: New Biographical Evidence', *Renaissance and Modern Studies*, 7 (1963), 90–1.
[2] Henry Rack, *Reasonable Enthusiast: John Wesley and the Rise of Methodism* (London: Epworth, 1989), 45.
[3] George Stevenson, *Memorials of the Wesley Family: including biographical and historical sketches of all the members of the family for two hundred and fifty years* (London: S. W. Partridge [1876]), 156.
[4] Quoted by Brailsford, *A Tale of Two Brothers*, 16–17.

To marital storms were added other problems. Samuel was a devoted clergyman whose concern for the poor was one of his most attractive characteristics and one that his sons were to inherit. As a poverty-stricken student at Oxford he had given his last two pennies to feed a starving child[5] and in later years he sponsored the education of a poor youth through the university.[6] Unfortunately this nobility of spirit was not matched by financial common sense and he found it difficult to survive on his clerical income. In 1700 Samuel was forced to apply to the Archbishop of York for assistance,[7] and five years later he was imprisoned for debt, leaving his large family at the mercy of enemies, who had often threatened to throw them into the street.[8] Acute financial problems and the resulting insecurity formed an ever-present backdrop to Charles Wesley's early life. Family letters reveal that the Wesleys were sometimes hard pressed to feed their children,[9] and when Samuel's brother Matthew visited the rectory in 1731, he was shocked by its half-furnished condition.[10] To this precarious situation can be attributed the almost obsessive concern with financial matters exhibited by John and Charles throughout their lives; this was manifested in various ways, from their insistence on frugal living to their keeping of detailed personal accounts.

Samuel Wesley was a difficult man to like. For all his strong principles, compassion, ready wit, and keen sense of humour,[11] he was also inflexible, abrupt, and possessed of a fiery temper. In these personality traits as well as his poetic talent, Charles appears to have resembled his father. Samuel was not a man to allow common sense to stand in the way of a firmly held principle: on one occasion he forcibly ejected from his house the mistress of his aristocratic patron and lost a well-paid appointment as a result.[12] This rigidity of outlook

[5] John Newton, *Susanna Wesley and the Puritan Tradition in Methodism*, 2nd edn. (London: Epworth, 2002), 79.
[6] Luke Tyerman, *The Life and Times of the Rev. Samuel Wesley, M.A.* (London: Simpkin, Marshall, 1866), 374–5.
[7] Stevenson, *Memorials of the Wesley Family*, 79–80.
[8] Samuel Wesley sen., to William Wake, MS letter, 25 June 1705 (MCA: DDWF 1/2).
[9] Susanna Wesley to Samuel Annesley jun., Published copy letter, 20 January 1722. Susanna Wesley, *Susanna Wesley: The Complete Writings*, ed. Charles Wallace jun., (Oxford: Oxford University Press, 1997), 93–9.
[10] Tyerman, *Samuel Wesley*, 436–7.   [11] Newton, *Susanna Wesley*, 81.
[12] Ibid. 82.

and authoritarian manner made him unpopular with the people of Epworth, who were notoriously distrustful of outsiders and a match for their stiff-necked rector in stubbornness. Charles's sister Mehetabal described the inhabitants of the village of Wroot, who were also under her father's pastoral charge, in the following short poem:

> Debarred of wisdom, wit and grace
> High births and virtue equally they scorn,
> As asses dull, on dunghills born;
> Impervious as the stones, their heads are found;
> Their rage and hatred steadfast as the ground.
> With these unpolished wights, thy youthful days
> Glide slow and dull, and nature's lamp decays:
> O what a lamp is hid' midst such a sordid race![13]

Samuel with his non-local origins, Oxford education, and demands for tithes represented an alien and unwelcome intrusion into a close-knit rural community.[14] So strong was the hostility that his crops were damaged,[15] and when he was arrested in 1705 it was to the obvious delight of many of his parishioners.[16] To give an even more sinister twist to an already unpleasant picture, the fire that destroyed the rectory in 1709, almost taking the life of John Wesley in the process, may have been a result of arson.

Samuel's relations with his seven daughters were also difficult and he certainly gave them little reason to regard him with affection. He wrote on one occasion 'I creep uphill more than I did formerly, being eased of the weight of four daughters out of seven, as I hope I shall be of a fifth in a little longer.'[17] The girls spent long periods away from home, staying with relations or working in schools for a pittance, and only two of their marriages could be said to be anything other than disastrous, those of Mary and Anne, indicating that the others were either unlucky or had looked upon matrimony as an escape route. The oldest daughter Emily revealed something of the tension and despair that was part of their daily lives in a letter to her brother John:

---

[13] Quoted by Tyerman, *Samuel Wesley*, 389.
[14] Rack, *Reasonable Enthusiast*, 45–6.
[15] Stevenson, *Memorials of the Wesley Family*, 88.
[16] Samuel Wesley sen. to John Hutton, MS letter, 27 June 1705 (MCA: DDWES 6/1).
[17] Quoted by Gill, *Charles Wesley*, 25.

I think you are not well rewarded by my father for all you have done; he thinks you [are] not a good son or friend. Take what care you can of your own interests, our family are full of fine sanguine dreams, my old belief yet remains that my father will never be worth a groat...and we of the female part of the family consequently left to get our own bread, or starve...but life will be over in a few years and then sure all sorrow will end...now indeed to die seems to me not only tolerable but desirable, that it is as Hamlet says, a dissolution devoutly to be wished...[18]

EDUCATION AND SPIRITUAL NURTURING

Very little is known about Charles Wesley's earliest years or how he responded to life as a member of this fragile family. However unstable aspects of his upbringing might have been, two priceless gifts that Samuel and Susanna gave their offspring were a home schooling and a grounding in spirituality that was remarkably advanced for its time and place. With her husband busy with his parochial duties, Susanna took on the chief responsibility for raising the children and her distinctive methods have received attention from scholars who have seen in her system a forerunner of the principles of Methodist discipline.[19]

The central feature of Susanna's system was the imposition of tight control over every aspect of a child's life in order to break the will, which she described as the 'root of all sin and misery'.[20] In a famous letter of 1732 she described her child-rearing methods and repeatedly stressed the central importance of this point: 'This therefore I cannot but earnestly repeat, break their wills betimes. Begin this great work before they can run alone, before they can speak plain, or perhaps speak at all. Whatever pains it cost, conquer their stubbornness, break the will, if you would not damn the child...'[21] Physical discipline had a part to play in this process and by Susanna's own admission her children from the age of 12 months were taught to 'fear the rod and cry softly'.[22] However, her method did not depend solely on the

---

[18] Emily Wesley to John Wesley, MS letter, 31 December 1729 (MCA: DDWF 6/2).
[19] Susanna Wesley, *Susanna Wesley*, 367–8.   [20] Ibid. 370.
[21] Susanna Wesley to John Wesley, Published copy letter, 24 July 1732. Susanna Wesley, *Susanna Wesley*, 370.
[22] Ibid.

indiscriminate threat or use of corporal punishment but was instead the product of a rational and somewhat emotionally detached mind. Every hour of her children's lives was closely monitored and each action and word was subject to immediate correction. The result was a household containing a large group of boys and girls who were so quiet and restrained in their behaviour that it was almost as if no child lived there.[23]

Scholars are agreed that just as Charles resembled his father in his impetuous and rather choleric nature, John took after his mother;[24] like her, he was on the surface even-tempered and coolly analytical, and kept a tight rein on his emotions. He also inherited his mother's urge to control people and situations; one of his veteran preachers John Hampson remarked that 'opposition from his preachers or people, he could never brook. His authority he held sacred.'[25] The influence that Susanna had on Methodism through her son was never illustrated more clearly than on the occasion when John complained that he did not have more than six preachers whose wills were broken enough to serve him as his 'sons in the gospel'.[26] Charles too inherited an authoritarian streak but in his case it owed more to his father than to his mother.

Susanna also taught the children to read and write and again there was in her system the close attention to detail so reminiscent of her sons' future management of Methodism: 'The way of teaching was this. The day before a child began to learn, the house was set in order, everyone's work appointed them, and a charge given that none should come into the room from nine till twelve, or from two till five, which...were our school hours. One day was allowed the child wherein to learn its letters...'[27] As well as basic literacy skills the children were given an excellent classical education to the extent that

---

[23] Susanna Wesley, *Susanna Wesley*, 369.
[24] For example, Rack, *Reasonable Enthusiast*, 51.
[25] John Hampson, *Memoirs of the late Rev. John Wesley, A.M. with a review of his Life and Writings, and a History of Methodism, from its commencement in 1729 to the present time*, 3 vols. (Sunderland: printed for the author by James Graham, 1791), iii. 179–80.
[26] John Wesley to Edward Perronet, Published copy letter [20? July 1750]. John Wesley, *The Works of John Wesley*, xxvi. *Letters II, 1740–1755*, ed. Frank Baker (Oxford: Clarendon, 1982), 433.
[27] Susanna Wesley, *Susanna Wesley*, 371.

Charles's sister Mehetabel was fluent in New Testament Greek by the age of 8.[28]

Every aspect of the children's upbringing was dominated by religion and it was at Epworth that the search for salvation became the central concern of Charles's life. He and his siblings were taught to read using the Bible, starting appropriately enough with the first chapter of Genesis, but their spiritual education commenced several years before that point:

> The children of the family were taught as soon as they could speak, the Lord's Prayer, which they were made to say at rising and bed time constantly; to which as they grew bigger, were added a short prayer for their parents, and some collects, a short catechism, and some portions of scripture...They were very early made to distinguish the Sabbath from other days, before they could well speak or go. They were as soon taught to be still at family prayers, and to ask a blessing immediately after, which they used to do by signs, before they could kneel or speak.[29]

In addition to formal instruction, the children were given individual spiritual counselling. Every week on a specific day, each child had a private interview with Susanna—Charles's day was Saturday and these conversations were taking place by the time he was aged 4.[30] A defining characteristic of early Methodism was the Wesleys' insistence on the nurturing of inward spirituality through close personal inquiry conducted in closeted group meetings as well as probing conversations with the Wesleys and their preachers. It is perhaps too much to say that Susanna's interviews with her young sons were decisive in their promotion of this practice as the influence of Continental Pietists can also be discerned, but they probably predisposed John and Charles to recognition of its value.

Susanna's concern for her children's spiritual welfare extended beyond the confines of the parish—when her sons and daughters were away at school or staying with relatives, she wrote regularly to monitor their progress. The more substantial of these documents constitute catechetical treatises of considerable sophistication and

---

[28] Frederick Maser, *The Story of John Wesley's Sisters, or Seven Sisters in Search of Love* (Rutland: Academy Books, 1988), 51.
[29] Susanna Wesley, *Susanna Wesley*, 371.
[30] Susanna Wesley to Samuel Wesley sen., Published copy letter, 6 February 1712. Susanna Wesley, *Susanna Wesley*, 80.

they give an excellent insight into what was taught at the rectory.[31] It is clear from such primary sources that the lives of the Wesley children were almost entirely taken up by a daily round of family and private devotions, bible study, and regular counselling by their formidable mother. Less Godly pursuits such as idle play and childish chatter were frowned upon and the children were deliberately deprived of contact with other boys and girls of their own age. This added to the isolation of what must have already been an intense, almost claustrophobic existence, which in Charles's case lasted until the age of 8 when he was sent to Westminster School, exchanging one rigidly controlled environment for another.

Samuel's place in this process of educational and spiritual formation is less clear than that of Susanna, although in his published works he attached great importance to catechetical instruction, arguing that it should be practised at evening service on all Sundays and holidays.[32] He also led family prayers twice a day and the children spent their Sundays in the parish church attending on their father's preaching and participating in worship according to the Anglican Book of Common Prayer. As young men, his sons were accustomed to turn to both their parents for advice on spiritual matters and this practice would have been instilled from their earliest days.

THE CHURCH OF ENGLAND IN 1707

There has been emphasis in studies of the Wesley family on the influence of Dissent in the formation of the children's religious values. There is no doubt that this aspect was extremely important, but it is equally necessary to look at the place of the Church of England in the life of Epworth Rectory. This is particularly significant for any study of Charles Wesley for his allegiance to the Church has always been viewed as the bedrock of his faith and ministry.

Samuel and Susanna were devout Anglicans and subscribers to the political and religious views of the High Church party. This informal grouping of ministers and laymen held strict views on church

---

[31] See e.g. Susanna's exposition on the Apostle's Creed contained in a letter of 13 January 1710 to her daughter Susanna. Ibid. 379–407.
[32] Tyerman, *Samuel Wesley*, 387.

discipline and had been one of the dominant influences in the Church of England since the late seventeenth century. Among the characteristics of his ministry that identify Samuel as a High Churchman was his emphasis on the importance of the Sacraments epitomized by the practice of monthly Communion, the holding of weekly prayers on a Wednesday and Friday and regular catechizing.[33] He was also a strict disciplinarian who insisted on public penance for sexual misdemeanours, a practice that did not endear him to his parishioners.[34] Samuel's three sons all became High Churchmen in their turn, although John and Charles were to be far from conventional in their approach. The main alternative to the High Church party was the moderate Latitudinarians who regarded religion as essentially a matter of reason and sense. They abhorred extremism and were tolerant of diversity, reacting against the religious violence of the previous generation.[35] This willingness to entertain other points of view sometimes led to accusations of unorthodoxy by their more doctrinally rigid High Church critics.[36]

Politics played an important part in distinguishing the individuals and groups that made up the Church of England at the time of Charles Wesley's birth. Anglicans of Samuel and Susanna Wesley's persuasion believed that royal and episcopal authority was divinely sanctioned and that loyalty to God and king went hand in hand. Of course matters could never be that simple given the confused state of English affairs following the Glorious Revolution of 1688. Many High Churchmen considered the replacement of King James II by his daughter Mary and son-in-law William of Orange to be nothing less than an ungodly usurpation and this presented a grave issue of conscience. The bitterest rift within Samuel and Susanna Wesley's marriage was over this thorny question of who was the rightful sovereign and head of the Anglican Church. Samuel, despite his own views on the divinely ordained nature of royal authority, accepted

---

[33] Rack, *Reasonable Enthusiast*, 53.   [34] Tyerman, *Samuel Wesley*, 387.

[35] Rupp, *Religion in England 1688–1791*, 32–9; John Walsh and Stephen Taylor, 'Introduction: The Church and Anglicanism in the "Long" Eighteenth Century', in John Walsh, Colin Haydon, and Stephen Taylor (eds.), *The Church of England c.1688–c.1833. From Toleration to Tractarianism* (Cambridge: Cambridge University Press, 1993), 36–7.

[36] Rack, *Religious Enthusiast*, 25; Walsh and Taylor, 'Introduction: The Church and Anglicanism', 39–40.

William as king; Susanna on the other hand was a Nonjuror, which is to say that she actively withheld allegiance from William. In this she was at one with the several bishops and an estimated 300–400 inferior clergy deprived of their livings for refusing to swear an oath of loyalty to the new regime.[37]

The result of Samuel's accidental discovery in 1702 that his wife had the audacity to have an opposing viewpoint to the master of the house was an all too predictable explosion. The resulting separation lasted several months and involved attempts at mediation all the way up to the Archbishop of York and the Bishop of Lincoln.[38] This disagreement illustrates not only the temperamental relationship between Samuel and Susanna, but also the divided nature of English Church and society at the time of Charles Wesley's birth. Within the lifetimes of men and women who Charles would have known, English society had been torn apart by civil and religious strife. Families and communities experienced violent division over the interlocking questions of royal authority, parliamentary government, religious toleration, and the nature of the national Church. The gratuitous bloodletting that resulted had extended in 1649 to the person of the king himself. Even in the more settled times such as followed the restoration of Charles II in 1660 and the overthrow of his brother James in 1688, the spectre of civil and religious strife was never far away and was not entirely dispelled until after the Jacobite rebellion of 1745. The family into which Charles was born represented a microcosm of this conflict.

CHARLES WESLEY'S DISSENTING ANCESTORS

Charles's parents might have been supporters of the established Church and royal supremacy, but they had been raised to hold very different opinions. Samuel's father and grandfather, John and Bartholomew Wesley, had been Presbyterians, members of one of the several churches and sects that are often grouped together under the label 'Puritan' because of their common wish to purify the English Church of any vestige of popish ritual. The Wesleys had been church

[37] Rupp *Religion in England*, 5.   [38] Rack, *Reasonable Enthusiast*, 49.

ministers under the Commonwealth and were ejected from their livings in 1662 for refusing to conform to the Act of Uniformity. This statute, part of the raft of legislation that accompanied the return of royal government in 1660, reintroduced the Book of Common Prayer as the liturgy of a reconstituted national Church. John and his father had been supporters of Parliamentary rule and there is a story that Bartholomew had come close to arresting the future King Charles II after his failed attempt to seize power in 1651.[39] Nine years later the Wesleys submitted to Charles's return from exile but the reimposition of the Anglican prayer book with what many regarded as its Roman Catholic elements proved too much for their Puritan sensibilities. After his ejection Bartholomew quietly withdrew to life as a physician,[40] but his son John made a courageous and public stand for his beliefs. He continued to preach and lead dissenting congregations for which he suffered persecution and imprisonment, which probably contributed to his death in 1670 at the age of 34.[41] John's son Samuel was aged 8 at the time and his father's premature demise added to the burden of what must have already been an insecure childhood.

Susanna's father Samuel Annesley experienced similar difficulties.[42] He had also been a minister during the period of Parliamentary rule when Presbyterian influence within the English Church was at its height and had served as a naval chaplain during the war against King Charles I, but he may not have been as republican as this record might suggest—he publicly opposed the king's execution in 1649, describing it as a 'horrid murder' and also had a dangerously low opinion of Lord Protector Oliver Cromwell.[43] Like the Wesleys and many others, Annesley was ejected from his living in 1662 but was able to continue his public ministry, despite occasional harassment by the authorities. He lived long enough to be regarded as one of London's leading Nonconformist divines and a man of principle respected on all sides of the religious divide.

---

[39] William Matthews (ed.), *Charles II's Escape from Worcester: A Collection of Narratives assembled by Samuel Pepys* (London: G. Bell & Sons, 1967), 126.
[40] Beecham, *Samuel Wesley*, 83.   [41] Ibid. 83–5.
[42] John Newton, 'Samuel Annesley (1620–96)', *Proceedings of the Wesley Historical Society*, 45 (1985–6), 29–45.
[43] 'The arrantest hypocrite that ever the Church of Christ was pestered with.' Quoted by Newton, *Samuel Annesley*, 32.

Despite their staunch Puritan background, Samuel Wesley and Susanna Annesley at a young age independently transferred their allegiance to the Church of England. This statement of religious identity was for the young couple, just as much as for their parents, a stand that was born of conviction although the specific reasons why they crossed over remain unclear.[44] As is the nature of converts, Samuel and Susanna were enthusiastic in their new loyalty and this may have contributed to their reactionary leanings.

THE RELIGIOUS DIVERSITY OF EPWORTH RECTORY

Charles' parents made the controversial decision to turn their backs on their Puritan upbringing, but this is not to say that non-Anglican influence was entirely absent from Epworth Rectory. For all her High Church and Tory opinions, there was much about Susanna specifically that was the product of an exceptionally wide Christian and intellectual tradition. Her strict routine of daily devotions set against the background of a regimented household is seen as typically Puritan and has parallels in the literature of the period. The words of advice written in 1670 by the Puritan Sir Edward Harley to his daughter Brilliana might have almost come from Susanna Wesley's pen:

> You must be careful to keep the family in good order and that all come to prayers constantly night and morning and the prayers be in seasonable time. Be you very watchful over yourself that not anything divert you from your morning and evening worship of God in secret and constant reading the scripture and some other good book... Tell your brothers that I hope they will be careful in learning their book, praying and singing their catechisms every day.[45]

Susanna's spiritual writings display a bewildering range of influences that include Roman Catholic mystics, deists, Anglican divines, Cambridge Platonists, and Presbyterian ministers.[46] She appears to have been particularly impressed by the work of the Roman Catholic

---

[44] Newton, *Samuel Annesley*, 39; Beecham, *Samuel Wesley*, 85–6.

[45] Quoted by J. T. Cliffe, *The Puritan Gentry Besieged 1650–1700* (London: Routledge, 1993), 138.

[46] Newton, *Susanna Annesley*, 136–9.

Lorenzo Scupoli on Christian perfection, a doctrine that was to occupy a central place in Methodist spirituality. Her chosen denomination might have been the Church of England, but her spiritual curiosity roamed far and wide and nourished the exceptionally wide outlook possessed by her children.

If Susanna represented the non-Anglican element of Charles's religious education, her husband Samuel has come to symbolize that of the Church of England in its most rigid form. It is unclear what if any residual influence his Puritan upbringing had on his personal outlook as very little manuscript material survives that casts light on his innermost spiritual concerns. The impression that we glean from Samuel's contemporaries is that he was a man resolutely fixed in his High Church viewpoint. His published work such as the controversial *A Letter from a Country Divine* of 1702 leaves no doubt as to where the author stood on the question of the Church, Nonconformity, and republicanism. This particular publication led to a bitter pamphlet war with Dissenters who viewed Samuel, perhaps understandably, as an unprincipled turncoat.[47] As one of the editors of the *Young Students' Library*, a selection of extracts from a range of learned works, Samuel's selection of theological material was entirely Anglican with a strong bias towards the High Church.[48]

As one-dimensional as Samuel Wesley may appear compared with Susanna, he nevertheless made an important contribution to the shaping of his sons' convictions. In politics Samuel was a Tory but had no sympathy with the exiled Stuarts unlike his wife and eldest son Samuel junior;[49] in this allegiance to the Hanoverian line and submission to secular authority, John and Charles were to follow closely in his footsteps. John summed up their viewpoint and cited a specific paternal legacy in a letter of 1775: 'I am an High Churchman, the son of an High Churchman, bred up from childhood in the highest notions of passive obedience and non-resistance.'[50] Charles's poetry espouses similar sentiments although revealing an attachment to the royal cause that was as much a matter for the heart and soul as well as

---

[47] Beecham, *Samuel Wesley*, 92–8.   [48] Tyerman, *Samuel Wesley*, 464–6.
[49] Rack, *Reasonable Enthusiast*, 51.
[50] John Wesley to the Earl of Dartmouth, Published copy letter, 14 June 1775. John Wesley, *The Letters of the Rev. John Wesley, A. M. sometime Fellow of Lincoln College, Oxford*, ed. John Telford, 8 vols. (London: Epworth, 1931), vi. 156.

the head. In his poem written to celebrate the birthday of George II, Charles stressed a direct link between God and king:

> With joy we see th' auspicious day return
> When Heaven on Brittain smil'd and George was born
> Born for the general good, by fate design'd
> A parent, King, a patron of mankind!
> Long may he bless the Nations with his sway,
> See the calm sunset of his glorious day
> With golden beams thro' all the horizon shine
> And late return to Heaven in Majesty divine![51]

This transcendent tradition of loyalty to the crown and strict non-involvement in party politics helped Methodism to deflect criticism during the eighteenth century and was passed down through the Wesleyan strand of the movement well into the Victorian period.

Samuel also bequeathed to his sons a devotion to the King James Bible, the Book of Common Prayer and a love of the Church of England as an institution. Despite the twists and turns of Evangelical conversions, Continental influence, and Anglican-inspired persecution, John and Charles were never to shake off the typically High Church belief that the Anglican Church was Christian, Primitive, and Apostolic with roots that went back to the patristic age. This stance was to have a considerable influence on the movement that the brothers founded.

As different as their specific contributions appear to have been, it would be a mistake to assume that there was a sharp divide between Samuel and Susanna on the question of their children's upbringing. They were, after all, both Anglican converts from a similar background and of broadly the same doctrinal persuasion. Both for example regarded the Lord's Supper as a 'sovereign means of grace' and this high sacramental tradition, which can be observed in certain Puritan groups as well as the Anglican High Church, was passed down to John and Charles.[52] Samuel would have been fully aware of what Susanna was teaching in the nursery, and as the undisputed master of the house (at least in his own mind), he must have approved; for her part, Susanna was a staunch supporter of the discipline of the Church and

---

[51] Charles Wesley, MS hymns on festivals (MCA: CW box 5).
[52] Newton, *Susanna Annesley*, 144–8.

shared her husband's views on many of its aspects. The Wesley parents, for all the tensions and difficulties of their marriage, were in fact complementary halves of a very effective partnership. It is worthwhile to note that John and Charles, the two children whose personalities most resembled their mother and father respectively, had a similarly tense though fruitful and close association. It is perhaps no coincidence that Charles, not long before his death, used phrases from the Anglican marriage service to describe his relationship with John.[53]

THE COMPLEX CHARACTER OF THE ANGLICAN CHURCH

The religious convictions that the Wesleys inherited from their parents were an eclectic mix of High Church Anglicanism infused with Puritan elements and tempered by influences from other Christian traditions. This may seem an unusual and rather confusing combination but it was in fact symptomatic of the wider Anglican ethos in the early eighteenth century. One of the effects of over one hundred years of controversy and intermittent violent upheaval was to make the Church of England home to so many different viewpoints that the boundaries between Establishment and Dissent became blurred.[54]

Neither the High or Latitudinarian wings of the Church were formally organized or rigidly defined, with the result that it was possible for many shades of opinion to exist within them. The Nonjurors, as has already been noted, represented a radical group on the fringes of the High Church with controversial views on the legitimacy of the successors to King James II. Some Nonjurors withdrew from mainstream Anglicanism altogether and established an episcopate of their own, which they regarded as the true Church of England, but others, including Susanna Wesley, stayed within the Anglican ranks. At the other end of the spectrum were the Cambridge Platonists, an eminent group of intellectuals with connections to the Latitudinarians. As

---

[53] 'Whom God hath joined, let no man put asunder. We have taken each other for better for worse...' Quoted by Gill, *Charles Wesley*, 199.
[54] W. M. Jacob, *Lay People and Religion in the Early Eighteenth Century* (Cambridge: Cambridge University Press, 1996), 7.

their name suggests, they promoted a Christian variant of classical and medieval philosophy.[55]

Churchmen from Samuel Wesley's generation often held a mix of opinions drawn from across this exceptionally broad denomination.[56] Cambridge Platonism influenced the Nonjuror William Law[57] while the Latitudinarian John Tillotson, as Dean of Canterbury, introduced a weekly Eucharist, a practice that was more commonly associated with the High Church.[58] On the other hand, some High Churchmen placed stress on careful preparation for taking Communion rather than frequency of celebration—Samuel Johnson for example received the bread and wine only once a year.[59] It is equally difficult to attach firm theological labels to the different groups. One significant area of debate centred on predestination, which had been a popular school of thought within the Church of England since the sixteenth century—two firm supporters of the alternative doctrine of free grace were Samuel and Susanna Wesley and this was passed down to their sons with significant effects for the section of the Revival that they were to lead.

The Puritan influence on the Church of England in the late seventeenth century was considerable and by no means confined to Susanna Wesley. Many Puritan ministers had charge of Anglican parishes during the Commonwealth and effectively formed the religious establishment. After the restoration of the king many denied the Act of Uniformity and lost their livings,[60] but others submitted and continued to exercise a Church of England ministry but in a Puritan fashion. One of many examples was Thomas Birch, Vicar of Preston, who it was claimed did not baptize in accordance with the custom of the Church and also held republican views. Another so-called 'Parish Puritan' was Isaac Archer the Vicar of Chippenham, who was prepared to read only parts of the Book of Common Prayer.[61] In counties where Puritanism had been strong, its influence over the Caroline Church remained visible long after

---

[55] Rupp, *Religion in England*, 30–2.   [56] Jacob, *Lay People and Religion*, 7.
[57] Rupp, *Religion in England*, 240.   [58] Rack, *Reasonable Enthusiast*, 19.
[59] Walsh and Taylor, 'Introduction: the Church and Anglicanism', 23.
[60] It is estimated that between 1660 and 1662 2,000 Puritan clergymen left the Church of England, either of their own volition or under duress. Ibid. 31.
[61] Cliffe, *The Puritan Gentry Besieged*, 92–3.

the return of the king. In 1680 the Bishop of Peterborough reported that thirty clergymen in Northamptonshire did not wear the surplice when officiating at services[62]—clearly such men were either Puritan sympathizers or were willing to bend to the wishes of congregations that regarded such vestments as a popish affectation. In some cases, like that of Thomas Birch, the patron of the benefice was a member of the Puritan upper class and used this legal right to appoint ministers of his own persuasion to Anglican parishes. Some former Puritans rose to high rank within the restored Anglican Church including the Bishop of Lincoln Thomas Barlow and Bishop John Hall of Bristol. The most eminent example of a former Puritan on the episcopal bench was John Tillotson who served as Archbishop of Canterbury between 1691 and 1694 and was a strong voice for toleration of the dissenting groups from which he had himself emerged.

Members of Nonconformist congregations frequently exhibited a dual loyalty, attending the parish church as well as their own meetings. This has a particular interest for students of Methodism as it provides precedents for what became standard practice for the Wesleys and their followers. One of the greatest of Puritan divines Richard Baxter described himself as a 'half-conformist' and he was by no means unique in this respect.[63] Some ministers who had been ejected took the opinion that while they had been forced for conscience sake to deny the Act of Uniformity, they still considered themselves part of a Church of England that was fundamentally sound. These men hoped for the day when liturgical and other requirements would be relaxed sufficiently to allow them to reunite with the Mother Church; in the meantime they led worship in private homes and encouraged their followers to attend Anglican services, sometimes leading them as a body to the church in a manner that is strongly reminiscent of Methodist practice fifty years later.

What was termed 'Occasional conformity' was sometimes a result of the legal requirement for holders of public office to take Anglican Communion—in the dissenting stronghold of Bridport for example,

---

[62] Ibid. 93.
[63] John Spurr, 'From Puritanism to Dissent', in Christoper Durston and Jacqueline Eales (eds.), *Culture of English Puritanism 1560–1700* (Houndmills: Palgrave Macmillan [1996]), 241–2.

the town's leading citizens were often pew-holders and churchwardens of the parish church as well as worshippers at the dissenting chapel.[64] Such bending of the rules aside, there can be little doubt that many people in the early eighteenth century saw no reason why they could not in all conscience frequent both the parish church and Nonconformist meeting.[65] It is true that Puritans both of the conforming and nonconforming stamp were subject to occasional harassment but the reality is that most people were sick of the violence associated with religious division. For the sake of peace in society at large the majority of Anglican clergy and laity were prepared to live and let live, especially after the granting of limited religious toleration in 1689.[66] High Churchmen often felt uncomfortable with such ambiguity but this attitude of pragmatic tolerance was an aspect of the Church of England that John and Charles Wesley, for all their own High Church convictions, were to use to full advantage.

CONTINENTAL INFLUENCE

With the return of a measure of religious and political stability after 1660, the English Church opened up to overseas influence. A significant introduction in terms of its effect on the growth and consolidation of Methodism was the concept of the religious society. Anthony Horneck, who had moved from his native Germany and taken Anglican Orders shortly after the restoration of Charles II, was the principal pioneer of this movement, although it is important to point out that the innovation was quickly and enthusiastically adopted by a significant number of home-grown clergy and laity.[67]

The societies consisted of small groups of laymen and supervising clergy whose avowed purpose was the promotion of holy living as a challenge to the moral laxity of Restoration England. Members met regularly to study the Bible and other devotional works as a means

---

[64] Paul Langford, *Public Life and the Propertied Englishman 1689–1798* (Oxford: Clarendon, 1991), 96.
[65] 'Confusion between Church and Dissent was commonplace.' Ibid.
[66] Walsh and Taylor, 'Introduction: the Church and Anglicanism', 53–9.
[67] Jacob, *Lay People and Religion*, 77–92; John Spurr, 'The Church, the Societies and the Moral Revolution of 1688', in *The Church of England c.1688–c.1833*, 131–2.

The Epworth Experience 19

of raising their lives to a higher level of public morality and personal holiness.[68] The societies were firmly attached to Anglican discipline and displayed affinity with such High Church principles as regular fasting and Communion,[69] although some High Churchmen were suspicious of such groups, seeing in them a disturbing reminder of the exclusive sects of the previous generation.[70] Samuel Wesley on the other hand embraced the new movement with enthusiasm and founded a society in Epworth.[71] It was Anglican societies of this type that were to form one of the foundation stones of early Methodist structure.

The religious societies were established against the background of the growth of Pietism in Germany. This movement had started in the Lutheran Church during the 1670s as an attempt to restore the primacy of the heart over the mind in matters of religion.[72] By the 1730s Pietist influence had spread to the British Isles carried in particular by the Moravians whose use of England as a stepping-stone to the New World was to play a key role in the birth of the Evangelical Revival. Pietist emphasis on holy living and the nurturing of inward spirituality found a receptive audience within the membership of the religious societies and struck a chord with the Wesley brothers whose own upbringing in the bosom of the Anglican Church had laid stress on those same elements.

CONCLUSION

The Church of England in the generation before the Revival has traditionally been viewed as existing in a state of spiritual and institutional lethargy.[73] Attacked by deists and Whig politicians,[74] undermined by internal conflict and affected with such weaknesses as pluralism and

---

[68] Richard Heitzenrater, *Wesley and the People Called Methodists* (Nashville: Abingdon, 1995), 21–4.
[69] Ibid. 22.
[70] Jacob, *Lay People and Religion*, 78–9; Tyerman, *Samuel Wesley*, 216–17.
[71] Jacob, *Lay People and Religion*, 81–2.
[72] Heitzenrater, *Wesley and the People Called Methodists*, 19–20.
[73] 'Conventionally the period between the death of Anne and the 1830s is regarded as a period of slumber in the established Church, enlightened only by the Methodist and Evangelical revivals.' Jacob, *Lay People and Religion*, p. ix.
[74] For a discussion of the widespread anticlericalism of the era, see ibid. 44–51.

non-residency, there was a great deal that was wrong with the Church, but there was also an openness that contributed to an atmosphere unusually receptive to revival. It is easy to view the Anglican Church as a monolithic instinctively conservative institution rigidly attached to the Thirty-Nine Articles and the Book of Common Prayer, but the eighteenth-century reality was far more complex. Anglicans in 1700 could hold a range of radically different theological opinions and disagree strongly and openly on aspects of liturgy and worship but continue as loyal members of the one denomination. When viewed against this inclusive background, the fact that Methodism was born in the Church of England and found a home within it for so long becomes easier to explain.

Epworth Rectory could not be described as a carefree place in which to spend a childhood. Beset by financial difficulties and surrounded by hostile neighbours, Charles and his siblings lived a confined and strictly controlled existence. With the possible exception of John, none of the children in later life appear to have remembered their childhood home with much affection. When Samuel junior and John were each in turn offered the possibility of succeeding their father as Rector of Epworth they reacted as if it were a poisoned chalice, much vaunted filial piety aside.[75] Yet despite such negative connotations, the Epworth experience with all its rich diversity represented an ideal preparation for the founders of Methodism. John and Charles Wesley were raised as High Anglicans with an instinctive attachment to the discipline and ritual of the Church, but they also received a deep grounding in a spirituality that crossed denominational barriers and were brought up to place loyalty to God above all other concerns. For Charles in particular there was to be considerable tension between these various elements of his religious identity, but there was never a breaking point and Methodism became the product of a synthesis that first started to take shape in the unlikely confines of a Lincolnshire backwater.

[75] Tyerman, *Samuel Wesley*, 417–19, 422–3; Rack, *Reasonable Enthusiast*, 93–4.

2

Brothers in Arms: The Early Relationship and Shared Ministry of John and Charles Wesley

The most important relationship of Charles Wesley's life was with his brother John. His bond with his wife Sarah, who he married relatively late in life, was exceptionally strong but in terms of longevity, depth of conflicting emotion, and impact, the fraternal relationship had singular significance. This was true not only for the Wesleys but also for the Methodist movement of which they were the co-founders. Charles's biographers have acknowledged the importance of the brotherly link, with particular regard to the ten years from 1738, a decade that saw the birth of the Revival in England and the emergence of a specific Wesleyan wing of the Evangelical movement. Scholars have in fact been at pains to show that in spite of disagreement in later years over such issues as the Church of England, the brothers remained close until the end of their lives.[1]

Except in regard to his hymns, Charles Wesley has never been viewed in isolation from John. This is understandable given their kinship and important place within the Revival's leadership, but many aspects of the brothers' relationship remain incompletely understood. Among the specific areas to which this judgement applies is Charles's apparent dependence on his domineering brother, their latent rivalry, and the mutual fear that other relationships would challenge their special understanding. Examination of these areas is important for an appreciation of the impact that their complementary and conflicting

---

[1] For example, Gill, *Charles Wesley*, 200; Brailsford, *A Tale of Two Brothers*, 276.

personalities had on the Revival. This chapter will chart the evolution of the brothers' relationship from their days at school and university through the first decade of Methodism's existence until the end of the 1740s at which point their relationship changed forever.

FAMILY AND SCHOOL

The roots of the close fraternal tie can be traced to a shared upbringing that was special, one might even say abnormal. Strict and devout child-rearing was not of course unique to Samuel and Susanna, but their mixture of discipline and spiritual preparation against the background of an isolated and precarious family situation resulted in the Wesley children becoming exceptionally close. The bond between John and Charles was always potentially the strongest as the age difference between them was just four years, while their brother Samuel junior was considerably older. The relationship with their sisters, while affectionate and mutually supportive, was not one of equals. As the males of the family, John and Charles enjoyed a superiority that was predetermined by society, and their professional lives overlapped in ways that were not accessible to their sisters. This common background and experience contributed to a closeness of understanding that they were never to replicate with anyone else. No one understood John Wesley to the same degree as Charles, while for his part John held his sibling in high regard; despite bitter clashes in later life, Charles remained one of the few men capable of swaying his imperious brother from a particular course of action.

After the claustrophobic closeness of their childhood in Epworth, the boys were sent to separate boarding schools in London. At the age of 8, Charles made the long journey to Westminster not far from Charterhouse where John had been a pupil for two years. We have little first-hand information concerning Charles's schooldays as none of his letters survive from that period. In later life he referred in passing to the corporal punishment that was standard in the schools of his day[2] and it is perhaps significant that he educated his own sons

---

[2] 'If Robin *will* not be led, he must be driven. I mean whipped through Westminster or some other great school.' CW to Mary Jones, Xerox copy letter [7 November] 1749 (MCA: DDCW 1/27).

entirely at home. Whatever the nature of his later misgivings about the public school system, he flourished at Westminster, displaying the academic prowess and strength of character that came with the Wesley name.

In 1721 Charles achieved the enviable status of King's Scholar, which brought with it free board and education together with the likelihood of a university scholarship. Four years later he became Captain of the School, an honour accorded to the most promising senior pupil. His contemporaries included the sons of aristocratic and gentry families and for Charles, the son of a penniless country minister, to win this distinction speaks volumes for the quality of his character. At Westminster Charles was under the supervision of his brother Samuel who was a teacher at the school and with whom he lodged for five years.[3] Given their father's financial embarrassment, Samuel junior subsidized his brother's education and in Samuel senior's words, was 'a father to your brothers and sisters'.[4] It is doubtful whether financial constraints would have allowed Charles to make the long journey home at all during his ten years in London.

Until he left Charterhouse for Oxford in 1720 John was only a short distance away from his brothers and spent his free time with Samuel and his family. Despite such contact, there is no doubt that it was Samuel junior who was the principal influence in Charles's life at this time. Samuel was a convinced High Churchman and may have shared his mother's passive loyalty to the exiled Stuarts.[5] He was a friend of the extreme High Church bishop Francis Atterbury and in later years was sharply critical of the irregularities attendant on the early stirrings of revival.[6] The natural attachment to Anglican doctrine and discipline that Charles brought with him from Epworth would have been reinforced by close contact with his oldest brother. In his future ministry Charles was to stray in quite radical ways from conventional High Church practice but he was never to entirely divest himself of its influence and for that Samuel must take some of the credit.

[3] Gill, *Charles Wesley*, 32.
[4] Quoted by Maldwyn Edwards, *Family Circle: A Study of the Epworth Family Household in Relation to John and Charles Wesley* (London: Epworth, 1949), 101.
[5] Vivian Green, *The Young Mr Wesley: A Study of John Wesley and Oxford* (London: Epworth, 1963), 56.
[6] Samuel Wesley jun. to JW, MS letter, 16 April 1739 (MCA: DDWF 5/15).

OXFORD AND THE HOLY CLUB

In 1726 Charles was awarded a scholarship to Christ Church Oxford, typically securing first place among successful candidates from his school.[7] In going up to Christ Church he was following family tradition—his brothers had both been undergraduates there and in the year of Charles's matriculation John moved to occupy a Fellowship at nearby Lincoln College. Charles would have found Christ Church a congenial place for a man of his background. Traditionally one of the most prestigious and Tory inclined of the Oxford colleges[8] it leaned towards high Anglicanism, very much in keeping with the rest of the university.[9]

Spiritual matters were not first on the list of Charles's concerns during his first year. By his own admission and in time-honoured undergraduate tradition, he celebrated his new-found freedom by indulging in 'diversions' such as playing cards, party-going, and at a slightly later date flirting with an actress.[10] None of these amounted to a great deal and there can be little doubt that by most standards Charles was an unusually upright and devout young man. He had in any case little money with which to indulge himself and, to his occasional chagrin, an older brother in the Lincoln College Senior Common Room who, when he was not absent in Epworth, kept a watchful eye over his sibling.[11] This in itself would have been enough to dampen the high spirits of most undergraduates.

By his second year the reality of Charles's situation was starting to sink in. He was depressed by the state of his finances,[12] which even with a scholarship were precarious, and he was also uncomfortably

---

[7] Gill, *Charles Wesley*, 33–4.   [8] Rack, *Reasonable Enthusiast*, 69.
[9] 'The flavour of Oxford churchmanship was neo-Jacobite and neo-Laudian.' Vivian Green, *Religion at Oxford and Cambridge: A History c.1160–c.1960* (London: SCM, 1964), 178.
[10] Green, *The Young Mr Wesley*, 142; CW to JW, MS letter, 5 June 1729 (MCA: DDCW 1/2).
[11] 'He pursued his studies diligently and led a regular harmless life; but if I spoke to him about religion, he would warmly answer "What, would you have me to be a saint all at once?" and would hear no more.' Quoted by Green, *Young Mr Wesley*, 142.
[12] CW to JW, MS letter, 20 January 1728 (MCA: DDCW 1/1).

aware that he was in a state of spiritual lethargy.[13] He therefore turned his back on his former amusements and threw himself into his studies and devotions. Charles derived particular comfort from weekly attendance at Holy Communion and was able to influence two or three fellow students to accompany him. It was in this rather low-key fashion that the famous 'holy club' started to take shape.

In a letter written many years later, Charles described the early days of what is sometimes seen as the birth of Methodism: 'I went to the weekly Sacrament and persuaded two or three young scholars to accompany me, and to observe the method of study prescribed by the Statutes of the University. This gave me the harmless nickname of Methodist. In half a year my brother left his curacy at Epworth and came to our assistance...'[14] Over the course of the next six years until the departure of the brothers for North America, the holy club, or Oxford Methodists as they were also known, expanded in size, activities, and notoriety. At its peak in the early 1730s it consisted of a network of student groups dispersed among several colleges. They engaged in intense bible study and other serious reading and were considered noteworthy for their rigid observance of church fast days and attendance at divine service. Their Christianity also had a practical aspect expressed by giving to the poor and visits to the town's prisons.[15]

Recent research has cast doubt on the traditional picture of the Oxford Methodists as a tightly organized group subject to the supervision of first Charles Wesley and then his brother John. The reality appears to have been that the meetings were informal in nature and that membership was fluid.[16] John Wesley was certainly one of the most influential participants and was at the centre of what Heitzenrater has termed a 'core society', but he could not be said to have exercised formal leadership over the entire group.[17] Charles

---

[13] 'I am not ashamed to desire your prayers. Tis owing in great measure to somebody's (my mother's most likely) that I am come to think as I do, for I cannot tell myself how or when I first awoke out of my lethargy—only that it was not long after you went away.' CW to JW, MS letter, 5/22 June 1729 (MCA: DDCW 1/2).
[14] CW to Dr Chandler, MS letter, 28 April 1785 (MCA: DDWes 1/38).
[15] Green, *The Young Mr Wesley*, 153–6, 175–9.
[16] Benjamin Ingham, *Diary of an Oxford Methodist Benjamin Ingham, 1733–1734*, ed. Richard Heitzenrater (Durham: Duke University Press, 1985), 6–9.
[17] Ibid. 8–9.

too was a prominent member and was talked about in college for his 'preciseness and pious extravagance'.[18] He also exercised a strong sway over individual students such as Benjamin Ingham[19] and John Gambold,[20] showing early signs of a personal flair for the exercise of spiritual direction.

The pattern of religious observance practised by the brothers and their friends was rooted in the High Church with more than a touch of Nonjuror influence. This can be seen from the earliest days when the holy club first became identifiable through the practice of regular Sacramental attendance; other typical High Church characteristics such as the observance of Wednesday and Friday fasts were also adopted. Two of the men named by John Wesley as major contributors to the Oxford Methodist system were the Nonjurors John Clayton and Thomas Deacon.[21] In particular, Clayton's concern that the Church should be restored to the doctrinal and devotional purity of its early history, made a deep impression on John Wesley and hence on the Methodist quest for a return to 'primitive' Christianity.[22]

The intensive regime of study, private devotions, attendance at worship and performance of good works was regarded as a vehicle to promote holy living with the end view of achieving 'perfection'.[23] Stress was placed on meditation as part of a constant process of spiritual self-examination. The reading favoured by Oxford Methodists included cross-denominational works of a mystical nature by a number of influential writers including Ignatius Loyola, Thomas à Kempis, Madame Guyon, William Law, Richard Baxter, and Lorenzo Scupoli.[24] There existed a wide common ground between the spiritual aims of the club and the religious values instilled into the Wesley brothers at Epworth. The importance of this small group of students was not confined to the Wesleys or the movement that they went on to found. Several other Oxford Methodists made significant contributions to the Evangelical Revival in both Britain and North America including John Gambold, Benjamin Ingham, and George Whitefield.

[18] Quoted by Green, *The Young Mr Wesley*, 170.
[19] Ingham, *Diary of an Oxford Methodist*, 46.
[20] Green, *The Young Mr Wesley*, 170.   [21] Rack, *Reasonable Enthusiast*, 90–1.
[22] Green, *The Young Mr Wesley*, 168–9.
[23] Ingham, *Diary of an Oxford Methodist*, 31–2.   [24] Ibid. 32–3.

The holy club aroused mixed reactions within the university and the Church. Some senior figures such as Bishop Potter of Oxford were supportive,[25] but others were distinctly lukewarm. This may seem strange as the club's Anglican credentials were beyond question and leaned towards the conservative wing of the Church establishment. The sight of young students flaunting their faith and good works in a rather sanctimonious fashion always inspires some derision, but there was a more serious side to the hostility. It was felt by some that the Oxford Methodists were too extreme in their ascetic lifestyle and that their constant self-examination and intense inner focus could have an unhealthy affect on impressionable young minds. Religious mania or 'enthusiasm' as it was often termed was a constant fear for an older generation raised in the shadow of sectarian strife.

Ammunition was given to the club's critics by the tragic death in 1732 of William Morgan. He had been one of the earliest and most dedicated members of the group and had initiated the work in the prisons.[26] Morgan was also of an unstable temperament and may have been prone to religious mania; according to one account of his final illness he 'used frequently to say that enthusiasm was his madness, repeated often "Oh religious madness"...'[27] This unfortunate youth might have descended into derangement without the unwitting help of the holy club, but the resulting scandal left a stigma attached to the label 'Methodist'. In 1743, more than a decade after Morgan's death, the satirist Thomas Este referred to the Methodists of his own day as that 'swarm of vile canting hypocrites' who had been a 'nuisance at our universities'.[28]

THE DEEPENING BOND BETWEEN JOHN AND CHARLES WESLEY

Another important development of Charles's Oxford years was the replacement of Samuel junior's influence by that of John, which coincided with Charles's decision that he must reform his ways and forge

---

[25] Green, *The Young Mr Wesley*, 141.   [26] Ibid. 154–5.
[27] Quoted ibid. 166.
[28] Thomas Este, *Methodism Displayed: a farce of one act. As it was intended to be performed at the Moot Hall in Newcastle* (Newcastle: Thomas Este, 1743), 20.

a deeper relationship with God. He quickly placed himself under John's supervision with regard both to academic matters and spiritual growth, one of the first of many to follow that path. This is first documented in a letter that Charles sent to John in June 1729: 'Tis through your means I firmly believe, God will establish what he has begun in me and there is no one person I would so willingly have to be the instrument of good to me as you—I verily think dear brother, I shall never quarrel with *you* again till I do with my religion, and that I may never do.'[29]

John's displacement of Samuel junior in Charles's loyalties did not go unnoticed by their oldest brother and his wife Ursula. During a visit made by Charles to Westminster during the college Christmas break of 1727, Samuel remarked in a letter to John that he 'was so entirely infected with your gravity that every motion and look made me almost suspect it was you.'[30] Ursula was more visibly resentful and attempted, according to Charles's account, to sow dissension between her brothers-in-law. So great was the tension that Charles breathed a sigh of relief at his return to the penurious freedom of Christ Church.[31] Samuel and Ursula were not the only ones to notice the deepening bond between John and Charles: John Gambold, their colleague in the holy club, remarked 'I never observed any person have a more real deference for another, than [Charles] had for his brother... He followed his brother entirely. Could I describe one of them, I should describe both.'[32]

It is perhaps understandable that Charles should have started to look more towards John as a role model. They were much closer in age and shared a life at Oxford that overlapped in many areas: Samuel by contrast was a married man and had left the enclosed college world behind him years before. He had been a father figure to his brother at a time when one was certainly needed and Charles no doubt felt a debt of gratitude, but the younger Wesley was no longer a schoolboy and had reached an age where placing distance between himself and his childhood was an expression of adult independence. However, there is considerable evidence to indicate that Charles's deference to

[29] CW to JW, MS letter, 5/22 June 1729 (MCA: DDCW 1/2).
[30] Samuel Wesley jun. to JW, MS letter, 6 January 1728 (MCA: DDWF 5/7).
[31] CW to JW, MS letter, 20 January 1728 (MCA: DDCW 1/1).
[32] Quoted by Tyson, *Charles Wesley*, 8.

John reached an unhealthy level and lasted for an unusually long time. It was John who persuaded Charles against his own judgement to enter the Anglican ministry in 1735,[33] and it appears that he also used emotional blackmail to pressure his younger brother to leave Oxford later that year and accompany him to Georgia.[34] As an old man looking back on his life, Charles acknowledged the extent of John's hold: 'I took my degrees; and only thought of spending all my days in Oxford: But my brother who always had the ascendancy over me, persuaded me to accompany him and Mr Oglethorpe to Georgia. I exceedingly dreaded entering into Holy Orders; but he overruled me here also.'[35]

If Samuel junior had been mildly irritated in the late 1720s by Charles's devotion to John, his unease by 1735 was so great that he attempted no disguise of his feelings. In October just before his brothers' departure overseas he wrote a scathing letter to his one-time charge:

> I knew you was not in your own power, else your common sense if not love to me would have inclined you to stay for my advice when you had once asked for it...I saw I could no more prevail on you to stay than the sirens could Ulysses...Jack [John Wesley] knew his strength and used it. His will was strong enough to bend you to go, though not me to consent. I freely own twas the will of Jack, but am not yet convinced twas the will of God.[36]

In later correspondence he accused John of stealing their brother away from him.[37] Samuel's distress was exacerbated by the fact that his brothers' departure for North America left him with sole responsibility for the upkeep of their recently widowed mother and unmarried sister Kezia, which point he was quick to point out to his brothers.[38]

Charles's apparent difficulty in asserting himself where John was concerned is all the more intriguing when one considers that he was

---

[33] CW to Dr Chandler, MS letter, 28 April 1785 (MCA: DDWes 1/38).
[34] 'You [Charles] say he [John] would not have gone without you. Was that his zeal? His apostleship? Did it depend on a younger brother's resolution?' Samuel Wesley jun. to CW, MS letter, 11 October 1735 (MCA: DDWF 5/11).
[35] CW to Dr Chandler, MS letter, 28 April 1785 (MCA: DDWes 1/38).
[36] Samuel Wesley jun. to CW, MS letter, 11 October 1735 (MCA: DDWF 5/11).
[37] 'nor will any unkindness every disturb me, after you have robbed me of Charles'. Samuel Wesley jun. to JW, MS letter, 29 April 1736 (MCA: DDWF 5/12).
[38] Ibid.

himself a naturally dominant personality. Any son of Samuel and Susanna, a Captain of Westminster School and founding member of the holy club could hardly be described as weak or retiring: indeed, the very strength of the partnership between two such powerful characters as John and Charles Wesley was to be a key component of Methodist success.

A considerable part of the explanation for the unusually strong hold that John had on his brother's loyalty can be found in the older man's charisma. John Wesley was one of that rare breed of men who can not only sway people by personality, but inspire devotion even in difficult circumstances; this facet of his character was reinforced after his Evangelical conversion in 1738, but it can be detected before that date. Such was John's magnetic quality that Richard Morgan entrusted a second son to his care even after his older boy William had died through what many, including for a time Richard himself, had believed to be the unnatural influence of the Oxford Methodists.[39] One can add the influence of the Epworth family circle—John was very like his mother in terms of personality and outlook and Charles's inability to shake off John's dominance until middle age, and then not entirely, might have its roots in the rigidity of his upbringing and the similarity between a controlling parent and brother.

OVERSEAS MISSION AND SPIRITUAL CRISIS

In December 1735 John and Charles sailed for the North American colony of Georgia. In taking this radical step, Charles appears to have been persuaded by his brother's determination to resolve spiritual doubt through immersion in a new sphere of God's work. What is clear is that Charles was deeply troubled at leaving Oxford and that he shared John's uncertainty whether he would be saved. The following passage from a letter written on the voyage reveals a man in the throes of acute depression:

God has brought me an unhappy, unthankful wretch hither, through a thousand dangers, to renew his complaints, and loathe the life which has been preserved by a series of miracles... In vain have I fled from myself to America; I still groan under the intolerable weight of inherent misery. If I

[39] Green, *The Young Mr Wesley*, 166.

have never yet repented of my undertaking, it is because I could hope for nothing better in England—or paradise. Go where I will, I carry my hell about me...[40]

If Charles had known what was in store for him, he would have had good reason to feel depressed. His stay in Georgia was extremely unhappy, marked by ill health, primitive living conditions, and quarrels with colonists who rivalled the Epworth parishioners in their dislike of High Church pretension.[41] Deeply disillusioned, Charles tendered his resignation in July 1736 and arrived back in England in December. John, who had experienced even greater disappointment, followed him just over a year later.

The brothers' failure to make an impact in the mission field added to mounting spiritual uncertainty to create a background conducive to the dramatic conversions that they experienced in the spring of 1738. More will be said in the next chapter about those events but in the specific context of the development of the brothers' relationship, it should be said that as they approached that crossroads John and Charles were in a state of almost perfect unison. At Epworth and Oxford they had been exposed to the same influences and had responded in a similar vein. John was showing himself to be the stronger character but Charles was not far removed and was equally focused on the search for personal salvation. In terms of intellect and energy the brothers were well matched and at this crucial point in their lives shared a similar perspective on the Anglican Church and the wider Christian community. They were exploring the same routes of inner focus and holy living and they both experienced at virtually the same time the personal knowledge and conviction that they would be saved by faith alone. The stage had been set for the appearance of one of the greatest of Evangelical partnerships.

THE BIRTH OF METHODISM

In the aftermath of their conversions, Charles followed John into open-air preaching and the itinerant ministry, content to defer to his brother's lead. John preached in the open air for the first time

---

[40] CW to 'Varanese' [Sarah Chapone], MS letter, 5 February 1736 (MCA: MA9725).
[41] Gill, *Charles Wesley*, 51–60; Baker, *Charles Wesley as Revealed*, 20–31.

in April 1739 and Charles joined him in this new and radical venture on 29 May. At once, the Wesleys found themselves preaching to large crowds and receiving considerable popular attention. Working initially in cooperation with their friend and fellow Oxford Methodist George Whitefield, the brothers coordinated their itinerant ministries to ensure maximum effectiveness.

In the first eighteen months of their open-air evangelism, they concentrated their attentions on Bristol, London, and the densely populated countryside between. They travelled back and forth, preaching en route, and by operating independently ensured a regular presence in both cities. Typical of this period was Charles's visit to the capital and its surrounds between 3 April and 18 June 1740[42] when he regularly preached several times a day to crowds of up to nearly ten thousand. During those months, his brother was visiting Bristol and South Wales, although he did make an unscheduled visit to the capital in April because of problems in the Fetter Lane congregation.[43] John returned to London on 5 June two weeks before Charles left to take his place in Bristol, allowing ample opportunity for consultation. John stayed in London until 1 September when he departed to join his brother in Bristol.[44] Charles's peripatetic ministry is exemplified by the twelve months from March 1740:[45] he was in Bristol and its vicinity for a total of approximately four months, London for nearly six months, and the Cardiff area for two weeks. Confirmation of the systematic nature of the brothers' itinerancy can be found in Susanna Wesley's complaint that as one of her sons arrived in London, the other left.[46] In later years, after their relationship soured, John accused his brother of not working in close harmony with him since the earliest years of their Evangelical ministry. The record of Charles's activities during the 1740s shows that this charge was the product of anger rather than recollection—during those vital early

---

[42] CWJ, 3 April–18 June 1740.
[43] John Wesley, *The Works of John Wesley*, xix. *Journal and Diaries II, 1738–1743*, ed. W. Reginald Ward and Richard Heitzenrater (Nashville: Abingdon, 1990), 146–8.
[44] Ibid. 151–66.
[45] Based on Charles's manuscript journal and correspondence.
[46] Susanna Wesley to CW, Published copy letter, 27 December 1739. Susanna Wesley, *Susanna Wesley*, 181.

years he was as active as John and their partnership was characterized by close coordination.

By the end of 1739 the Wesleys had established the first Methodist preaching houses at the New Room in Bristol and the Foundery in London.[47] These became the home of the Anglican religious societies in those two cities that placed themselves under the brothers' supervision and from this point it is possible to speak specifically of a Wesleyan movement within a wider Evangelical revival. As Methodism put down firm roots in its two early centres, the brothers began to sow the Gospel seed further afield. As early as October 1739 John embarked on a five-day preaching tour of Wales and in June 1741 he visited the Midlands at the invitation of the Countess of Huntingdon. In the spring of 1742 he made his first preaching tour of the north of England.[48] Charles was content at this stage to allow his brother to take the initiative elsewhere in the country. The fact that he looked after existing societies, principally in Bristol and London, meant that John had the luxury of being able to embark on such journeys, confident in the knowledge that his brother was keeping a close eye on Methodism in its first heartland.

It was not long before Charles was also venturing outside the initial area of activity. He spent two weeks preaching in South Wales in November 1740[49] and returned there for short visits twice the following year.[50] In late 1742 he visited the Midlands and the north of England, thereby beginning the far-reaching tours that were to be the dominant feature of his ministry during the rest of the decade. During the period 1743 to the end of 1749, Charles visited the Midlands five times; the north of England five times; Wales eight times; the southwest of England three times, and Ireland three times. Each journey typically lasted from three to eight weeks and involved preaching up to four daily sermons.[51]

The effectiveness of his personal ministry can be traced in the letters he received from devoted followers. Charles is addressed by such admiring and respectful salutations as 'Ambassador of Christ

---

[47] Heitzenrater, *Wesley and the People Called Methodists*, 103 and 109–11.
[48] Ibid. 134–7.   [49] CWJ, 6–19 November.
[50] CWJ, 13–18 July and 8–19 September 1741.
[51] For example, CWJ, 27 October 1743 and 18 May 1746.

and well-beloved in the Lord'[52] and 'My dear father in God'.[53] The tone and content of this correspondence illustrate the regard with which he was held and the deep impression made by his evangelism.[54] A considerable number of conversions were directly attributed to his labours and the concluding sentence of Margaret Austin's letter of 19 May 1740 is representative of many; 'Awakened by the Reverend Mr Whitefield: Convicted by the Reverend Mr John Wesley: Converted by the Reverend Mr Charles'.[55]

The Wesleys were both gifted preachers although John's brother appears to have had the edge in this respect. Mary Thomas wrote to Charles in May 1742 and commented on the difference, providing us with an opportunity to judge the brothers' effectiveness against their contemporary George Whitefield:

When Mr Whitefield came first to town I went to hear him, I very much approved of his doctrine. When I heard him preach the last sermon at Rosegreen and telling that there was one coming after him [John Wesley] whose shoe laces he was not worthy to unloose. I found that was he that stood by him [John Wesley]. I found great love in my heart to him after that. The first opportunity I had, I went to hear Mr John Wesley and my conscience soon told me that it was the true Gospel of Christ that he preached ... when you came first to Bristol, I seemed to like you better than your brother. I thought your way of delivery was finer than his ... [56]

While it is difficult to reach a definitive conclusion concerning the merits of one preacher over another, it is clear from the primary sources that Charles compared very well with his brother and their associates. This is all the more impressive when one remembers that Whitefield is considered by many to have been one of the great preachers of the Christian Church. John acknowledged his younger brother's strength in this area: 'You are made as it were for this very thing. Just here you are in your element. In connexion I beat you; but

---

[52] Ann Martin to CW, MS letter, 1740 (MCA: EMV 4).
[53] Maria Price to CW, MS letter, 18 May 1740 (MCA: EMV 12).
[54] For example, 'I began to pray for the 2 Mr Wesleys, *but more for that dear soul Mr Charles for he had plucked my soul out of hell and I am sure I can not forget him so long as I live.*' [Sister?] Ibison to CW, MS letter, 23 May 1740 (MCA: EMV 8).
[55] Margaret Austin to CW, MS letter, 19 May 1740 (MCA: EMV 1).
[56] Mary Thomas to CW, MS letter, 24 May 1742 (MCA: EMV 128).

in strong pointed sentences you beat me.'[57] The Methodist preacher John Pawson, who could in no wise be labelled a friend of Charles Wesley, also testified to his effectiveness: 'His word I often thought was like a two edged sword. It cut and wounded every way and few could stand before him unaffected.'[58]

Charles's contribution was particularly significant, as these first ten years of Methodism's existence were painfully difficult. The Wesleys and their followers endured persecution and engaged in fierce conflict with Calvinist Evangelicals. The controversy within the Revival and the complex question of Anglican reaction will be looked at in detail in the next chapter but suffice it to say for now that the early spirit of Evangelical cooperation was short lived and that the Methodists sorely tested Anglican patience.

Charles no less than his brother proved himself a courageous and determined man during these difficult years. In one six-month period in 1743, he reported in his journal no fewer than nine instances of obstruction, physical attack, or intimidation.[59] The entry made on 18 July 1743 is representative:

> When we came to the place of battle, the enemy was ready, set in array against us. I began the 100th psalm and they beating their drum and shouting. I stood still and silent for some time... then offered to speak to some of the most violent; but they stopped their ears and ran upon me crying I should not preach there, and catching at me to pull me down. They had no power to touch me... I shook off the dust of my feet and walked leisurely through the thickest of them, who followed like ramping and roaring lions...[60]

This fortitude in the face of adversity represented the positive side of the uncompromising and principled character that Charles inherited from his father. His leadership in the face of physical danger was an example to the people around him and bolstered their own commitment. Here he was not simply John's loyal subordinate, but a role model in his own right.

---

[57] JW to CW, MS letter, 27 June 1766 (MCA: DDWes 3/27).
[58] Quoted by Luke Tyerman, MS folio entitled 'Copies of Original Letters and other Documents relating to Methodism collected from various sources', 19th century (MCA: MS 657B), 71.
[59] CWJ, 15 January–28 June 1743.   [60] CWJ, 18 July 1743.

METHODIST WORSHIP MODELS AND PASTORAL OVERSIGHT

Open-air preaching was only one of the foundation blocks of early Methodism. Had it not been for the fact that this was allied to the development of a sophisticated administrative and pastoral framework, the Wesleys would have left no more lasting legacy than did George Whitefield. The years from 1739 to 1744 saw the introduction of the most important features of Methodist organization and worship, such as the society, the love feast, band and class meetings, lay preaching, and the Conference.

Charles Wesley's specific contribution to this process has not been documented in detail, which is understandable as there is no evidence to indicate that he was personally responsible for any major innovation. However, it should not be forgotten that the same applies to his brother. It is difficult to think of one major feature of Methodist practice that was not borrowed from other denominations, or suggested by individuals other than the Wesleys.[61] The love feast and the bands were taken from the Moravians;[62] the religious society originated within the Anglican Church and was again influenced by the Moravians; while the class system and quarterly meetings were the suggestions of Captain Foy and John Bennet respectively.[63] Lay preaching appears to have been a spontaneous development and was at first opposed by John Wesley,[64] while the Conference was a logical result of the need for deliberation. This is not to diminish the significance of the brothers for they were the driving force behind the adoption of such measures. Their energy and foresight was crucial to the very existence of Methodism while their ability to utilize the talents of others was proof of their capacity for leadership.

Charles Wesley was no radical innovator, but he did have a vital role to play in the working out of the Wesleyan Methodist system.

---

[61] 'He [JW] may have lacked a creative mind, but he was a genius at adaptation, a masterly opportunist, an inspired borrower.' Vivian Green, *John Wesley* (London: Thomas Nelson & Sons, 1964), 155.

[62] *A Dictionary of Methodism in Britain and Ireland*, ed. John A. Vickers (Peterborough: Epworth, 2000), 18 and 213.

[63] Ibid. 69 and 286.   [64] Rack, *Reasonable Enthusiast*, 210–11.

The Shared Ministry of John and Charles 37

Little record survives of discussions between the brothers regarding the introduction of administrative structures and forms of worship, but it is inconceivable that such conversations did not take place, given the closeness of their ministries. Charles, no less than his brother, was instrumental in the imposition of discipline and practice. His tours of the country were not just about preaching, but were also concerned with inspection and examination—as important as active evangelism for the consolidation of faith. Mary Thomas's letter of 1742 provides us with an illustration of this aspect of his work:

> You ordered the society to come and speak with you which I found a great grief to me for I was ashamed to think I was no better but I came as I was and you asked me if I was justified and I said no, you told me I was in a state of damnation which words pierced my heart though it were what I had heard many times yet it never pierced my heart so much as it did then.[65]

Charles's journal contains many other examples of this close and uncompromising attention to pastoral oversight; one such entry occurs on 28 June 1740: 'Met the bands in Kingswood and reproved Hannah Barrow before them all. She would not be convinced of her pride; but was *sure* she had the witness of the spirit and the seal and what not. I tremble to think what will be the end.'[66] Such strict spiritual examination was a vital aid to conversion and one that the brothers had learned to value at Epworth and Oxford.

The initial awakening by means of a sermon was simply the first step in a process that could last for years as Methodists were taught to view their spiritual road as a rock-strewn path marked by certain clear pointers towards salvation. Conversion testimonies tend to show the same identifiable stages, as the individual was first convinced of his or her damned condition, received assurance of God's saving grace and was finally purged of sin. The following excerpts of a letter of May 1742 from Elizabeth Sayse to Charles illustrate the several stages in this quest for salvation:

> About five years ago, I went to hear Mr Whitefield preach...and thought that strange things were brought to my ears...but my understanding was not opened...when Mr [John] Wesley came, I went to hear him in Nicholas

---

[65] Mary Thomas to CW, MS letter, 24 May 1742 (MCA: EMV 128).
[66] CWJ, 28 June 1740.

Street Society but at that time the Word had little effect on me. But at his preaching at Clifton Church the Word came very sweet and with power and I shed tears... I went constantly to the Societies... When you expounded on Isaiah, it all seemed very sweet, but when you... said that we deserved to be damned, I thought I might be excepted... But soon after I saw that my inward parts were very wickedness... In this state I continued for several weeks... until it pleased God... in great mercy passed by me... and said unto me Live; which was at your repeating the 11th verse of the XXXIII chapter of Ezekiel... I gladly received the exhortation and could with great joy testify, that I had redemption in his blood.[67]

Such testimonies make it clear that Charles Wesley made a real difference to people's lives. He may in fact have been better suited than his brother to guide people through the difficult transition associated with the 'new birth'—John was often criticized for attaching too much credence to spiritual claims, particularly when relating to sanctification.[68] Charles on the other hand showed a keen awareness of the potential pitfalls of charismatic Christianity. This is illustrated by an entry from his journal for 8 June 1743:

[I] spoke to the bands severally and tried if their faith could bear shaking. We have certainly been too rash and easy in allowing persons for believers on their own testimony; nay and even persuading them into a false opinion of themselves. Some souls tis doubtless necessary to encourage; but it should be done with the utmost caution—To tell one in darkness, he has faith, is to keep him in darkness still, or to make him trust in a false light a faith that stands in the words of men, not in the power of God.[69]

The criticism of John may have been implied on that occasion, but on 5 February 1743 Charles left no doubt as to his awareness of his brother's naivety:

One among the classes told my brother she had a constant sense of forgiveness and he let her pass. I could not help proving her farther: and then the justified sinner appeared full of the gall of bitterness, said again and again, of a sister present, 'I do not love her, I hate her' etc. I assured her, if an angel from heaven told me she was justified, I would not believe him; for she was a murderer. As such we prayed for her... I fear we have many such believers among us.[70]

[67] Elizabeth Sayse to CW, MS letter, May 1742 (MCA: EMV 126).
[68] Rack, *Reasonable Enthusiast*, 541.   [69] CWJ, 8 June 1743.
[70] CWJ, 5 February 1743.

The Shared Ministry of John and Charles

This subtle difference between the brothers had little practical significance when their ministries were complementary, but it does illustrate the important point that Charles was not blind to John's faults. Throughout the decade of the 1740s, John remained the dominant partner but his younger brother was starting to show signs of frustration with the balance of their relationship. One of Charles's letters to John from July 1746 documents very well these twin aspects:

> I find it utterly in vain to write to you upon anything whereon we are not already agreed. Either you set aside the whole by the short answer that I am in an ill humour, or take no notice at all of my reasons, but plead conscience. [I] have so little success in my remonstrances that I have many times resolved never to contradict your judgement as to any one thing or person.[71]

This undercurrent of latent rebellion was the herald to bitter clashes in later years.

Charles was equally devoted to other aspects of pastoral care. When not engaged in preaching or leading worship, he was regularly to be found with the sick and dying,[72] visiting prisons,[73] and accompanying condemned convicts to their execution.[74] His deep determination to evangelize in all conditions and circumstances is illustrated by an encounter that enlivened Charles's journey to London by public coach on 27 July 1738:

> I preached faith in Christ. A lady was extremely offended, avowed her own merits in plain terms; asked if I was not a Methodist; threatened to beat me. I declared I deserved nothing but hell; so did she; and must confess it before she could have a title to heaven. This was most intolerable to her. The others were less offended... a maid servant devoured every word.[75]

Charles Wesley made a vital contribution to the birth and consolidation of the Methodist movement. Energetic, courageous, and blessed with keen spiritual insight, he was a brilliant servant of Christ and an equal partner to his brother in the hard and dangerous work of the Revival. The fact that there were two Wesleys working in close concert gave them a tremendous advantage over other Evangelicals. The lasting value of Charles's poetry is well recognized, but it is

---

[71] CW to JW, MS letter [15 July 1746] (MCA: DDCW 6/12).
[72] For example, CWJ, 14 May 1741 and 29 September 1744.
[73] For example, CWJ, 7 November 1738 and 9 September 1741.
[74] For example, CWJ, 12 September 1741.   [75] CWJ, 27 July 1738.

worth remembering that most people during the early years would have known Charles better as a preacher, pastor, and leader. What Charles's contribution meant to John on a personal level will now be examined.

THE PERSONAL BOND BETWEEN THE WESLEY BROTHERS

John Wesley throughout his life had few people with whom he was truly intimate. He was in certain respects an insensitive, almost inhuman figure, somewhat removed in important respects from the popular and persistent image of the Methodist leader as a saintly patriarch. Brought up in an atmosphere of strict control and entire subordination to the will of God, John had difficulty in sustaining close personal relationships.[76] His marriage to Mary Vazeille was as much a casualty of his absolute refusal to be swayed from his chosen path as it was of her emotional insecurity. John's correspondence contains several instances of his inability to relate to the feelings of others. One such was sent in November 1742 to his sister Martha upon the death of her last surviving child: 'I believe the death of your children is a great instance of the goodness of God towards you. You have often mentioned to me how much of your time they took up. Now that time is restored to you, and you have nothing to do but to serve our Lord without carefulness and without distraction.'[77] This disturbing level of emotional detachment may have been a result of the Wesleys' upbringing. Maser comments on the lack of love within the family[78]—the children were imbued with the virtues of duty, loyalty, and obedience, but not necessarily of love, either of one another or of other people. This aspect of John Wesley did not escape contemporary comment: John Hampson, a former Wesleyan itinerant made the intriguing charge that Wesley's much-praised philanthropy stemmed more from a sense of Christian duty than genuine

---

[76] Rack, *Reasonable Enthusiast*, 542.
[77] JW to Martha Hall, Published copy letter, 17 November 1742. John Wesley, *The Works of John Wesley*, xxvi. 90–1.
[78] 'Fundamentally, both Susanna and Samuel, Sr. seemed to lack the spirit of love...one cannot help but feel that both lacked that warmth of love and human understanding.' Maser, *Seven Sisters*, 111.

compassion.[79] Hampson was alienated from the Methodists when he wrote those words, but John's insensitivity is well documented from other sources, including his own pen. Hampson also stated that John 'had no attachments, so far as we have been able to discover, that partook of the genius of friendship. His regard for some individuals, proceeded less from personal, than from public considerations. All his views were of this kind. His first object, was the success of Methodism.'[80]

John Wesley's isolation was exacerbated by his leadership position. He brooked no rival and therefore tolerated no intimate. It is perhaps no coincidence that on the few occasions that he shared his feelings it tended to be with women,[81] which was a reflection both of the female-dominated Epworth household and also perhaps of the fact that women could not challenge his leadership. The one exception was his brother in the twenty years from their time at Oxford until Charles's marriage in 1749. During that momentous period the two forged a seemingly unbreakable bond founded on a common background, education, and spiritual mission. In some respects they were temperamentally alike, as one would expect from brothers; they were fearless, energetic, and completely devoted to the work of God and both possessed an unshakeable will where principle was involved. They also inherited their father's temper, but whereas Charles periodically exploded, John was a master of control both of himself and others.[82]

The talents of the brothers were complementary. John was the supreme organizer and master of detail, driving and inspiring his followers to superhuman efforts. Charles's particular strengths appear to have been those of a preacher and pastor, although he too displayed a capacity for practical leadership and a remarkable commitment to unstinting travel and hard work. He could have been pre-eminent in his own right but was instead the perfect colleague; the brothers' special relationship ensured that Charles could be relied upon to remain loyal and be a confidant as well as a sturdy right hand.[83] He

---

[79] Hampson, *John Wesley*, iii. 199.   [80] Ibid.
[81] Rack, *Reasonable Enthusiast*, 545; Green, *John Wesley*, 127.
[82] 'A remarkable feature in Mr Wesley's character, was his placidity. His temper was naturally warm and impetuous. Religion had, in a great degree, corrected this; though it was by no means eradicated.' Hampson, *John Wesley*, iii. 179.
[83] 'John, despite disagreements, always tended to be more candid about his inner life in his letters to Charles than to anyone else.' Rack, *Reasonable Enthusiast*, 251.

was the Agrippa to John Wesley's Augustus and for all John's searching in his later years, he never found anyone who could quite fill the place that his brother had once occupied.

John Wesley was not one for revealing his innermost feelings and the letter that he wrote to William Holland on 6 February 1748 has particular significance as an evaluation of his brother's worth in the tenth year of the Revival and little more than twelve months before their relationship changed forever: 'The plain reason why I bless our Lord daily for the assistance of my brother Charles is because I know him to be an able minister of the New Testament, of the spirit which maketh alive, and one that exercises himself to have a conscience void of offence toward God and toward man.'[84] In this concise testimonial, John summarized Charles's outstanding contribution to the birth of Methodism and hinted at his own heartfelt appreciation of his brother's support. It is a warmer eulogy than the one that he was to give on the occasion of Charles's death forty years later, but it is noticeable that his praise is stated entirely with regard to ministerial value. For Charles's importance on a personal level, one must turn to a letter written to another layman just over a year later in October 1749 in the immediate aftermath of the first serious storm in the brothers' relationship: 'To you, therefore, I can freely speak my mind, as knowing it will go no further. Since I was six years old I never met with such a severe trial as for some days past...the whole world fought against me; but above all my own familiar friend...'[85]

After 1749, John Wesley never again enjoyed a relationship with anyone that was as special as that which he had once shared with his brother. His detachment became complete, a man who in Green's memorable words was 'granite in aspic'.[86] Charles was also damaged by their alienation and although he was to find domestic contentment with a woman whom he loved deeply, he too missed the old intimacy with John. The extent of the pain and hurt that this breakdown caused to both men and the significant ways that their mistrust impacted on Methodism will form an important theme of the rest of this book.

[84] JW to William Holland, Published copy letter, 6 February 1748. John Wesley, *The Works of John Wesley*, xxvi. 278.
[85] JW to Thomas Bigg, Published copy letter, 7 October 1749. John Wesley, *The Works of John Wesley*, xxvi. 388–9.
[86] Green, *John Wesley*, 127.

3

Cooperation, Conflict, and Controversy During the Early Years of the Revival

The ten years from 1739 witnessed an extraordinary explosion in popular religion as a tidal wave of revival swept the British Isles. At the start of this period the Wesley brothers were not regarded as pre-eminent leaders but were rather members of a small group of predominantly young Anglican clergymen who commenced an itinerant ministry at about the same time. Several of these men, such as Benjamin Ingham and George Whitefield, had been associated with the Wesleys in the holy club, but there were others who had no Oxford connection. In Wales, the curate of Llangeitho Daniel Rowland and the layman Howell Harris embarked on mass evangelism in 1735–6 before Whitefield and the Wesleys commenced field preaching and independently of them. Rowland and Harris owed their inspiration to the Anglican minister Griffith Jones who had preached in the open air as early as 1714. Further afield in New England, what Americans term the 'Great Awakening' started in 1734–5 with the work of the Congregationalist Jonathan Edwards, while in Germany the growth of Pietism paved the way for the widespread adoption of its particular brand of religious renewal in Britain and North America.

The fact that the first stirrings of revival were not confined to one place or orchestrated by a single individual or group helps to account for its rapid expansion from several points of local origin over a wide geographical area from Central Europe to the Eastern seaboard of North America. Historians continue to debate the diffuse origins of the Revival and the extent of the mutual influence and interaction of its various agents, but the important point to note here is that John and Charles Wesley were not its creators or its leading lights in those very early years. By 1760 however, the brothers were firmly established as the principal exponents of Evangelical religion in Britain and Ireland and were advancing down a road that was to see Wesleyan Methodism acknowledged as the Revival's most important legacy.

There were several keys to this personal success, such as organizational ability and preaching skills, but these features were not unique to the Wesleys. All the main branches of the Revival in Britain were built on the foundation of a highly effective preaching ministry.[1] Nor was the system that the brothers imposed on their followers very much different in its fundamental character from that adopted by other Evangelical groups. The Wesleyans, Moravians, and Calvinistic Methodists all developed on similar lines, relying to a considerable extent on the basic structure of society, and small cell group. The same organizational and worship terms occur across the Evangelical spectrum such as love feast, band, society, and 'preaching house', which helps to explain the eighteenth-century tendency to group all Evangelicals together under the 'catch-all' term Methodist. It was only towards the end of the period that Methodism and Wesley became virtually synonymous. One facet that did set the Wesleys apart from their contemporaries was their unusually forceful leadership style. To their array of other talents was added an uncompromising and at times ruthless imposition of personal authority and this proved fundamental in the formation of a specific Wesleyan Methodist identity. The brothers' exceptional drive enabled them to establish and lead a movement that by the end of their lives had overshadowed other Evangelical groups in their native islands and was starting to spread across the rest of the English-speaking world.

At the same time as stamping their imprint on the Revival, the Wesleys also clashed with champions of their own denomination inimical to what was viewed as undisciplined and theologically dangerous enthusiasm. The troubled decade of the 1740s saw division between old friends and colleagues within Evangelical ranks and also with

[1] The Moravians were opposed to an outdoor preaching ministry but were not averse to taking over societies established by that means. Podmore argues convincingly that the English Moravian Church in 1760 was almost entirely based on the pioneering efforts of just four field preachers. Colin Podmore, *The Moravian Church in England, 1728–1760* (Oxford: Clarendon, 1998), 97–9.

Anglicans who reacted violently against this disturbing phenomenon. The Wesleys were in the frontline of both these battles and were often not only the initiators of conflict, but the beneficiaries of it, as confrontation gave shape and definition to their movement and promoted its public image. This chapter will examine the part played by Charles and his brother in the controversies of these stormy but singularly fruitful years.

The three main bodies of British Evangelical opinion were represented by the Arminianism of the Wesleys, the Calvinist wing led chiefly by George Whitefield, and the Moravians, whose supporters included the Anglican ministers Benjamin Ingham and John Gambold. In looking at the differences that shattered Evangelical unity, it is necessary to detail some of the defining characteristics of these groups and the close albeit uncomfortable relationship between them.

THE MORAVIANS

The Moravians were one of the driving forces behind the birth of the Revival in England, possessing an influence that far outweighed their numbers. In the words of one recent authority:

Without the Moravians, English Church history would have been very different. It was the influence of a Moravian, Peter Böhler, that prompted the heart-warming experience, which transformed John Wesley from a tortured High-Church Oxford don into a revivalist leader, and it was from the Fetter Lane Society which Böhler founded that the Revival burst out in 1739.[2]

The Moravians or *Unitas Fratrum* as they are more properly termed originated in what is now Czechoslovakia as an offshoot of the fifteenth-century Hussite reformation. After centuries of persecution, they were driven from their homeland and in 1722 found a refuge on the German estate of the Lutheran Count Zinzendorf.[3] Under his wing the demoralized refugees were organized into a new religious society with beliefs and practice that were influenced by Pietist concern with holy living coupled with a classic Lutheran emphasis on justification by faith.[4] This does not appear to have marked a radical

[2] Ibid. 1.   [3] Ibid. 5–6.   [4] Ibid. 16–17.

break with the Moravians' own religious past but rather represented in some measure a return to sixteenth-century practice.[5] Imbued with confidence by their institutional reawakening, Moravian representatives made several visits to England between 1728 and 1737.[6] Their intention was not the planting of congregations in Britain itself, but rather the establishment of fellowship with other Christians and to request permission to participate in the Georgia colony.

The Moravians found a warm welcome in Britain where their proud Protestant lineage and experience of recent persecution aroused a mixture of respect and sympathy. There were also developments in London in which the Moravians themselves could show a keen fraternal interest. The Anglican religious societies pioneered years before were focal points of grass-roots spirituality, and their concern with personal holiness represented common ground with the German visitors. Also, several former Oxford Methodists were active as ordained Anglican ministers in and around the city.[7] These men brought with them from university their own experience of a pietistic pursuit of Godliness nourished by deep meditation in small groups. Present in the capital were several ingredients of revival, for which the Moravians were to provide a catalyst.

Moravian influence over the Wesleys is well known. The first encounter occurred during the voyage to Georgia where the Germans' humility, seriousness, and faith made a deep impact on John Wesley.[8] Charles's first impressions are more difficult to gauge as his extant journal begins only in March 1736 and he makes little mention of the Moravians until his return home from America at the end of that year. In London on 19 January 1737 Charles met Count Zinzendorf and four days later was introduced to Bishop Nitschman.[9] In the weeks

---

[5] 'Zinzendorf came across accounts of the discipline and practices of the Unitas Fratrum by Comenius (1592–1670)...and discovered similarities with the system he had established.' Podmore, *The Moravian Church in England*, 6.

[6] Ibid. 8–28.

[7] In addition to the Wesleys themselves who were frequent visitors after their return from North America, Thomas Broughton was the curate of the Tower and George Whitefield served a curacy in London for two months in 1736. Ibid. 35.

[8] For example, JWJ, 25 January 1736. John Wesley, *The Works of John Wesley*, xviii. *Journals and Diaries I, 1735–1738*, ed. Reginald Ward and Richard Heitzenrater (Nashville: Abingdon, 1988), 142–3.

[9] CWJ, 19 and 23 January 1737.

that followed he was involved in discussions concerning the Moravian role in the Georgia colony;[10] inevitably, he also conversed with the Germans on spiritual matters and was struck by their piety and the atmosphere of their worship.[11]

The Wesley brothers came increasingly under German Pietist influence in the months leading up to their conversions. They had returned from North America full of self-doubt and were unusually susceptible to outside influence. After his own arrival back in England in February 1738, John had several meetings with the Moravian Peter Böhler and his preaching began to feature typical Pietist themes such as justification and the new birth.[12] Charles was also introduced to Böhler and on 20 February 1738 started to help his new friend to learn English.[13] Through such contacts Charles was drawn deeper into Moravian spirituality and came to accept the importance of salvation by faith alone, although he was initially reluctant to accept any critique of his own spiritual state.[14] On 11 May he had his first encounter with John Bray, who was in Charles's words 'a poor ignorant mechanic who knows nothing but Christ'.[15] Bray was to be the agent of Charles's conversion and while he was not formally a Moravian, was very much guided by their beliefs. It is not surprising therefore that Charles's conversion on 21 May 1738 was expressed in terms that Moravians would have expected from their own converts: 'I saw that by faith I stood; by the continual support of faith, which kept me from falling though of myself I am ever sinking into sin.'[16] John Wesley's more famous Aldersgate experience followed a few days later and the language used to describe that event is again indicative of Moravian influence.[17]

Several weeks before these conversions, another significant event took place, namely the founding of the Fetter Lane congregation. This came about when several members of London's religious societies

---

[10] For example, CWJ, 1 February 1737.
[11] 'I was present at their public services, and thought myself in a quire of angels', CWJ, 23 January 1737.
[12] Rack, *Reasonable Enthusiast*, 138.   [13] CWJ, 20 February 1738.
[14] 'Some time ago I had taken leave of P. Böhler, confessed my unbelief and want of forgiveness, but declared my firm persuasion that I should receive the atonement before I died.' CWJ, 11 May 1738.
[15] Ibid.   [16] CWJ, 21 May 1738.
[17] Podmore, *The Moravian Church in England*, 42.

began to meet for the purpose of fellowship. On 1 May 1738, it was decided on Böhler's advice to form a new group consisting of certain select members including John Wesley.[18] Rules and worship practices were adopted based on Moravian models, such as the band, the love feast, and an emphasis on mutual confession.[19] The Fetter Lane Society represented a grafting of Moravian practices onto a predominantly Anglican membership and constituted an important halfway point in the evolution of what became Methodism.

As harmonious as relations appeared to be in the summer of 1738, the roots of division can be detected. The Wesley brothers accepted certain Moravian teachings and were impressed by aspects of their organization, but they remained Anglican clergymen and unaccustomed to play a secondary role in spiritual matters to foreigners and laymen. Suspicion and resentment of outside influence quickly surfaced. Ironically, the fact that the Germans did not exercise direct control of the Fetter Lane congregation exacerbated the situation, as some of their English followers started to interpret doctrine in a more extreme fashion than the Moravians themselves. Early in 1739, a section of the society started to display tendencies to separation from the Church of England and Charles Wesley felt constrained to warn against any such move.[20] At the end of April there was an outbreak of lay preaching, inspired by the argument of the layman John Shaw in favour of the priesthood of all believers, and within a short space of time the Fetter Lane Society experienced its first schism.[21]

Concurrent with these developments was the emergence of a serious theological difference. The Moravians taught that those without faith should refrain from striving for it as this could impede the workings of the Holy Spirit: excessive prayer, Bible reading, and even regular Communion should therefore be avoided. People should instead remain 'still' and wait for the gift of faith.[22] Again, certain members at Fetter Lane took this doctrine to an extreme, influenced by the teachings of the French Prophets whose charismatic practices

---

[18] Heitzenrater, *Wesley and the People Called Methodists*, 79.
[19] Rack, *Reasonable Enthusiast*, 141.   [20] CWJ, 28 February 1739.
[21] Podmore, *The Moravian Church in England*, 53.   [22] Ibid. 60.

were gaining supporters in London's volatile religious atmosphere.[23] To the Wesleys, stillness was a denial of the function of the Church and raised the spectre of antinomianism; the situation was not helped when the Bishop of London warned them on this specific point.[24] The controversy led ultimately to the Wesleys leaving Fetter Lane with their supporters in July 1740.[25]

Theological differences apart, it is debatable how long the Moravians and the Wesleys could have worked in close collaboration. The Germans were hostile to the concept of active evangelism, particularly the practice of open-air preaching,[26] and this fundamental difference in approach must in time have led to a parting of the ways. It is also difficult to escape the conclusion that John Wesley's inability to tolerate rivals had a part to play. He was critical of the Moravians as early as September 1738,[27] and the following month German visitors to Fetter Lane commented on his 'reserved and secretive' reaction to them.[28]

In the aftermath of the division, Moravian attempts at rapprochement were rejected, despite their acceptance that the Fetter Lane leadership had been at fault.[29] In March 1741 Charles referred to his brother's ambition; 'Are you not afraid lest they [the Moravians] should eclipse your own glory, or lessen your own praise?'[30] Despite this criticism, his own alienation from the Germans and their English supporters had kept pace with that of his brother. On 7 January 1739 Charles expressed discontent at some of the 'orders which Bray etc were imposing on the society'.[31] He was particularly concerned by some of the mystical leanings of his Fetter Lane associates—on 11 December 1738 he carried out an impromptu exorcism of a convert

---

[23] The French Prophets began to urge abstention from Communion on those who had received the gift of faith, which was certainly something the Moravians did not teach. Ibid. 62–3.

[24] CWJ, 21 February 1739.

[25] Podmore, *The Moravian Church in England*, 70.   [26] Ibid. 54.

[27] JW to the Moravians, Published copy letter [27–8] September 1738. John Wesley, *The Works of John Wesley*, xxv. *Letters I, 1721–1739*, ed. Frank Baker (Oxford: Clarendon, 1980), 566–7.

[28] Quoted by Podmore, *The Moravian Church in England*, 44.

[29] Ibid. 73–4.

[30] CW to JW, Published copy letter [10 March 1741]. John Wesley, *The Works of John Wesley* xxvi. 53.

[31] CWJ, 7 January 1739.

to the French Prophets[32] and the following month tried to persuade his fellow clergyman George Stonehouse to 'throw away his mystics'.[33] The fact that he objected to trends within the Fetter Lane membership on a point that was of particular concern to him shows that he was not simply falling into line with John. The question of public lay ministry was also raised several times, with Charles and John vehemently opposed to lay administration of the Sacraments.[34]

The Wesley brothers were quickly outgrowing their original Evangelical circle. They were preaching in the open air by the spring of 1739 and before the end of that year opened the New Room in Bristol and commenced work on the Foundery in London. The astonishing success of this public ministry would have reinforced their natural leanings towards an independent course. The Moravians had in effect outlived their usefulness, although it should also be said that the brothers retained admiration for aspects of the *Unitas Fratrum*.[35]

GEORGE WHITEFIELD AND THE ARMINIAN–CALVINIST SPLIT

Theological differences and a considerable element of personal rivalry were also at the centre of the conflict between the Wesleys and their old friend George Whitefield. This particular division, even more than the split with the Moravians, was one of the defining moments in Methodist history. In its aftermath the Revival as a mass movement divided and the Wesleys emerged from Whitefield's shadow. It also illustrates in clear fashion the brothers' ruthless handling of real or potential rivals.

George Whitefield was a younger contemporary of the Wesleys at Oxford and a fellow member of the holy club. He began his meteoric rise to fame in 1736 when sermons preached during a short-lived curacy in London, some on the Pietist theme of the 'New Birth',

---

[32] CWJ, 11 December 1738. [33] CWJ, 2 January 1739.
[34] CWJ, 17 April 1739.
[35] Podmore, *The Moravian Church in England*, 75–8.

caused a major stir.[36] No stranger to controversy, Whitefield found himself barred from many pulpits after his return from Georgia in December 1738.[37] The roots of this hostility can be traced back to his earlier London ministry, the popularity of which had aroused jealousy on the part of other clergymen:[38] his high-profile fund-raising for charity schools and the Georgia poor also provoked suspicion of his integrity in certain quarters.[39] Whitefield should bear part of the blame for the bad feeling that he inspired. In the preface to his printed sermon of 1738 on *The New Birth*, he expressed the hope that his fellow clergymen would start to preach more like him and 'that they would not, out of a servile fear of displeasing particular persons, fail to declare the whole will of God'.[40] This statement from a minister who was only in his early twenties caused quite a few hackles to rise and is an early example of the insensitivity amounting to spiritual arrogance that was to be a feature of many Evangelicals, including the Wesleys. Whitefield's popularity reached even greater heights after he preached in the open air for the first time in February 1739[41] and within a few months his sermons were attracting crowds of up to ten thousand.[42]

Just as the Moravians inspired the Wesleys to pursue their own spiritual path, so Whitefield was the prime mover in pushing the brothers towards a mass ministry. John and Charles preached their first open-air sermons in England after observing Whitefield at first hand and he introduced them to audiences in and around Bristol and London. He also placed his societies under John Wesley's direction prior to his return to North America in August 1739.[43] How close the three evangelists were in the early years of the Revival is revealed by the testimony of lay converts—letters from the period 1739–40 regularly refer to hearing the Wesleys and Whitefield preach in relatively quick succession. For example, Mary Ramsey of London heard Whitefield for the first time on 2 June 1739, after which

---

[36] Arnold Dallimore, *George Whitefield; The Life and Times of the Great Evangelist of the 18th Century Revival*, 2 vols. (Edinburgh: Banner of Truth Trust, 1970), i. 104–5 and 124.
[37] Ibid. 218–19.   [38] Ibid. 134–6.
[39] 'Some called me a spiritual pick-pocket and others thought I used some kind of charm to get the people's money.' Quoted ibid. 135.
[40] Quoted ibid. 134.   [41] Ibid. 254–6.   [42] Ibid. 263.
[43] Ibid. 389.

she regularly attended his sermons; she heard John Wesley on 4 September that same year and periodically thereafter; and she first attended on Charles Wesley's preaching at an unspecified date in February or March 1740. As Ramsay said, 'I can but admire the wisdom of God in seeing how he sends out the labourers one after the other.'[44]

Whitefield's ardent recommendation of the Wesleys is also mentioned in the primary sources. In a letter of 24 May 1742 Mary Thomas recalled hearing Whitefield preach three years earlier at Rose Green in Bristol and his referring to 'one coming after him whose shoe laces he was not worthy to unloose':[45] John Wesley is not specifically named in the letter although other sources make the identification certain.[46] One might almost say that the Wesleys entered mass evangelism on Whitefield's coat-tails and at the very least they benefited from close association. It is important to note that at this early stage in the Revival, Whitefield was without doubt its principal exponent in England. The subsequent eclipse of his reputation by that of John Wesley was the product of a combination of factors that included the older man's superior powers of organization, his focus on a national as opposed to a transatlantic ministry and the tendency of some historians to concentrate on Wesley to the virtual exclusion of his contemporaries.[47]

Despite the close personal ties between the three men, the first stirrings of controversy were not slow to appear. The fundamental difference was theological in nature, with coal heaped upon the flames by the Wesleys' forcefulness. Whitefield was a proponent of the Calvinist doctrine of predestination, which at its most fundamental stated that God saved only a part of mankind, termed 'the elect'. Whitefield argued that holiness was a mark of election and that because we do not know the identity of these chosen few, the Christian message must be made available to all. The Wesleys held

---

[44] Mary Ramsay to CW, MS letter, 4 June 1740 (MCA: EMV 13).
[45] Mary Thomas to CW, MS letter, 24 May 1742 (MCA: EMV 128).
[46] Dallimore, *George Whitefield*, i. 274.
[47] 'Wesley and his biographers never really did him [George Whitefield] justice and indeed tended to obscure the fact, very obvious in contemporary accounts, that Whitefield and not Wesley was seen by the public as the real leader of the movement at this stage.' Rack, *Reasonable Enthusiast*, 191.

the diametrically opposing view that salvation is freely offered to everyone and that each individual ultimately has the choice of heaven or hell. In their teaching of this doctrine, the brothers followed in the footsteps of the Dutch theologian Jacob Arminius (1560–1609), which is why the Wesleys and their followers were sometimes termed 'Arminian' Methodists. The brothers were extremely hostile to Whitefield's doctrine of 'election', claiming that its logical conclusion was the invalidation of preaching, as the elect are predetermined. This dispute became the great theological battleground of the Revival, one that divided families and destroyed friendships.

A short time before their difference in opinion became public in the spring of 1739 Whitefield was expressing concern over what he rightly perceived to be a gathering storm in relations with his old friends and college mentors. In a letter to the layman James Hutton, John Wesley reported:

> our brother Whitefield here [Bristol], and our brother Chapman since, had conjured me to enter into no disputes, least of all concerning predestination, because this people were so deeply prejudiced for it. The same was my own inclination. But this evening [23 April] I received a long letter...charging me roundly with 'resisting and perverting the truth as in Jesus' by preaching against God's decree of predestination. I had not done so yet, but I questioned whether I ought not now to declare the whole counsel of God.[48]

This formed the background to arguably the most important sermon that John Wesley ever preached, namely that on 'Free Grace', delivered in Bristol on 29 April 1739. In this work, Wesley launched a blistering attack on predestination, describing it as blasphemy for its representation of 'the most Holy God as worse than the devil; as both more false, more cruel, and more unjust'.[49] Without naming Whitefield, Wesley declared his intention to 'join issue with every asserter of it'[50] and pressed the matter further by publishing the sermon just a few weeks later.[51] It is indicative of Wesley's insensitivity that he saw nothing wrong in joining Whitefield in open-air preaching in London,

---

[48] JW to James Hutton and the Fetter Lane Society, Published copy letter, 30 April 1739. John Wesley, *The Works of John Wesley*, xxv. 639.
[49] John Wesley, *The Works of John Wesley*, iii. *Sermons III, 71–114*, ed. Albert Outler (Nashville: Abingdon, 1986), 555.
[50] Ibid. 556.   [51] Ibid. 542.

six weeks after he had described his friend's views as blasphemy.[52] Whitefield, who was apparently unaware of events in Bristol,[53] expressed pleasure at introducing his 'honoured and revered friend' to a large crowd at Blackheath.[54]

After Wesley's return to Bristol, Whitefield learned of the sermon on 'Free Grace' and wrote what could be considered in the circumstances a mild letter of protest.[55] During his absence in North America, he continued to plead with Wesley to avoid controversy,[56] but his supporters in England were not so reluctant to take up the gauntlet. The talented lay preacher John Cennick emerged as the champion of the Calvinist wing of the Revival in Whitefield's absence. He clashed with the Wesleys in public[57] and after a period of rising tension, abandoned his connection with the brothers in March 1741.[58]

Charles's views on predestination were perfectly in accord with those of his brother,[59] and the role that he played in the controversy was no less significant. In his journal, he testifies to his own forbearance[60] and regret at controversy[61] yet failed to acknowledge the connection between his opponents' anger and the content of his own sermons. These included a particularly controversial effort preached on the occasion of the death of the Calvinistic Methodist William Seward in 1740. Charles took the opportunity provided by

---

[52] JWJ, 14 June 1739. John Wesley, *The Works of John Wesley*, xix. 69.
[53] Dallimore, *George Whitefield*, i. 315.
[54] George Whitefield, *George Whitefield's Journals* (London: The Banner of Truth Trust, 1960), 288.
[55] 'I hear, Honoured Sir, that you are about to print a sermon against predestination. It shocks me to think of it! What will be the consequences but controversy? If people ask my opinion, what shall I do?... Silence on both sides will be best. It is noised abroad already that there is a division between you and me, and my heart within me is grieved.' Quoted by Dallimore, *George Whitefield*, i. 315.
[56] Ibid. 571–4.   [57] For example, CWJ, 4 November 1740.
[58] JWJ, 6 March 1741.
[59] For example, 'who can stand before envy, bigotry and predestination?' CWJ, 30 November 1740.
[60] 'Had a Conference in K. [Kingswood] with Mr Cennick and his friends but could come to no agreement, though I offered entirely to drop the controversy if he would.' CWJ, 2 December 1740.
[61] 'I acknowledged the Grace given to our dear Brother [Howell] Harris and excused his estrangement from me through the wickedness of his Counsellors.' CWJ, 28 June 1741.

Seward's martyrdom at the hands of anti-Methodist rioters to speak with 'unfeigned concern of our dear departed brother' and also to preach universal redemption[62]—a conjunction that the dead hero would have found highly objectionable. In public statements and private conversations, Charles made perfectly clear his views, referring to predestination as 'the snare of the fowler'[63] and its advocates as 'miserable comforters'.[64] This willingness of the Wesleys to provoke, and often initiate, heated debate while blaming the opposition for the consequences, was a character trait that is only recently beginning to be recognized.[65]

The development of the relationship between Charles and Whitefield is interesting. His comments about his old friend in the first months of the Revival are invariably warm[66] and as late as September 1740, his letters to Whitefield remained cordial despite the prevailing tension,[67] but as the dispute intensified, Charles became hostile. In January 1741, Charles told his brother 'If [George Whitefield] has declared against the truth, G W will come to nothing. Therefore leave him.'[68] This was written before Whitefield's return from North America after an absence lasting eighteen months and was not therefore based on a personal encounter. Charles's hostility did not lessen after Whitefield's return to England following his triumphant North American preaching tour. He complained to John that their former close associate was not to be trusted and that he had preached predestination in front of what Charles considered a Wesleyan congregation[69]—apparently unable to recognize that this kind of provocation was precisely what the brothers had been doing for some time.

A letter written to John in September 1741 illustrates the volatility of Charles's temperament:

Do you know the value of souls, precious immortal souls, yet trust them within the sound of predestination?... To trust [George Whitefield] while the wound he has made is yet unclosed... Stop the plague *just now*, or it will be too late. Send me word first post that you have warned our flock from

---

[62] CWJ, 28 October 1740. [63] CWJ, 28 May 1741.
[64] CWJ, 23 July 1741. [65] John Wesley, *The Works of John Wesley*, iii. 542–3.
[66] CWJ, 4 August 1739.
[67] CW to George Whitefield, MS letter, 1 September 1740 (MCA: DDCW 6/34).
[68] CW to JW, MS letter [10 January 1741] (MCA: DDCW 1/11).
[69] CW to JW, MS letter [16–17 March 1741] (MCA: DDCW 1/12).

going to hear the Other Gospel? O how you are outwitted... renounce your credulity, and [George Whitefield] till he renounces reprobation... Send me word, I say, by next post... or I shall on the first preaching night renounce [George Whitefield] on the housetop!⁷⁰

During the twelve months that followed, Whitefield complained in writing to John of his brother's obstructive tactics, which included arranging worship events at the same time that Whitefield was preaching in the vicinity.⁷¹ On another occasion, Charles refused Whitefield's offer of assistance in administering Communion and brusquely warned the messenger, not to listen to Whitefield preach.⁷² Later in life, Charles was referred to as a 'rough worker' when dealing with opposition;⁷³ that this aspect of his personality was apparent from the very beginning of his Evangelical ministry is clear from examination of these first disputes with the Calvinists.

John did not annotate Whitefield's letters of complaint, nor did he apparently take issue with Charles, leading to the assumption that he supported his brother's actions. Charles's aggression has been portrayed as forming a contrast to his brother, who tended to exude an aura of mild yet principled reason,⁷⁴ but it appears that both Wesleys were equally ruthless. John's reluctance to curb his impetuous brother's 'rough work' provides a glimpse into the political side of his character and one is faced with the possibility that it suited John to allow Charles to confront their rivals. For a later example of his Machiavellian touch, one can cite his willingness to stand back and allow Charles to take on the chief responsibility for disciplining the preachers, despite the damage to his brother's popularity that he must have known would result. Charles's iron fist might have made the stronger impression on Methodist scholarship, but that should not distract attention from what lay inside John's velvet glove. In this

---

⁷⁰ CW to JW, MS letter [28 September 1741] (MCA: DDCW 1/13).
⁷¹ George Whitefield to JW, Published copy letter, 21 December 1742. John Wesley, *The Works of John Wesley*, xxvi. 97–9.
⁷² George Whitefield to JW, Published copy letter, 11 March 1742. John Wesley, *The Works of John Wesley*, xxvi. 74.
⁷³ Quoted by Baker, *John Wesley and the Church of England*, 178.
⁷⁴ 'Wesley's emotional temperament... seemed to be a miracle of calm, controlled serenity.' Rack, *Reasonable Enthusiast*, 540.

respect as in so many others, they formed equal halves of an effective partnership.

Was Charles justified in acting with what appears to have been a mixture of theological and personal animosity? Certainly, the dispute evoked very strong reactions on both sides: Charles's journal records several instances of his being subjected to verbal abuse by his opponents,[75] while Whitefield felt constrained in 1741 to respond to the Wesleys in print.[76] Predestination was a fundamental issue, one on which there could in reality have been no long-term compromise within a single Evangelical movement. The Anglican Church had traditionally contained Arminians and Calvinists within its ranks, but in the first half of the eighteenth century their differences did not tend to be aired before unlettered crowds eager for the Word of God in all its aspects; the Methodist societies on the other hand, demanded clarification from their leaders and the resulting polarization led inevitably to division.

As fierce as the Calvinists could be in defence of their principles, it has to be said that the Wesleys appear to have taken the initiative in making public the differences. They showed little hesitation in attacking their opponents and resorting to tactics that were on occasion of questionable morality. These included John Wesley sending a copy of his printed sermon on Free Grace to Alexander Garden, Whitefield's main opponent in North America.[77] Whitefield was drawn into the controversy but with apparent reluctance; he urged Wesley to desist from provocation[78] and tried to enlist the support of at least one mutual friend to the same end.[79] The sentiments he expressed towards the brothers on a personal level were invariably friendly, even in the face of their rather obvious antagonism.[80] The fact that their friendship managed to survive in the long term

---

[75] For example, CWJ, 25 May 1741.
[76] George Whitefield, *A Letter to the Reverend Mr John Wesley, in answer to his sermon entitled 'Free Grace'* (London: printed by W. Strahan for T. Cooper and sold by R. Hett, 1741).
[77] Dallimore, *George Whitefield*, i. 579.   [78] Ibid. 571–2.   [79] Ibid. 571.
[80] 'I love you most tenderly, and wish the work of our Saviour may prosper much in your hands. I mentioned your success in the north at our last letter-day, and prayed most earnestly for you.' George Whitefield to JW, Published copy letter, 21 December 1742. John Wesley, *The Works of John Wesley*, xxvi. 97.

was due in large measure to Whitefield's willingness to forgive and forget.

WIDESPREAD OPPOSITION AND THE ANGLICAN REACTION

Additional evidence of the brothers' combative instincts comes from a number of primary sources arising from events during the 1740s. One such manuscript documents the activities of the Anglican minister Benjamin Ingham, another former member of the holy club and Moravian sympathizer. In this detailed and unpublished account of the Revival's first decade, Ingham's associate William Batty explicitly links the Wesleys with controversy and division as exemplified by the following extracts:

> In July 1742 the Moravian united brethren came into Yorkshire, and some time after, John Wesley at the request of John Nelson and then there began to be differences and division in Yorkshire as well as in London.[81]

> [William] Darney now began to introduce Mr Wesley's preachers in opposition to BI [Benjamin Ingham]... so that frequently when [William] Batty had preached at Roughlee on a Sunday at 2, they preached in the other end of the house when the meeting broke up.[82]

> The work of the Lord would have prospered better in this country [Lincolnshire] had not J. Wesley made separation...[83]

It was not just Evangelicals who felt the cutting edge of the Wesley character; in 1766, Samuel Newton, the Congregational minister in Norwich, complained bitterly that 'for more than twenty years... Methodism has thinned your auditories [and] broke in upon the order of your churches'.[84]

---

[81] [William Batty], MS 'Church History collected from the memoirs and journals of the Rev. Mr Ingham and the Labourers in connection with him', 14 July 1779 (MCA: MAM 11b), 6.
[82] Ibid. 12–13. [83] Ibid. 12.
[84] Quoted by Cyril Jolly, *The Spreading Flame: The Coming of Methodism to Norfolk* (Dereham: [Cyril Jolly], c.1970), 23.

One might argue that documents such as the Ingham manuscript were written from a broadly anti-Wesley perspective and should therefore be treated with caution, but statements by the brothers' allies paint a similar picture. Selina Hastings, Countess of Huntingdon, wrote to John Wesley on 24 October 1741 that Charles had taken a step that would certainly meet with John's approval, namely 'his declaring open war with [the Moravians]'.[85] This underlines the point that Charles no less than his brother was in the thick of the fight and indeed seemed to relish the challenge. The impression given from a variety of sources from differing viewpoints is that the appearance of the Wesleys and their preachers was often akin to the arrival of a succession of stormy petrels.

The Wesleys' fellow clergymen also had occasional cause to regret the turbulent brothers' offers of assistance. In 1742 Charles was invited by the churchwarden of Wednesbury in Staffordshire to evangelize the parish.[86] The vicar Edward Eggington was initially welcoming and entertained John Wesley when he visited in January 1743.[87] Within three months however, Eggington had turned hostile after the Wesleyan itinerant Robert Williams preached a highly inflammatory sermon to his parishioners: 'Look upon your ministry: there are dicers and carders, some blind guides and cannot see, some dumb dogs and will not bark. It might be better if all dumb ministers were hanged up in their church.'[88] On 15 April 1743 John Wesley was again in Wednesbury and listened to Eggington preach what he termed a 'wicked sermon...delivered with...bitterness of voice and manner'.[89] In his journal, Wesley acknowledges Williams's 'inexcusable folly' in provoking the minister, but made no reference in his published account of the Wednesbury riots to the circumstances that contributed to the outbreak.[90] The anti-Methodist disturbances that erupted in the parish and adjacent townships between May 1743 and

---

[85] Selina Hastings to [JW], MS letter, 24 October 1741 (MCA: Folio of Letters of the Countess of Huntingdon, 1).
[86] Charles Goodwin, 'Vile or Reviled? The Causes of the Anti-Methodist Riots at Wednesbury between May, 1743 and April, 1744 in the Light of New England Revivalism', *Methodist History*, 35:1 (October 1996), 17–18.
[87] Ibid. 19–20.   [88] Ibid. 20.   [89] Ibid.
[90] John Wesley, *Modern Christianity Exemplified at Wednesbury and other adjacent places in Staffordshire* (Newcastle upon Tyne: printed by John Gooding, 1745).

March 1744 were among the most violent in the annals of British Methodism.

The provocative actions of the Wesleys and their preachers came as a shock to their contemporaries. Despite the brothers' repeated declarations of Anglican allegiance, they thought nothing of preaching in other ministers' parishes, introducing new worship forms and indulging in public criticism of the Church and its clergy. In contrast to the quietly rebellious Parish Puritans and Nonjurors of fifty years before, the Evangelicals flaunted their defiance of Church of England mores in the most public fashion, while at the same time claiming to be good sons of Mother Church. This contradictory conduct by Evangelical Anglicans provoked considerable anger from within their own denomination expressed in a flood of anti-Methodist literature. Many of these publications were attacks on the enthusiasm that Methodist preaching inspired and which was so reminiscent of the destructive sectarianism that had turned English society upside down a hundred years before. In 1741, the Bishop of Lichfield addressed his clergy on the subject:

> I cannot think it improper to obviate the contagion of those *enthusiastical* pretensions that have ... betrayed whole multitudes either into an unreasonable presumption of their salvation, or into melancholy, if not desponding opinions... *Enthusiasm* indeed, when its false pretensions are detected, in the course of things is very apt to create *infidelity*; and infidelity is so shocking a thing.[91]

An angry letter of May 1740 from a layman reinforced very vividly the same point that some Christians regarded Methodism as nothing less than an abomination:

> Lord Jesus's cause...constrains me to speak...to cry aloud against these lying dreamers, who cause his people to err & thereby to pervert their ways; these false dissembling hypocrites, who by falling into divers strange postures, & their frightful shrieks and groans, & other ridiculous gestures, would make the world sensible, that the work of conversion is manifestly wrought upon their souls.[92]

---

[91] [Richard Smalbroke], *A Charge deliver'd to the reverend the clergy in several parts of the Diocese of Lichfield and Coventry in a triennial visitation of the same in 1741* (London: printed for J. and P. Knapton, 1744), 1–2.

[92] Anonymous to the 'Ministers called Methodists', MS letter, 31 May 1740 (MCA: EMV 144).

Other critics focused their attention on the wayward nature of Evangelical churchmanship and in the process tried to place distance between the Anglican Church and this new group of religious firebrands. Bishop Edmund Gibson in his 1744 tract *Observations upon the Conduct and Behaviour of a Certain Sect, usually distinguished by the name of Methodists* was swift to point out the irregularities of Methodist practice with regard to preaching, Communion, and worship. He tartly observed that 'the *Leaders* of these people would act a far more consistent and uniform part, if they would either renounce communion with the Established Church, or oblige themselves and their followers to have a greater regard to the *rules* and *orders* of it'.[93]

The point should be stressed that not all Anglicans were opposed to the Methodists. Sympathy for the Wesleys and Whitefield extended all the way up the Church hierarchy[94] and this division within Anglican ranks contributed to the confused and troubled relationship between the Church of England and its Evangelical children. The Anglican–Methodist issue became a running sore and posed an ever-deepening dilemma as the years passed and the Wesleys' movement put down roots in towns and villages throughout the land.

The combative stance exhibited by the brothers in their dealings with fellow Evangelicals, Dissenters, and Anglicans was in part at least a product of the conviction that they were engaged in a battle for souls, for the success of which they would answer before the throne of God. Their strenuous Evangelical empire-building should be viewed against this mindset. In addition to founding their own societies, they took over groups established by others, thereby promoting the Wesleyan movement's rapid and sometimes undisciplined expansion. The case of William Darney is a good illustration of this strategy at work; Darney was an illiterate pedlar and a pioneer of the Revival in Lancashire and Yorkshire, founding a large number of societies.[95] In 1747 he placed himself and his followers under the Wesleys' control,

---

[93] [Edmund Gibson], *Observations upon the Conduct and Behaviour of a Certain Sect, usually distinguished by the name of Methodists* (London: ?printed by E. Owen, 1744), 6.

[94] For example, John Potter, Archbishop of Canterbury between 1737 and 1747, was sympathetic towards the Wesleys. Baker, *John Wesley and the Church of England*, 59.

[95] J. W. Laycock, *Methodist Heroes in the Great Haworth Round 1734 to 1784* (Keighley: Wadsworth 1909), 39–44.

considerably strengthening the movement's presence in what was to become a Methodist heartland.[96] There was never any question of authority being shared as a result of such takeovers—John Wesley was insistent that he and his brother knew what was best for the Methodist movement and that preachers and people alike were under his personal charge.

The Wesleys were not the only Evangelicals to indulge in controversy or take over societies founded by others. The wider Methodist scene in the 1740s was characterized by shifting alliances and bitter disputes interspersed with regular attempts to unite in a common cause. The brilliant lay preacher John Cennick for example was affiliated at different times during one five-year period with the Wesleys, the Calvinists and the Moravians. Evangelicals of every theological stamp shared the conviction that they were doing God's will and this lent their ministry a sharp edge and tendency towards independent action. If the Wesleys were in the long term more successful than their contemporaries in building an Evangelical denomination out of this fluid and volatile mix, part of the explanation lies in their superior qualities of leadership and uncompromising attitude.

In their disputes with the Moravians, Whitefield, and indeed virtually everyone on the contemporary religious scene, it could be argued that the Wesleys were simply clear-sighted. For the Revival to take root, it needed strong leadership, which they were able to provide; it also required a doctrine and a structure, and again, they were swift to fill the gap. There was, however, a less positive side to their forcefulness and one could even argue that John Wesley consciously set out to displace his rivals; even the most charitable interpretation is that he could always find a reason why he should be in charge. Charles in his own way was equally domineering. He might have willingly abrogated first place in the Methodist hierarchy to John, but there was no doubt in his mind as to who should sit at his brother's right hand. As long as these two remarkable men worked in concert, they formed an unstoppable partnership: old friendships and spiritual mentors were not allowed to stand in the way of the imposition of their authority over the Methodist movement. It is true that their calling was a high one and their leadership produced inestimable benefit but there was a less

---

[96] Laycock, *Methodist Heroes*, 53.

praiseworthy side of their characters, one which Methodist historians have been reluctant to point out. This is of particular significance to any in-depth examination of Charles, for the aspect of his nature that produced the heroic period of his ministry in the 1740s was also at the root of the later troubled relations with his brother and the preachers. His fierce resilience, uncompromising stands for principle's sake, and personal charisma were to be turned against the man who had once been his closest friend and colleague.

4

Charles Wesley the Paradoxical Anglican

The question might legitimately be asked when considering the early years of the Methodist movement how the Wesley brothers could accommodate their radical ministry with their Anglican orders and continued membership of the Church. This is particularly the case with Charles, whose championship of the Church of England was the defining characteristic of his later ministry. His absolute refusal to countenance the secession of the Methodists from the Anglican Communion, stated with particular emphasis in the years after 1750, was to poison his relationship with a number of the preachers and cause severe strain with his brother. His aggressive advocacy of the Church also flavoured the way that he has been viewed by Methodist scholarship—his principal biographer Thomas Jackson described Charles as the 'most rigid and unbending Churchman in the Methodist body',[1] while one recent study referred to his refusal to 'step outside the discipline of the Church of England'.[2] In one sense, it is understandable that scholars have unanimously accepted that Charles Wesley was devoted to the Church in which he was raised; after all, he declared as much himself repeatedly and with characteristic vigour. In his journal entry for 3 July 1743, he expressed his 'inviolable attachment to the Church of England'[3] and he never appeared to shift from that fundamental position.

There was however, as with many things about this complicated man, a contradiction that demands clarification, and which puts this

---

[1] Jackson, *Charles Wesley*, ii. 474.
[2] Robin Leaver, 'Charles Wesley and Anglicanism', in S. T. Kimbrough jun. (ed.), *Charles Wesley: Poet and Theologian* (Nashville: Kingswood Books, 1992), 157.
[3] CWJ, 3 July 1743.

much-vaunted loyalty in a different light. During the crucial decade of the 1740s there was little about Charles Wesley's ministry that would have suggested unbending devotion to Anglican discipline, and for all his protestations of loyalty his drift away from the Church in practice was unmistakable. In the aftermath of his conversion, he found much to dislike about his fellow Anglicans, whether it was a minister complaining of the increase in communicants because of the activities of the Evangelicals,[4] or the rank hypocrisy of some that attended worship.[5]

He could be blunt in his criticism; on one occasion in 1748, he took issue with the future Primate of Ireland for his complaint of the lay preachers' lack of education, replying 'so the dumb ass rebukes the prophet'.[6] He was even threatened with excommunication in a personal interview with the Archbishop of Canterbury for the crime of preaching in other ministers' parishes; Charles stood his ground and wrote in his journal for that day 'I felt nothing in my heart but peace'.[7] Such a direct confrontation with the most senior person in the Church hierarchy hardly supports the view that Charles was unconditionally devoted to the 'old ship'. Nor was this uneasy relationship with the Church of England an exclusive characteristic of Charles's early Evangelical years—until the end of his long life, he regularly contravened Anglican practice by encouraging lay preaching and preference for work in a Methodist circuit rather than a parish.

In seeking to explain the contradictory stance adopted by Charles Wesley with regard to the Church of England, it becomes clear that his conversion experience represented a fundamental turning point with regard both to personal faith and the way that he viewed the Church. In the aftermath of May 1738, Charles experienced a change in religious identity, but crucially without breaking the link with his own past. He had been raised as a conservative Anglican, although his membership of the holy club shows that he was unconventional in his approach and open to new ideas; after his conversion, Charles became a radical conservative influenced by the High Church but inspired by the new wave of Pietist thought and innovative forms of worship. The movement that he helped to create was a product of this

[4] CWJ, 13 October 1739. [5] CWJ, 27 October 1739.
[6] Gill, *Charles Wesley*, 233. [7] CWJ, 19 June 1739.

mix of tradition and innovation. Methodism was built on a Church of England foundation and on the basis of attachment to the Church, yet it was far removed in many areas from what Charles's father Samuel would have recognized or approved of. This apparent contradiction gave rise to many questions concerning the true nature of Methodism and it became an issue that plagued the brothers throughout their careers. It is necessary therefore to examine the nature of Charles Wesley's changing churchmanship and the impact of the brothers' Anglican background on the early Methodist movement, starting with the effect of their nurturing in the High Church tradition.

HIGH CHURCH INFLUENCE

Charles and John were raised to be loyal to Church and King and this view was reinforced by their experiences at Oxford. As influential as other strains of religious thought and practice became in their lives, the brothers always retained a strong vestige of this background and placed it to good use in their Evangelical ministries. The High Church placed emphasis on discipline and the maintenance of private and public morality and this was echoed in the brothers' management of Methodism. It was very easy to transgress the Wesleys' rigid codes of behaviour and the extensive tours made by the brothers were often accompanied by expulsions from the societies. In March 1743 for example, John observed that sixty-four people had been expelled from the Newcastle society during the previous three months for offences ranging from Sabbath-breaking and selling alcohol to 'lightness and carelessness'.[8] Charles was no less backward in enforcing proper conduct, expelling fifty from the Bristol society in May 1747.[9] This firm hand was no doubt made necessary by Methodism's expansion and the lack of clerical helpers to share the workload, but it was also part of the High Church ethos and came naturally enough to the sons of the Rector of Epworth.

The brothers made other impositions on their followers that were grounded in conservative Anglicanism. John Wesley's manuscript

[8] JWJ, 12 March 1743. John Wesley, *The Works of John Wesley*, xix. 318.
[9] CWJ, 29 May 1747.

annotation to his copy of the *Rules of the United Societies* laid down the following requirements for membership of a Methodist band:

1. To be at [parish] church, and at the Lord's Table every week...
2. To attend the ministry of the Word every morning...
3. To use private prayer every day and family prayer if you are the head of a family...
4. ...
5. To observe as days of fasting or abstinence all Fridays in the year.[10]

One can easily identify elements from this list that fit comfortably into a High Church context, such as the insistence on weekly Communion and the use of family prayers, while fasting had been a feature of the brothers' own spiritual life since at least their days at Oxford.

It is with regard to the Sacraments and specifically Holy Communion that the influence of Epworth Rectory over Methodism is at its most visible. Charles's parents set great store by regular attendance at the Lord's Table and emphasized the need for communicants to be in a proper frame of mind and spirit for what the High Church considered the most important act of Christian worship.[11] In his book *The Pious Communicant rightly prepared*[12] Samuel Wesley justified the practice of frequent observance and made suggestions as to how one should prepare for the celebration. John and Charles inherited this eucharistic concern to such a degree that it became a central component of Methodist doctrine. The devotion displayed by the holy club to regular and careful attendance at the Lord's Table earned them the nickname 'Sacramentarians' and it was through Charles's unusual practice of weekly celebration that Oxford Methodism had its beginnings.[13] In an undated sermon or treatise on Acts 20: 7,[14]

---

[10] MS annotation to John Wesley's *Rules etc of the United Societies* ([London]: 1743) (MCA: MAW G 43B).

[11] 'The eucharist was the apex of High Church and Non-juror worship.' Robert Cornwall, *Visible and Apostolic: The Constitution of the Church in High Church Anglican and Non-Juror Thought* (Newark: University of Delaware Press, 1993), 136.

[12] Samuel Wesley, *The Pious Communicant rightly prepared, or a Discourse concerning the Blessed Sacrament* (London: printed for Charles Harper, 1700).

[13] CW to Dr Chandler, MS letter, 28 April 1785 (MCA: DDWes 1/38).

[14] Charles Wesley, *The Sermons of Charles Wesley*, ed. Kenneth Newport (Oxford: Oxford University Press, 2001), 277–86.

Charles expounded his mature views on the Eucharist with particular regard to the necessity for a weekly observance. In a manner typical of the High Church, he points to scripture and ancient Christian practice in support of his contention[15] and it is noteworthy that he cites the *Apostolic Constitutions* to which the Nonjuror John Clayton first introduced the Wesleys at Oxford.[16]

Conservative Anglicans believed that Communion was a means of bringing spiritual refreshment and comfort to the soul[17] and this is reflected in Wesleyan doctrine. In his sermon on *The Duty of Constant Communion* John Wesley stated: 'As our bodies are strengthened by bread and wine, so are our souls by these tokens of the body and blood of Christ. This is the food of our souls: this gives strength to perform our duty and leads us on to perfection...'[18] High Church Sacramental theology and observance was adopted by the Wesleys with such fervour that in the words of John Rattenbury the revival they led 'might as truly be called Sacramental as Evangelical'.[19] Charles himself took Communion far more frequently than even the majority of High Church ministers would have deemed strictly necessary—in the Christmas week of 1738 for example he attended the Lord's Table on no fewer than six successive days.[20]

For Charles, the taking of the elements represented a mystical experience during which the doors of heaven itself were opened. His conviction that the Eucharist when properly celebrated was a channel for the transmission of grace was no mere academic notion but a deeply personal experience. This is seen many times in his letters and journal from which the following extracts are taken:

[I] received the never-failing blessing at the Sacrament. Our prayer after it always opens heaven.[21]

[I] found the great blessing after the Sacrament, an ordinance which God always magnifies and honours with his special presence...[22]

---

[15] Charles Wesley, *The Sermons of Charles Wesley*, 286.
[16] Rack, *Reasonable Enthusiast*, 90.
[17] Cornwall, *Visible and Apostolic*, 138–9.
[18] John Wesley, *The Works of John Wesley*, iii. 429.
[19] John Rattenbury, *The Eucharistic Hymns of John and Charles Wesley* (London: Epworth, 1948), 3.
[20] CWJ, 25–30 December 1738.   [21] CWJ, 10 February 1745.
[22] CWJ, 7 April 1745.

My subject at Spitalfields Chapel was, Let us therefore come boldly to the throne of grace that we may obtain mercy etc... [Brother] Richardson assisted me to administer to above 1200 communicants...[23]

The central importance of Communion to the Wesleyan wing of the Revival is corroborated by manuscript testimonies written by the brothers' followers. For some it represented the moment of conversion itself—the preacher Thomas Tennant upon being given the bread and wine 'was enabled to believe that Christ died for me, and was filled with peace in the Holy Ghost'.[24] For others, regular observance made an important contribution in their struggle towards conversion; Thomas Middleton felt at chapel services in London that 'my heart was poured out before the Lord: it was full and ready to break, and particularly at the Lord's Table...'[25] The mystical aspect of Charles's own celebratory experience can also be detected in a passage from a letter written by Elizabeth Halfpenny: 'Being at Kingswood on Sacrament day, in an instant, was brought to my view, by the eye of faith, the form of a tall person in his surplice: his hair was white and seemed to move on the ground with his back towards me, but he was soon vanished.'[26]

Inextricably bound up with the supreme spiritual significance attached to the Eucharist was the vital role performed by the officiating minister. The High Church stressed the necessity of proper celebration by an episcopally ordained priest who alone, in their opinion, was qualified to act in a sacerdotal role and draw down the grace and favour of God.[27] This view was carried over by the Wesley brothers into Methodism where over time it became a bone of contention and a steadily widening point of fracture with the Church of England. The fact that only Anglican priests were allowed to administer the bread and wine drastically curtailed the opportunities for Methodists seeking to attend Communion outside London—in some areas they were

---

[23] CW to Sarah Wesley, MS letter, n.d. [post-1757] (MCA: DDCW 7/20).
[24] *The Lives of Early Methodist Preachers*, ed. Thomas Jackson, 3 vols. (London: Wesleyan Conference Office, 1871; repr. as a retypeset from the original 6 vols. of the 4th edn., Stoke on Trent: Tentmaker Publications; Lewes: Berith Publications, 1998), iii. 383.
[25] Thomas Middleton to CW, MS letter, 8 October 1743 (MCA: EMV 111).
[26] Elizabeth Halfpenny to CW, MS letter, May 1742 (MCA: EMV 87).
[27] Cornwall, *Visible and Apostolic*, 123–6.

barred from the parish church while in other parts of the country, weekly and even monthly celebration was rare.[28]

In one sense, the Wesleys were hoist on their own High Church petard. They urged their followers on to 'constant communion' and taught the spiritual benefits of proper celebration, but that served to expose what some Methodists viewed as the inadequacies of the Established Church and its clergy. Over time, a section within the societies began quietly to make their own arrangements by taking the bread and wine from Methodist preachers, despite their lack of clerical orders. John Wesley never abandoned his view that ordination was necessary to act as mediator of divine grace,[29] but he did after years of strenuous mental gymnastics finally conclude that he was as qualified to ordain as any bishop;[30] thus a separate Methodist ministry and Church was born. It is ironic that John Wesley's High Church stance with regard to the Lord's Supper became a parting of the ways for the Anglicans and the Methodists. Charles Wesley on the other hand, while he was willing enough to depart from many points of Anglican practice, never compromised on what he viewed as the essential requirement for the participation of a specifically Anglican ministry in the Methodist mission. The various Sacramental and ordination controversies and their role in the unravelling of Methodism from the Church will be covered in greater detail later.

THE WIDER RELIGIOUS INFLUENCE IN THE MAKING OF METHODISM

Any attempt at identifying the specific contribution made by the different sections of the Anglican community to the evolution of Methodism is rendered complicated by difficulties in defining what constituted typical Church of England belief and practice in the early eighteenth century. Anglicans might hold High Church views in some respects but not in others, and there was broad agreement between the different parties on important points of doctrine and practice.

---

[28] John Bowmer, *The Sacrament of the Lord's Supper in Early Methodism* (London: Dacre, 1951), 6–8.
[29] Ibid. 149–52. [30] Rack, *Reasonable Enthusiast*, 294–6.

Most Latitudinarians and Dissenters would have been as concerned with the necessity of maintaining a strict moral code within society as their High Church brethren, and there was a strain of Puritanism that espoused a Sacramental theology that was close to the High Church model. Some other aspects of Methodism's Anglican character such as the use of the Book of Common Prayer or the Wesleys' practice of wearing full canonicals when leading worship may not indicate anything more than an inheritance from the broader Anglican mainstream.

This blurring of distinctions makes it difficult to draw firm conclusions about the exact starting point for some areas of Methodist ecclesiology. The Wesleys certainly received their Sacramental doctrine and views on secular authority from a High Church source, but the origin of other Methodist building blocks are not so easy to trace with exactitude. It should also be remembered that individual members of the societies, some of whom were Dissenters or Roman Catholics, would have quietly accepted or rejected aspects of the Wesleys' teaching based on their own experience and background. Over the course of several decades this invisible pressure from the grassroots had as great an effect on the construction of Methodist identity as the more public actions of the leadership. The Wesleyan wing of the Revival was not simply a modification of one particular denominational tradition, but was rather a weaving together of many different strands. In the rest of this chapter, some of these other influences will be examined, with particular regard to the grafting of radical practice onto the brothers' High Church sensitivities and the extent to which this was accepted and even encouraged by Charles Wesley.

The Wesleys' dissatisfaction with the state of the Church, coupled with the driving force of their new-found faith, found expression in the adoption of practices that were most untypical of Anglican ministers. In addition to Sacramental services that followed the forms laid down in the Book of Common Prayer and the insistence that Methodists attend their parish church, the brothers introduced meetings that had little or no Anglican precedent. The very concept of a religious society was, as we have seen, a relatively recent introduction to the English Church and one that was regarded with suspicion by some High Church ministers.

The Wesleys further divided the societies into bands and classes, which were intimate gatherings of small groups under the supervision of a lay leader with an established reputation for piety. This process of rapid development represented a part of what Walsh and Taylor have termed a radicalization of the Anglican model.[31] The bands were introduced as early as 1739 as a direct borrowing from the Moravians and were for the encouragement and guidance of people who had already been converted and were seeking to attain higher levels of holiness on the path to perfection. By way of contrast, was the weekly class meeting, which commenced in 1742 and was originally a mechanism for raising money. Within a short time, the classes were also being used for spiritual examination and the giving of advice and correction where necessary. Unlike the bands, conversion was not a prerequisite for class membership and it became possible therefore for the Wesleys to insist that all their followers meet in this fashion. Within a few years, membership of the Methodist societies was defined by possession of a class ticket, which could be taken away for backsliding and other infringements of the rigid code of discipline that was central to the early Methodist system.[32]

The lovefeast and watchnight were different types of meeting altogether and satisfied the need for informal fellowship on a wider society level. The lovefeast originated as a communal meal of bread and water accompanied by prayer, conversation, singing, and the giving of testimonies. It was another feature of Methodism that was borrowed from the Moravians, although it is also referred to in the New Testament, which gave it the additional attraction of representing a return to primitive Christianity. At the watchnight meetings, Methodists spent part of the night in a vigil of prayer, praise, and thanksgiving. Like the class meetings the watchnight appears to have started in Bristol independently of the Wesleys, although again there is some Moravian and New Testament precedent.[33]

Another Wesleyan innovation was the covenant service and this has special interest as the only Methodist meeting that drew specifically on a Puritan source. The idea of a divine contract whereby grace is given through Christ in exchange for faith and obedience is part of

---

[31] Walsh and Taylor, 'Introduction: The Church and Anglicanism', 18.
[32] Rack, *Reasonable Enthusiast*, 240–2.   [33] Ibid. 411–12.

Charles the Paradoxical Anglican 73

mainstream Christian theology and one that was particularly influential in Puritanism, where it took the form of a personal commitment entered into by an individual. John Wesley drew heavily on the writings of Richard and Joseph Alleine, who had been ejected in 1662, for his views on the covenant, but in 1755 he took the concept one step further with the introduction of a covenant service during which the assembled congregation gave their assent as one body to a binding agreement with God.[34]

THE USE OF HYMNS IN WORSHIP

An important feature of all Methodist gatherings was the singing of hymns and this was another practice that had roots in the Pietist and dissenting traditions. Hymns made their first appearance in English Protestant worship in the late seventeenth century with the work of the Baptist minister Benjamin Keach. Both Anglicans and Dissenters had written hymns for devotional use prior to this but it was Keach who introduced hymn-singing to services.[35] Writers of hymns who followed Keach's example in the early eighteenth century were almost exclusively Nonconformists and included Philip Doddridge, Anne Steele, and Joseph Stennett. The best known and most talented was Isaac Watts, an Independent minister who authored six hundred hymns to become known as the 'father of English hymnody'.

The use of hymns in services was not generally accepted even by Nonconformists and was positively disliked by many in the Church of England well into the nineteenth century. Public hymn-singing came under suspicion because of its dissenting associations and was placed by conservative churchmen into the same 'enthusiastic' category as extempore preaching and prayer.[36] The practice favoured in Anglican churches was the singing of metrical psalms, which while adapted for

---

[34] Leslie Church, *More about the Early Methodist People* (London: Epworth, 1949), 249–50; Rack, *Reasonable Enthusiast*, 412–14.
[35] Richard Watson, *The English Hymn: A Critical and Historical Study* (Oxford: Clarendon, 1997), 110.
[36] Susan Tamke, *Make a Joyful Noise unto the Lord: Hymns as a Reflection of Victorian Social Attitudes* (Athens, Ohio: Ohio University Press, 1978), 19–23.

congregational use, remained close to the biblical source and were not therefore as prone to the promotion of wild flights of fancy.

John Wesley's fascination with religious song as an aid to spiritual growth can be traced back to his contact with the Moravians while on passage to Georgia.[37] The German Pietists were the inheritors of a rich tradition of the use of hymns in public worship dating back to the time of Martin Luther, and Wesley was so impressed by what he witnessed on board the ship *Simmonds* that within a year he had compiled a collection of hymns for publication in Charlestown, South Carolina.[38] This slim but important volume contains work by an eclectic mix of contributors including Isaac Watts, the Roman Catholic John Austin, George Herbert, Samuel Wesley senior, and John Wesley's own translation of German originals. The Charlestown hymnal has the distinction of being not only the first of many such collections produced by the Wesleys, but also the first hymn-book produced specifically for use by an Anglican congregation.[39] One of the complaints made against Wesley to the Grand Jury for Savannah was that this most unusual High Churchman had deviated from Anglican principles by introducing 'into the church and service at the altar, compositions of Psalms and Hymns not inspected or authorized by any proper judicature'.[40]

Hymns by Charles Wesley did not appear in print until 1739 although he was certainly writing religious poetry well before that date.[41] In a letter written from Georgia to the wife of Governor Oglethorpe,[42] Charles refers to being inspired by his wild surroundings to write a 'hymn' but it is likely that this was intended for personal use rather than congregational worship. He showed no such restraint after his Evangelical conversion in May 1738 and starting with the publication the following year of *Hymns and Sacred Poems*,

---

[37] Rack, *Reasonable Enthusiast*, 123.
[38] *A Collection of Psalms and Hymns*, compiled by John Wesley (Charles-Town: printed by Lewis Timothy, 1737).
[39] John Wesley, *John Wesley's First Hymn-Book: A Facsimile with Additional Material*, ed. Frank Baker and George Williams (London: Wesley Historical Society Publication 6, 1964), p. ix.
[40] JWJ, 22 August 1737. John Wesley, *The Works of John Wesley*, xviii. 555.
[41] Charles's earliest extant religious verse dates to 1728. Rack, *Reasonable Enthusiast*, 256.
[42] Baker, *Charles Wesley as Revealed*, 25.

verse written specifically for use in services flowed from his pen. Charles's compositions formed the backbone of Methodist hymnals well into the twentieth century and so profound was the spiritual and theological content of the best of his work that according to one non-Methodist critic they 'prefigured the constitution of the new [Methodist] Church and formed the manual of its spiritual discipline'.[43]

The hymns of Charles Wesley were a vital ingredient in Methodism's success as a popular religious movement. Immediately accessible to people of all levels of education, easy to remember and fun to sing, they were heard not just in chapels, but in the workplace, the home, and the street. Between 1739 and the end of the century the Methodists published a multitude of separate collections on a bewildering array of themes ranging from earthquakes to children, together with volumes intended for specific services and general usage. The income produced from the sale of hymn-books made a significant contribution to Connexional finance—in 1791 a detailed inventory of the contents of the Methodist Book Room recorded over 11,000 hymnals in the warehouse awaiting distribution together with several thousand more available for sale in the shop.[44] Such print runs attest to the phenomenal popularity of Methodist sacred verse and help to explain how hymns such as 'O for a Thousand Tongues to Sing' entered the mainstream of popular culture.

Anglican Evangelicals such as Augustus Toplady and John Newton noted the success enjoyed by the singing Methodists and started to write and publish their own collections for use in parish churches. The struggle towards acceptance of hymns in the Church of England was long and hard; as late as 1820 the Bishop of Peterborough condemned their use because there was no provision for them in the Book of Common Prayer,[45] but by the end of the nineteenth century the singing of hymns had become a standard feature of Anglican worship and could be regarded as Methodism's most important gift to her parent denomination.

[43] Louis Benson, *The English Hymn: Its Development and Use in Worship* (Philadelphia: The Presbyterian Board of Publication, 1915), 244.
[44] MS inventory of books belonging to John Wesley, 27 April 1791 (MCA: Wesleyan Conference collection).
[45] Tamke, *Make a Joyful Noise unto the Lord*, 27.

PREACHING AND PRAYER

As radical as the Wesleys' services and meetings seemed to their contemporaries, it was in their ministry of the 'Word' that the most controversial departures from the Church of England took place. Open-air preaching, while not in itself contrary to canon law, was a sensitive area, touching as it did on public order and the traditional alliance between Church and State. In the turbulent and often violent world of Georgian England, the sight of large crowds of the lower orders being whipped into a state of high emotion by charismatic preachers was certain to cause concern on the part of the authorities. Confusion and suspicion were exacerbated by the fact that two of the most successful of these evangelists were self-proclaimed Tory stalwarts and ministers of the established Church. It is hardly surprising that some critics found sinister significance in the fact that the Wesley family had Nonjuror and Jacobite connections.[46]

The employment of lay itinerants was even more distasteful to champions of the Establishment.[47] Reverend John Lewis in a letter of October 1747 to John Wesley criticized his encouragement of 'unlearned mechanics to usurp the ministerial office' describing it as an 'indefensible point'.[48] There can be no doubt that Lewis was correct in his assessment, as lay preaching was certainly in breach of the Thirty-Nine Articles that Charles and his brother had sworn to obey at the time of their ordination.[49]

It has been stated, or at least implied, that Charles was more reluctant than John to accept the validity of this lay call to preach,[50] but there is evidence to indicate that he was in fact more receptive. It

---

[46] Rack, *Reasonable Enthusiast*, 172.

[47] For example, 'Another error is their permitting unlearned men without ordination, to go about preaching the Gospel.' Nathan Fletcher, *A Methodist dissected; or, a description of their errors* (York: printed by Caesar Ward, 1749), 14.

[48] John Lewis to JW, MS letter, 5 October 1747 (MCA: Collection of letters to JW).

[49] Article XXIII: 'It is not lawful for any man to take upon him the office of public preaching, or ministering the Sacraments in the Congregation before he be allowed, lawfully called and sent to execute the same. And those we ought to judge lawfully called and sent, which be chosen and called to this work by Men who have public authority given unto them, in the Congregation, to call and send Ministers into the Lord's Vineyard.'

[50] Heitzenrater, *Wesley and the People called Methodists*, 115–16; Church, *More about the Early Methodist People*, 101; Laycock, *Methodist Heroes*, 12–13.

is true that one of Charles's grievances with the Fetter Lane Society in 1739 was the demand for lay preaching, but the issue there was complicated by the insistence of some at Fetter Lane on lay administration of the Sacraments, something to which Charles was resolutely opposed throughout his life. For an insight into his opinion of lay preaching in isolation, one should turn to his journal entry for 8 May 1740, describing an address given by the layman Howell Harris to the London Society:

> He declared his experience... O what a flame was kindled! Never man spake in my hearing as that man spake. What a nursing father has God sent us! He has indeed learnt of the good Shepherd to carry the lambs in his bosom. Such love, such power, such simplicity was irresistible... These words broke out like thunder 'I now find a commission from God to invite all poor sinners, justified or unjustified, to his altar'...[51]

It is true that Harris appears on this occasion to have been exhorting or testifying, as opposed to preaching from a scriptural text, which was a subtle distinction of great value to the Wesleys in their justification of lay ministry.[52] However, Charles could not have been unaware that his friend had been speaking in public both from a text and without for several years, a divine call to which Harris specifically referred in the above passage. At no point in their several meetings at this time did Charles express concern over such activities, and indeed it is clear that he held the Welshman in the highest regard; it was not long either before he was using the specific term 'preaching' to describe Harris's role in Methodism.[53] Charles might have questioned the ability of individuals, but he never declared against the validity of lay preaching per se. One might contrast this apparent indifference with John's reluctance to allow the practice, which he apparently

---

[51] CWJ, 8 May 1740.
[52] 'At their first setting out, they called themselves... Exhorters, rather than Preachers; a distinction, at least as they managed it, which I confess I don't very well understand...' [Robert Cruttenden], *The principles and preaching of the Methodists considered in a letter to the Reverend Mr***** (London: printed for James Buckland, 1753), 3.
[53] 'Had an opportunity to moderate the spirits of some, who were greatly exasperated against Howell Harris, for preaching predestination among them.' CWJ, 8 November 1740.

permitted only after an angry confrontation with his mother in early 1741.[54]

The acceptance of lay preaching by the Wesleys at such an early date was of vital significance for the spread of Methodism. There were Church of England ministers such as William Grimshaw and John Meriton who were prepared to contribute to the work of the Revival, but for Methodism to make any long-term impact it quickly became apparent that lay assistance was required, regardless of Anglican opposition. This was underlined by the importance that the brothers attached to their followers hearing the 'Word' on a regular basis— John Wesley specified a daily attendance in his *Rules of the United Societies*. Something that the brothers did not appreciate in this first rush of Evangelical success was that by elevating preaching to such a high level of importance, they were also paving the way for the lay purveyors of God's message to assume a special status in Methodist eyes.

Another controversial and related aspect of Methodism was the widespread use of extempore preaching and prayer. Impromptu preaching was not unknown in an early eighteenth-century Anglican context, but the normal practice was for sermons to be carefully prepared and either memorized or delivered from notes.[55] Alternatively, ministers would make use of the compositions of others; Charles Wesley for example transcribed several of John's sermons and preached them himself.[56] Public prayer was regarded in a similarly formal fashion and was based on the set forms laid down in the Book of Common Prayer.[57]

After their Evangelical conversions, the Wesley brothers started to preach and pray extempore following the direction of the Holy Spirit.[58] In the case of a sermon, this involved selecting a random biblical text at the last possible moment before beginning to speak, and then trusting to divine inspiration. In March 1740, Charles wrote to his brother concerning such an occasion: 'In the pulpit, I opened the book and found the place where it is written, "the Spirit of the

---

[54] Rack, *Reasonable Enthusiast*, 210.   [55] Rupp, *Religion in England*, 515.
[56] Charles Wesley, *The Sermons of Charles Wesley*, 78–81.
[57] Spurr, John, *The Restoration Church of England, 1646–1689* (New Haven: Yale University Press, 1991), 334.
[58] Charles appears to have commenced extempore preaching in July 1738. Charles Wesley, *The Sermons of Charles Wesley*, 35.

Lord is upon me, because he hath anointed me to preach the gospel to the poor, etc" I explained our Lord's prophetic office, and described the person on whom alone He could perform it. I found as did others that he owned me.'[59] With regard to public prayer, the Evangelicals continued to use the Anglican liturgy but supplemented by their own spur-of-the-moment compositions. Such discourses were a source of concern to the brothers' High Church friends who objected to their irregularity and encouragement of excess. John Clayton wrote to John Wesley in May 1739 cautioning him of the need for prudence and warning that his refusal to use notes was causing offence,[60] while Samuel Wesley junior brusquely told his brother 'to banish extemporary expositions and extemporary prayers',[61] but to no avail.

Extempore preaching and prayer had been commonplace in seventeenth-century Puritanism and were a cause of disquiet to Latitudinarian and Nonjuror alike for their reliance on unseemly emotion rather than reason and solid teaching.[62] If the brothers had restricted these activities to themselves and their ordained colleagues, it would probably have been regarded as little more than harmless eccentricity, but by encouraging laymen also to preach and pray in this fashion, the Wesleys provoked deep and widespread concern. Memories were revived of Puritan firebrands rocking the foundations of society with misplaced zeal for God; James Buller referred in typically High Church language to this lingering fear in his *Reply to the Rev. Mr Wesley's address to the clergy*:

Whilst the sons of *Belial* were undermining the *Church* and *State*, and unnatural subjects were most cruelly conspiring against the life of God's *Anointed*, our then most gracious Sovereign, *Charles the First*. Great was the *Company of Preachers*. Like the *frogs* in *Egypt* they *filled* the houses ... The *Colonels* and the *Captains*, the *Drummers* and private *Centinels* of the *Soldiery*, most audaciously became the *Trumpeters* of the Gospel; they effectively paved the way with their *tongues* for their *swords*. ... [63]

---

[59] CW to JW, Published copy letter, March 1740. Charles Wesley, *The Sermons of Charles Wesley*, 36.
[60] Rack, *Reasonable Enthusiast*, 141.
[61] Samuel Wesley jun. to JW, MS letter, 16 April 1739 (MCA: DDWF 5/15).
[62] W. Spellman, *Latitudinarians and the Church of England 1667–1700* (Athens, Ohio: University of Georgia Press, 1993), 124–7.
[63] James Buller, *A reply to the Rev. Mr Wesley's address to the clergy* (Bristol: printed by S. Farley, 1756), 19–20.

Unlettered laymen leaving their lawful occupation and tramping the countryside expounding the Gospel as the Spirit allegedly moved them was not simply a question of stepping on the toes of ordained clergymen, but had implications for public order. The Wednesbury riots represent just one example of what could happen when itinerant preachers went too far in their calls for people to repent.

The criticism in 1745 by the Anglican minister Henry Stebbing in his *Address to the Methodists* reflects this widespread perception that the Evangelicals were disturbers of the peace and wreckers of social harmony: 'Some of them [Methodists] have since run about the country, teaching and exhorting, without any orders or authority, learning or judgement; distressing the minds of the poor, ignorant well-meaning people; throwing some into despair, others into presumption and many into madness...'[64] Stebbing's accusations appear extreme, but the fact that his work went through five editions in as many years after first publication and fourteen editions by 1807 indicates the depth and longevity of fears concerning the Wesleys and their so-called Sons in the Gospel.

When reading accounts of early Methodist meetings, it is difficult not to feel some measure of sympathy with the brothers' critics. The Evangelicals encouraged emotional outbursts through their highly charged preaching and public prayer, and Charles Wesley himself acknowledged the potential dangers inherent in this inflammatory brand of popular religion. In 1740 he wrote to John from Bristol that 'the noises and outcries here are over. I have not spoken one word against them, nor two *about* them. The Devil grows sullen and dumb because we take no notice of him.'[65] Other instances of his concern with keeping fanaticism in check are scattered throughout the journal, as on 6 May 1741 when he 'cautioned the unstable and comforted the feeble-minded'.[66]

The best example of Methodism out of control occurred in London in 1763 when the preacher George Bell was arrested for disturbing

---

[64] [Henry Stebbing], *An earnest and affectionate address to the people called Methodists* (London: printed by J. Oliver, 1745), 38.
[65] Quoted by Baker, *Charles Wesley as Revealed*, 36.   [66] CWJ, 6 May 1741.

the peace of the King's subjects.[67] Bell had claimed to be in a state of sinless perfection, a condition regarded as the Holy Grail of Methodist spirituality. Unfortunately he took the Wesleys' teachings to extravagant lengths and in the months leading up to his arrest claimed the power to heal the sick and raise the dead.[68] Bell achieved great personal influence and enjoyed the approbation of John Wesley until a short time before the final *denouement*.[69] Bell's downfall occurred when his prophecy that the world would end on 28 February 1763 resulted in mass panic in the streets of the British capital. John Wesley not surprisingly distanced himself from his one-time protégé, but too late to prevent letters appearing in the popular press denouncing Methodism as the 'the most destructive and dangerous system to government and society that ever was established'[70]—not the type of publicity that would have endeared the Wesleys to their colleagues and superiors in the Anglican ministry. The fact that the London society lost a quarter of its membership in the immediate aftermath of the controversy indicates that many of the Wesleys' own followers also took fright at the direction their movement was taking.[71]

Charles Wesley took a strong line against claims of extreme spiritual revelation and he was certainly more aware than his brother of the threat posed by preachers such as Bell.[72] At the same time, however, Charles was himself encouraging his followers to step over the boundaries of what many Anglicans, including his own father and oldest brother, would have considered seemly or safe behaviour. His preaching and prayer were passionate in their content and delivery and often produced strong reactions. The following was recorded in Charles's journal for 22 April 1741: 'I sharply reproved three or four inflexible pharisees; then prayed the Lord to give me words of consolation and immediately I was filled with power which broke out as a mighty torrent. All our hearts caught fire as in a moment, and such tears and strong cryings followed as quite drowned my voice.

---

[67] Gareth Lloyd, 'A Cloud of Perfect Witnesses: John Wesley and the London Disturbances 1760–1763', *The Asbury Theological Journal*, 56/2 (Fall 2001/Spring 2002), 117–36.
[68] John Walsh to CW, MS letter, 11 August 1762 (MCA: EMV 134).
[69] Lloyd, 'A Cloud of Perfect Witnesses', 126–8.   [70] Ibid. 130.
[71] Ibid. 129.   [72] Ibid. 123–4.

I sat still while the prayer of the humble pierced the clouds...all present received an answer of peace.'[73]

Charles Wesley, for all his High Church upbringing and reputation as an Anglican loyalist, breached the conventions and discipline of his denomination on a daily basis across such key areas as liturgy, preaching, and subservience to Episcopal authority. The closer that one examines the detail of his activities, the more radical he appears and the less like his historical image and High Church stereotype.

CHARLES WESLEY AND THE 'MOTHERS IN ISRAEL'

Another area in which Charles displayed a startling degree of toleration was his willingness to allow women to play an active role in Methodist affairs. This important aspect of his ministry has never been addressed in the standard biographies and it is valuable therefore to examine now as a final example of Charles Wesley's radical churchmanship.

One of Charles's closest friends was Sarah Perrin, with whom he enjoyed an extensive correspondence for over thirty years. In 1741, Perrin wrote to Charles describing her personal contribution to the work of the Revival:

> here [Leominster] seems to be some good stirring. Many of the Church of England meet often together to talk of the things of God. They invited me to come among them. I have been with them several times...I earnestly desire I may lay no stumbling block in their way but that the master...may give me words for their edification...one evening I gave them the sermon upon salvation by faith, they much approved of it. I read the hymn to them...they said it comforted them.[74]

Perrin was clearly exercising a semi-public ministry at a very early date. Depending on the way that this passage is interpreted, she could even be said to have been preaching, and that would have been unheard of in a contemporary Anglican setting. Perrin referred to

[73] CWJ, 22 April 1741.
[74] Sarah Perrin to CW, MS letter, 1741 (MCA: 'Letters to CW II'), 5.

her public ministry on other occasions in her letters to Charles.[75] The most striking example was written on 12 June 1750 when she described exhorting several times a week in Leominster[76] and to Charles's successful prayers that she might be blessed with wisdom, presumably in her utterances.[77] This constitutes one of the earliest unambiguous references to Methodist women exhorting in public.

The fact that Perrin was a convert from the Quakers who had long accepted female ministry may account for Charles's toleration. There are unfortunately no extant letters from Charles to Perrin, although we can deduce from indirect evidence that he had no major objection to her irregular activities. His annotation on the letter of 1741 consists simply of her name, and the tone of her correspondence does not suggest that this was an uncomfortable subject. As for general Anglican opinion about the role of women in the Church, this is summed up by a comment made to Charles in 1771 by the Irish minister and later bishop Thomas Barnard that women 'should not forget that their office is to *wash the feet* and not direct the paths'.[78] It is interesting that Charles's annotation on Barnard's letter suggests approval of his view,[79] indicating that in this area he grew more conservative with the passage of years.

THE ANGLICAN–EVANGELICAL DIVIDE

Charles Wesley was far from being a typical churchman despite his historical image, which is in large part based on his actions and statements in later life. This could cause confusion to his contemporaries: during his visit to Ireland in 1748, he commented 'It is worth

---

[75] For example, Sarah Perrin to CW, MS letter, 2 May 1741 (MCA: 'Letters to CW II'), 6.

[76] 'he [God] gave me utterance more than an hour. I exhorted them to repentance and to come to knowledge of God by the remission of sins... I have ever seen myself the most unfit to exhort having neither mouth nor wisdom, yet several times of late I could not refrain.' Sarah Perrin to CW, MS letter, 12 June 1750 (MCA: 'Letters to CW II'), 55.

[77] 'You had need indeed to pray for wisdom for me. They increase that come to hear.' Ibid.

[78] Thomas Barnard to CW, MS letter, 18 August 1771 (MCA: DDPr 1/3).

[79] 'Barnard. Wise remark of honourable women.' Ibid.

observing that in Kinsale I am of every Religion. The Presbyterians say I am a Presbyterian; the church-goers, that I am a minister of theirs; and the Catholics are sure I am a good Catholic in my heart.'[80] Far from being concerned that he was difficult to recognize as an Anglican minister, Charles seemed proud of the fact. This cavalier attitude towards his denominational identity was something that Charles shared with people from all sections of the Evangelical community. The willingness of the Wesleys and their associates to venture outside denominational constraints in the most public fashion was one of the aspects that distinguished them from their more conventional brethren.

The Methodists did not differ from the Church of England in matters of doctrine, and far from rejecting her Sacraments and public worship they embraced them with a degree of enthusiasm that other Anglicans found rather unsettling. Nor was the pursuit of inward holiness incompatible with the tenets of the Church; High Churchmen such as Samuel Wesley senior and Latitudinarians such as John Tillotson would have all claimed to be focused on this quest. There were differences in emphasis between Evangelicals and other Anglicans exemplified by the use of such terms as the 'New Birth', but these should perhaps more properly be termed variations rather than departures from the Anglican norm. There was in fact no aspect of the Wesleys' teaching that was not either contained within the doctrines of the Church of England or so radically different that it could not have been accommodated within this exceptionally broad denomination. The brothers' older contemporary Archbishop William Wake proudly noted that:

The moderation of the Church of England has been very exemplary... and we have felt the good effect of it in that peace we enjoy among our ministers, notwithstanding their known difference of opinion in many considerable articles of Christian doctrine. The Thirty-nine Articles... we have left every one to interpret them in his own sense; and they are indeed so generally framed that they may, without any equivocation, have more senses than one fairly put upon them.[81]

---

[80] CWJ, 8 September 1748.
[81] Quoted by Paul Avis, *Anglicanism and the Christian Church*: Theological Resources in Historical Perspective (Minneapolis: Fortress, 1989), 138.

Wake was writing before Methodism was founded, but his references to 'moderation' and 'peace' provide a key to understanding why the Wesleys provoked such fierce opposition. The Evangelicals were viewed in many quarters as dangerous radicals, not because of their beliefs, although the Wesleyan concept of perfection did raise a few eyebrows, but because of their practices. They were obviously discontented with the Church as it stood, but instead of moving into nonconformity, they abused traditional Anglican toleration and seemed set on undermining the Church from within, very much like the Puritans of an earlier era. They imposed meetings that had no place in Anglican structure, adopted practices that owed more to Dissent than the Establishment, and showed scant respect for their colleagues and superiors in the ministry. This is not to argue that the institution of the Church of England was negative in its attitude towards innovation or dead to the stirrings of popular piety. The religious societies of the late seventeenth century are an example of Anglican openness to new ideas, while the Wesleys' experiments with holy living at university were tolerated and even welcomed in certain quarters. It was when the Wesleys and their fellow Evangelicals took promotion of personal holiness out of the Oxford colleges and fashioned a mass ministry that the flashpoint occurred.

The Evangelicals were not the only Anglicans to stray outside normal Church of England practice, and indeed the point has already been made that in the half-century after the restoration of the monarchy it would be difficult to define what constituted such practice. At the parish level there was great diversity exemplified by the fact that some ministers wore a surplice, others did not; in some churches, the Eucharist was celebrated once a month, and in others, once a quarter; the parish Puritans had a dual identity that encompassed attendance at the parish church as well as more private gatherings and to the outrage of the High Church, many individuals embraced the practice of occasional conformity in order to avoid civil penalties. At the other end of the Anglican spectrum, Nonjurors such as Susanna Wesley sought the advice of their own bishops outside the Church of England over such intimate matters as the state of her marriage.[82] The Anglican leadership had been able to hold these many disparate

---

[82] Susanna Wesley, *Susanna Wesley*, 34–9.

strands of the denomination together because few people showed any inclination to take religious differences into the street and thereby run the risk of inciting disturbance and persecution. The civil authorities too had learned to turn a blind eye to quiet breaches of Anglican conformity. Practical toleration was the prevailing sentiment of the early eighteenth-century Church and a source of pride to men such as William Wake.

This uneasy consensus was disturbed by the arrival of the Evangelicals on the religious scene at the end of the 1730s. It had been possible to ignore such groups as the discreet parish Puritans, but the loud and turbulent Methodists were a different matter. Whitefield and the Wesleys beseeched the Almighty and celebrated their spiritual triumphs before crowds of thousands and were followed by an ever-growing band of lay preachers. They trumpeted their views, one might say their defiance, through a multitude of publications that were aimed primarily at the common man rather than the Church and social elite, and when the brothers were called to account for their actions, they refused to give way, confident in the knowledge that they were doing God's work.

The Wesleys also made use of an uncommon talent for picking over fine points of discipline in order to find a convenient loophole. John Wesley for example, justified his practice of preaching in other ministers' parishes because of his status as a Fellow of Lincoln College.[83] It is worth pointing out that Charles as a mere 'student of Christ Church' did not have that argument available to him, but preached anyway. This level of public intransigence came as a shock to the bishops: in 1738 Charles had a stormy interview with the Bishop of London during the course of which he bluntly challenged his superior to invoke his authority and prevent him from preaching. It was the bishop who backed down with the telling words: 'O why will you push things to an extreme? I do not inhibit you.'[84]

Anglican toleration did of course have its limits and there are many first-hand accounts of Methodists being persecuted, but it is important not to exaggerate this campaign of violence and harassment; incidents tended to be localized in nature and were driven by the

---

[83] Baker, *John Wesley and the Church of England*, 71.
[84] Quoted by Gill, *Charles Wesley*, 77.

irritation of individuals rather than the policy of Church and State. Much of the active persecution was also confined to the first decade of Methodism's existence, although hostility and dislike remained for many years. The Anglican response was rendered confused by the fact that the Church of England itself was divided over its reaction to revival. The rank and file of the Wesleyan societies was drawn largely from Anglican congregations and there were sympathizers among the bishops, parochial clergy, and gentry. Even people who were inimical to the Evangelicals tended to stop short of calling for the suppression of the movement or their expulsion from the Church, perhaps fearful that such action would lead to yet greater division and sectarian feeling.

There is no doubt that Charles Wesley was indeed a paradoxical Anglican, but his view of God and the Church was shared by many within the Methodist movement and the broader Anglican community. The Church of England was so wide in its boundaries that people could legitimately regard themselves as true Anglicans while at the same time building a loyalty to another body that was rapidly forging its own identity. In one sense, Methodism was one of the fruits of that spirit of Anglican toleration and inclusiveness that had evolved through bitter experience. For Charles Wesley and the majority of Methodists there was no inherent contradiction in their stance, particularly during the first twenty years of the Revival. They placed obedience to God above unthinking subservience to denomination and were able to maintain loyalty to both. Yet there came a stage in Charles Wesley's life after which he tried to act as a brake on the process he had initiated and he may have even attempted to reverse it. One must ask when did his views change, and why? This must be looked at against the background of the evolution of the Wesleys' relationship with one another starting with their engagements and marriages.

5

Engagements and Marriages

Three distinct phases in Charles Wesley's Evangelical ministry can be identified. The first lasted for ten years from the birth of Methodism as a mass movement in 1739; during the decade that followed, the Wesley brothers worked in a state of almost perfect harmony, the product of a unique relationship grounded in shared experience and a common outlook. This golden age was followed by a period of upheaval marked by increasingly bitter disagreements between the two men and worry over developments within the movement that they had created. This transitional phase lasted for seven years from 1749 and concluded with Charles Wesley's retirement from the itinerancy. His adoption of a settled lifestyle and assumption of the mantle of champion of the Anglican–Methodist link marked the onset of the third and final stage of Charles's Methodist ministry which lasted from 1756 until his death in 1788.

The scholarly coverage of the fifty-year span of Charles's involvement with Methodism has often been uneven, with the greatest attention being paid to his heroic efforts during the 1740s and early 1750s.[1] The third phase of his ministry has often been dominated by Charles's family life, his hymns and, to a lesser extent, the fierce disputes over the separation question. The seven-year bridge between these two stages has always posed something of a problem for historians and has never been properly examined. Yet its importance is self-evident—in 1748, as Charles entered the ninth year of his ministry as a Methodist preacher, there seemed little reason to doubt that his

---

[1] For example, in John Telford's biography of Charles Wesley published in 1900, the last thirty years of his subject's life are covered in just 51 pages out of a total of 309. Telford, *Charles Wesley*, 201–15 and 255–92.

life would continue in its by now familiar path, but an event was about to take place that signalled a fundamental change, one that in its own way was as far-reaching as his conversion. The marriage of Charles Wesley and Sarah Gwynne in April 1749 was a watershed, one that was to have effects far beyond Charles's personal life. After his marriage, Charles reduced his itinerant ministry until it ceased altogether and this development reflected a change in priorities as he opted increasingly for a life of domesticity. This re-orientation adversely affected Charles's relationship with John and for the first time serious cracks in the fraternal bond appeared. There is also evidence to indicate that Charles's engagement and marriage caused his brother to take stock of his own personal life, with tragic and far-reaching consequences. Personal disagreements between the Wesley brothers were in turn aggravated by tension over the Methodist relationship with the Church of England and soon private and public areas of discord became inextricably intertwined. This chapter and the next will explore the dramatic events of these years, starting with the courtships and marriages of John and Charles Wesley.

THE ENGAGEMENT AND MARRIAGE OF CHARLES WESLEY

As a young man, Charles's views on his fitness for marriage are difficult to judge. In one journal entry, he claimed to be afraid of matrimony,[2] but this should perhaps be seen as an aspect of a nature that tended towards negativity. Against this should be set an obvious fondness for the company of women: Charles had a flirtatious manner and it appears that he was an attractive and passionate man. As an undergraduate, he had briefly been the romantic target of a designing actress called Molly Buchanan, who had apparently been the kept woman of the Duke of Richmond. As careful as Charles was not to get too involved, it appears from his letter to John Wesley describing the affair, that he rather enjoyed this brush with a genuine scarlet woman.[3] A few months after his dalliance with Buchanan,

---

[2] CWJ, 19 April 1748.
[3] CW to JW, MS letter, 5 June [1729] (MCA: DDCW 1/2).

family correspondence reveal that his visits to the girls' school where his sister taught may have been prompted by more than family duty. One of the teenage pupils referred to Charles, who was aged 22 at the time, as a 'saucy cur', while another pined for him after he left.[4]

Later in life, as a charismatic evangelist, Charles had a particular appeal for the opposite sex: James Hutton, a friend of the Wesleys, referred to the brothers in a letter of 1740 as 'dangerous snares to many young women; several are in love with them'. He also made the intriguing comment that he would not like any sister of his to marry John or Charles.[5] Based on such evidence, it appears that the Wesleys' charisma was grounded in more than spiritual gifts, and this sexual element to their attractiveness led on occasion to accusations of impropriety.[6] As groundless as these charges undoubtedly were, Charles's eventual engagement was a source of disappointment to at least one female Methodist, as well as his friend Edward Perronet, who, unlike James Hutton, had hoped that Charles would one day marry his sister. Despite such entanglements, Charles's only serious romantic commitment was to his future wife Sarah Gwynne.

Sarah was the daughter of Marmaduke Gwynne, a prominent Welsh landowner and a friend of Methodism during the movement's early years. Charles first made the acquaintance of his bride-to-be on 28 August 1747 when he paid a visit to the Gwynne family estate at Garth in Brecknockshire.[7] Sarah was his junior by nineteen years, but subsequent events indicate that the attraction between them must have been at first sight. After a stay with the family lasting several days, Charles left for Ireland from where he conducted a correspondence with Sarah that quickly became personal as well as pastoral. The fact that he was soon confiding his 'embryo intentions' to his

---

[4] 'Peggy has had the tooth-ache ever since he [Charles] went away. Miss Kitty is here by me, and says he is a saucy cur, and she will turn him off, because he never went to see her at Gainsborough.' Emily Wesley to JW, Photographic copy letter, 31 December 1729 (MCA: DDWF 6/2).

[5] James Hutton to Count Zinzendorf, Published copy letter, 14 March 1740. Quoted by Daniel Benham, *Memoirs of James Hutton: comprising the annals of his life, and Connection with the United Brethren* (London: Hamilton, Adams & Co., 1856), 47.

[6] Baker, *Charles Wesley as Revealed*, 54–5.   [7] CWJ, 28 August 1747.

brother shows the deep impression that the young Welsh woman had made.[8]

On 25 March 1748, Charles returned to Garth after a gruelling preaching tour. His health had been affected and he remained for nine days under Sarah's care.[9] While recovering from his illness, Charles proposed to Sarah Gwynne on 3 April 1748 and this is recorded in shorthand in his journal.[10] The proposal was accepted without hesitation and almost immediately a reaction set in, at least on Charles's part.[11] There is no doubt that the couple had strong feelings, but as Charles himself acknowledged on another occasion, it was part of his nature to be fearful.[12] There were also practical matters to take into account: Charles had no home or regular income, and this latter consideration would be a major obstacle in the way of gaining parental approval. Finally, there was John Wesley's reaction to bring into the equation, and this is more interesting still as Charles's marriage proved a significant turning point in the fraternal relationship.

When Charles first mentioned to his brother, prior to his proposal of marriage, that he had a strong attraction for Sarah Gwynne, the response was lukewarm,[13] although this is understandable as at that early stage in the relationship even Charles doubted that anything would result.[14] What is puzzling is that more than seven months elapsed between the proposal and John being informed of the engagement. It is true that the couple appear to have kept it a secret from most people and it is highly doubtful whether their 'understanding' could be said to have amounted to a binding commitment—for a

---

[8] Charles's reference to this conversation is retrospective in that he states that it had taken place during his preaching tour of Ireland between 9 September 1747 and 20 March 1748. CWJ, 19 April 1748.

[9] CWJ, 25 March 1748.

[10] 'At night my dearest Sally, like my guardian angel, attended me ... I asked her if she could trust herself with me for life and with a noble simplicity she readily answered me she could.' CWJ, 3 April 1748.

[11] 'Frightened at what I had said last night I condemned mine rashness and almost wished I had never discovered myself.' CWJ, 4 April 1748.

[12] 'Our different judgement of persons was owing to our different temper: his all hope, and mine all fear.' Quoted by Baker, *John Wesley and the Church of England*, 207.

[13] 'I had communicated my embryo intentions to my brother while in Ireland, which he neither opposed, nor much encouraged.' CWJ, 19 April 1748.

[14] 'It was then a distant first thought, nor likely ever to come to a proposal; as I had not given the least hint, either to Miss Gwynne or the family.' CWJ, 19 April 1748.

wealthy family like the Gwynnes, financial negotiations were a necessary prelude to a formal engagement and this would have been understood by both parties. Charles did however confide in his close friend Vincent Perronet on 19 April 1748[15] and the Bristol Methodist Elizabeth Vigor on 4 November.[16] He also appears to have made up his mind to speak to Sarah's mother as early as June 1748,[17] although he did not write to her formally concerning the matter for another six months.[18] The fact that Charles was actively making plans and was prepared to talk about his intentions, but not to his own brother and closest colleague, suggests a wariness concerning John's reaction.

Finally on 11 November, he made this journal entry:

My brother and I having promised each other (as soon as he came from Georgia) that we would neither of us marry, or take any step towards it, without the other's knowledge and consent, today I fairly and fully communicated every thought of my heart. He had proposed three persons to me, S.P., M.W., and S.G.: and entirely approved my choice of the last. We consulted together about every particular and were of one heart and mind in all things.[19]

In the months that followed, John was deeply involved in negotiations concerning the marriage settlement, and there is nothing in either Charles's plain-text journal or his correspondence until just prior to the wedding in April 1749, to indicate that his brother was anything other than totally supportive. However, there is evidence to indicate that John had deep misgivings from a very early stage: just five days after his brother was told of the engagement, Charles wrote the following shorthand entry in his journal: 'Talked with my brother about a provision in case I got married and he said the Church could not afford it. "Then" I thought, "the Church did not deserve a gospel minister." '[20] With this shorthand passage, a major deficiency of Charles Wesley scholarship is highlighted. Without access to the shorthand, his biographers have made inevitable mistakes concerning interpretation of key events in Charles's life and this is exemplified by their analysis of the Wesley brothers' relationship as they approached this crossroads. Brailsford for example states that 'John's heart warmed

---

[15] CWJ, 19 April 1748.
[16] CWJ, 4 November 1748.
[17] CWJ, 20 and 26 June 1748.
[18] CWJ, 2 December 1748.
[19] CWJ, 11 November 1748.
[20] CWJ, 16 November 1748.

towards the lovers, and he encouraged his diffident brother',[21] while Baker refers to Charles's choice of wife being confirmed by John Wesley,[22] implying that at that stage he was completely supportive. All these are reasonable assumptions to make from the evidence of Charles's plain-text journal and his letters, but a more complicated picture is revealed by the shorthand and this evidence of early hesitation will assume importance as the discussion of the Wesleys' marriages and their effect on Methodism takes further shape.

The practical objection to Charles's marriage on the grounds of finance will be examined shortly but it is important at this point to look at other possible explanations for John's lack of enthusiasm. His doubts may have been based on fear that the special bond with Charles was under threat, as he could not have been unaware that marriage would challenge his own central place in his brother's loyalties. Also, if he had suspected that Charles had proposed seven months previously, he would have had grounds for arguing that his brother had broken their agreement not to 'take any step towards [marriage]' without the other's consent. Charles had spoken of his plans to at least two mutual friends, Vincent Perronet and Elizabeth Vigor, and it is possible that John discovered or suspected what was going on prior to 11 November 1748. This puts into a different light the charge that is sometimes levelled at John Wesley, namely that he did not inform Charles at an early stage of his own marital intentions late in 1749. Charles's violent reaction to John's engagement to Grace Murray has been partly excused by this assumption that John had broken his word;[23] Charles himself complained that his brother had betrayed their agreement,[24] but without any acknowledgement that he had done likewise.

John did not refer to his worries about the impending wedding in his surviving personal papers. Indeed, he did not mention the engagement at all in his journal or extant letters, written between November 1748 and the day of the wedding itself five months later.

---

[21] Brailsford, *A Tale of Two Brothers*, 167.

[22] Baker, *Charles Wesley as Revealed*, 59–60.

[23] Brailsford, *A Tale of Two Brothers*, 189–90; Frank Baker, 'Poet in Love—The Courtship of Charles Wesley, 1747–49', *Methodist History*, 29:4 (July 1991), 238.

[24] 'All the security I desired...was his bare word, that he would not take a step of so general importance without advice.' CWJ, 13 December 1749.

This is a curious omission for a man who in his journal during this same period discourses on a wide variety of subjects from the literary merits of the *Iliad*[25] to his horse throwing a shoe.[26] It is true that the journal was written with publication in mind, but some reference to the forthcoming happy event might have been expected. The entry in which he describes conducting his brother's wedding service is also strangely impersonal: 'I married my brother and Sarah Gwynne. It was a solemn day, such as became the dignity of a Christian marriage.'[27] This may be simply another sign of the strange detachment from human feelings that was an aspect of John's personality, but it may also indicate a reluctance to face up to an issue with deep personal implications. It is perhaps appropriate to point out that John does not appear to have objected to Sarah on a personal level. Very little correspondence between them has survived, but there is nothing to indicate that their relationship was anything other than cordial, and after his brother's death in 1788, John was quick to offer help to his sister-in-law.

A vivid retrospective insight into John's intimate thoughts about his brother's marriage can be deduced from a pointed letter that he wrote to Charles at the time of his own engagement to Grace Murray, just a few months after Charles's wedding.[28] John argues that his marriage to Murray would not involve additional expense 'if I married one I maintain now, who would afterward desire nothing more than she had before'. Also, he had observed Murray from a close distance for several years and this had convinced him that she was suitable for marriage to a travelling evangelist: '[for] I particularly insist upon this. If I ever have a wife she ought to be the most useful woman in the kingdom—not barely one who probably *may* be so (I could not be content to run such a hazard).' As for Murray's humble birth, he considered this an irrelevance 'as it does not prevent either her grace or her gifts. Besides, whoever I marry, I believe it will not be a gentlewoman—I despair of finding any such so qualified.' This

---

[25] JWJ, 12 August 1748. John Wesley, *The Works of John Wesley*, xx. *Journal and Diaries III (1743–1754)*, ed. W. Reginald Ward and Richard Heitzenrater (Nashville: Abingdon, 1991), 238.
[26] JWJ, 21 February 1748. Ibid. 209.   [27] JWJ, 8 April 1749. Ibid. 266.
[28] JW to CW, Published copy letter [25 September 1749]. John Wesley, *The Works of John Wesley*, xxvi. 380–7.

incisive logic contained barely concealed criticism of Charles's own choice of bride, as Charles had known Sarah for only a very short time before he was confiding his 'embryo intentions' to his brother. Also, she was certainly a 'gentlewoman' from a family that required their daughter be maintained in a lifestyle that did not sit well with that of an itinerant preacher.

John's subtle way of criticizing his brother without the complication of a direct assault was a tactic that he was to use several times as their personal and public disagreements gathered pace and venom. In 1786 for example, he published a letter in the *Arminian Magazine* responding to Charles's objections to separation from the Church of England.[29] The tone of this public epistle is sharp with more than a hint of personal animosity, but does not contain any reference to his brother being the addressee. Charles could be just as careful in his own clashes with John; in 1785 he authored, under the nom de plume of a 'Methodist of the Church of England', a published attack on Thomas Coke, which also contained implied criticism of his own brother.[30] The beginning of this pattern of bitter controversy and indirect attack can be seen in John's letter justifying his choice of wife.

Money was certainly a factor in the start of the brother's alienation and was to prove a lasting source of resentment. Methodism had a particular appeal for the poor, with the inevitable result that Connexional finance was a perennial problem. Itinerant preachers were dependent on local societies for their support and those with families were subject to particular hardship,[31] which was a major reason why single men were preferred for the itinerant ministry. The settlement that was insisted upon by the Gwynnes before they consented to their

---

[29] The *Arminian Magazine, for the year 1786. Consisting chiefly of extracts and original treatises on universal redemption*, 8 (January 1786), 50–1.

[30] [Charles Wesley] 'A Methodist of the Church of England', *Strictures on the substance of a sermon preached at Baltimore in the state of Maryland before the General Conference of the Methodist Episcopal Church, on the 27th of December 1784 at the ordination of the Rev. Francis Asbury to the office of superintendent by Thomas Coke, LL.D., superintendent of the said Church* (London: G. Herdsfield, 1785).

[31] John Wesley's 'Rules of an Assistant' states: 'Take no money of any one. If they give you food when you are hungry or clothes when you need them, it is good. But not silver or gold. Let there be no pretence to say, we grow rich by the gospel.' Quoted by Albert Brown-Lawson, *John Wesley and the Anglican Evangelicals of the 18th Century* (Bishop Auckland: Pentland, 1994), 87–8.

daughter's marriage represented a significant burden, not just for the groom but also for his brother and the Methodist movement.

The final version of the marriage settlement, signed on 9 August 1749,[32] required that £2,500 be raised from the sale of publications and invested to produce an annuity in Sarah's name of £100.[33] The deed lists over sixty published works, the proceeds from which were to be temporarily transferred to two trustees. The titles included many of Charles's hymn-books, such as *Hymns and Sacred Poems* and *Hymns on the Nativity*, but works written by John are also well represented, including his published journal in four volumes, *The Character of a Methodist* and the *Sermon on Christian Perfection*. Until this time, the profits from the sale of these works had been devoted to furthering the Revival, and the loss of £2,500 was no small matter— during the winter of 1739 it cost just £700 to adapt the Foundery to use as the Methodist headquarters.[34] At a time when preachers could expect nothing beyond food on the table and clothes on the back, John's misgivings are understandable; certainly, he used this issue as a stick to beat his brother with in the years that followed.

There were also fears concerning the effect of marriage on Charles's commitment to the itinerancy, and in a meeting with the brothers, Sarah agreed that she would not require him to abandon this aspect of his ministry.[35] Her promise was without doubt sincere, but it was not long before domestic matters were proving an inevitable distraction.

John's doubts reached a climax as the wedding day approached. On 1 April 1749, as the brothers were preparing to leave Kingswood for the ceremony, to be held at Garth a week later, Charles wrote in his journal: 'Just as we were setting out...my brother appeared full of scruples; and refused to go to Garth at all; I kept my temper and promised, "If he could not be satisfied there, to desist." '[36] Tension between the two men increased as they neared their destination. Charles, not surprisingly, was in a hurry but discovered to his aggravation that John had arranged to preach at several places

---

[32] MS settlement upon the marriage of CW and Sarah Gwynne, 9 August 1749 (MCA: DDCW 6/87).
[33] Children of the marriage were also to benefit from the annuity.
[34] Heitzenrater, *Wesley and the People Called Methodists*, 110.
[35] CWJ, 19 February 1749.   [36] CWJ, 1 April 1749.

along the way;[37] at one point climbing to the top of an uninhabited Welsh mountain to do so.[38] This has been explained as an illustration of John's overriding commitment to evangelism,[39] but it can also be viewed as a pointed reminder to Charles as to where his priorities should lie. The fact that John was having second thoughts about the marriage settlement, which was agreed on in principle only on the day before the wedding itself, would have done nothing to ease Charles's nerves or his resentment. After a meeting with Sarah's mother,[40] John finally gave way with regard to the financial details and on the morning of 8 April 1749, Charles Wesley and Sarah Gwynne were married.

Charles Wesley's marriage was an event of central significance in his life and ministry. Leaving aside the obvious effect of having a wife and raising a family, the nature of his relationship with John and the Methodists was changed for ever. The tension between the brothers, apparent from 1749, was to a certain degree founded on Charles's awareness of his new domestic responsibilities and attempts to assert independence from his overbearing brother. At the same time, this was to clash with a part of his nature that was acutely protective of the brothers' special bond: for his part, John was to prove insensitive to the change in Charles's circumstances and seems to have always expected first call on his brother's loyalties. The most obvious result of Charles's marriage on his position within Methodism has been seen as its contribution to his eventual withdrawal from the itinerancy, but this process did not reach completion until 1756 and will therefore be examined in a later chapter.

JOHN WESLEY'S ENGAGEMENT AND HIS BROTHER'S REACTION

It appears that the tension between the brothers eased once Charles's wedding actually took place, but within a few months trouble again

---

[37] 'found my brother had appointed to preach in several places till Friday: which I did not take kindly'. CWJ, 2 April 1749.
[38] JWJ, 6 April 1749. John Wesley, *The Works of John Wesley*, xx. 265–6.
[39] Gill, *Charles Wesley*, 140.   [40] CWJ, 7 April 1749.

erupted from a totally unexpected source, namely John Wesley's engagement to Grace Murray. This rather strange affair provides further insight into the disturbed undercurrents of the fraternal relationship, as well as marking the first occasion that private tension spilled over into the public work.

A foretaste of Charles's views on the desirability of John entering into wedlock is provided by a conversation he had with George Whitefield which he subsequently reported to Sarah Gwynne in December 1748.[41] Whitefield had urged the Wesley brothers to marry, unaware that Charles was already engaged. Charles 'pleaded hard for my brother's exemption; but he would not hear of it'. It seems strange that Charles should have been determined that John should be excluded from finding domestic happiness at precisely the same time that Charles himself was striving for it. This reluctance may have been grounded in concern that his brother was simply not suited to matrimony; certainly, the disaster that was John's union with Mary Vazeille adds weight to the view that he was incapable of sharing his life in an equal relationship, but it appears that Charles had other more personal reasons for wishing his brother to remain unattached.

Even as the conversation between his brother and Whitefield was taking place, John had already taken his first steps towards engagement and marriage. In August 1748, while suffering from an illness in Newcastle, he was nursed back to health by Grace Murray, the housekeeper at the Orphan House. John later described his deepening feelings: 'I observ'd her more narrowly than ever before, both as to her temper, sense & behaviour. I esteem'd and lov'd her more & more. And, when I was a little recover'd, I told her, sliding into it I know not how, "If ever I marry, I think you will be the person." After some time I spoke to her more directly...'[42] One is tempted to speculate what misunderstandings might have been avoided if John had informed his brother at this stage, but he did not, and Charles did not find out about the match until he received in September 1749 a copy of a letter that John had sent to Grace's other suitor, John Bennet.[43] This was twelve months after John had tentatively declared his romantic

---

[41] CW to Sarah Gwynne jun., MS letter [23 December 1748] (MCA: DDWes 4/53).
[42] John Wesley, *John Wesley's Last Love*, ed. J. A. Leger (London: J. M. Dent & Sons, 1910), 1.
[43] Brailsford, *A Tale of Two Brothers*, 189.

interest in Murray. Charles's reaction to this bombshell revelation was extreme; in the two weeks following receipt of the letter on about 18 September, he travelled literally from one end of England to the other in order to prevent his brother's wedding from taking place.

Charles's objections were summarized by John in a letter that he wrote to his brother on 25 September 1749 following a tense meeting between the two men in Whitehaven.[44] Charles apparently feared that John's authority over the societies would be destroyed by the fact of Murray's humble birth, and the scandal that could be imputed by her having travelled with John to Ireland; more importantly, it was at least debatable that she was simultaneously engaged to the preacher John Bennet.

Charles's reasons were not entirely without a rational base. His brother's relationship with Murray had already been the source of jealous discussion within the societies, especially among the female members who did not wish to see one of their number singled out by their charismatic leader.[45] Murray's own lack of decisiveness when it came to choosing between Bennet and Wesley added to the turmoil;[46] Charles's misgivings were certainly shared by other people, including the preacher Christopher Hopper and the laywoman Jeanie Keith.[47]

During a meeting on 24 September to try to resolve the situation, the brothers agreed to submit to their friend Vincent Perronet's arbitration, but two days later Charles broke his word. Taking advantage of John's temporary absence, he left without warning for the village of Hindley Hill, where his brother had left his fiancée a week previously.

Given Charles's erratic behaviour during the Grace Murray affair, it is valuable to digress briefly in order to examine the reliability of John Wesley's manuscript narrative, which is the main source for the details of this episode.[48] Unfortunately there is little in the way of

[44] JW to CW, Published copy letter [25 September 1749]. John Wesley, *The Works of John Wesley*, xxvi. 380–7.
[45] Brailsford, *A Tale of Two Brothers*, 181, 185, 187.   [46] Ibid. 181–2.
[47] Simon Valentine, *John Bennet and the Origins of Methodism and the Evangelical Revival in England*, Pietist and Wesleyan Studies, 9 (Lanham, Md.: Scarecrow, 1997), 215.
[48] This manuscript was deposited at the British Museum in 1829 and was later transcribed and edited by J. A. Leger under the title *Wesley's Last Love*.

corroborating or conflicting contemporary evidence—there is a gap in Charles's journal between 16 September and 21 October 1749, while John Bennet makes little reference to the affair in his manuscript diary but directs the reader to a pocketbook which does not appear to be extant.[49] All things considered, the balance of probability appears to be in favour of John's recollection being substantially correct—the names, dates, and details of conversations are very specific, and the fact that the manuscript was not apparently intended for publication is additional weight in favour of its accuracy.

Immediately after his arrival in Hindley Hill, Charles confronted Murray. His opening words, as reported by his brother, illustrates his excited state of mind: 'About eleven my brother [Charles] came. He kist her and said "G. M. You have broke my heart." Then he dropped down.'[50] This extravagant initial reaction was not replaced by more sober reflection. Instead, Charles, once he had recovered his senses, exerted considerable pressure on Murray to accompany him to Newcastle where her other love-interest Bennet awaited her. John later discovered that his brother was so determined to destroy his engagement that he constantly changed direction to elude possible pursuit.[51] He also misled Murray in order to persuade her to go with him, telling her that they were going to meet John Wesley and giving her the impression that his brother had himself made this arrangement.[52] Upon her arrival in Newcastle, Grace Murray was married to Bennet on 3 October 1749; neither party were keen to go through with the ceremony and it took all of Charles's powers of persuasion before they consented.[53]

The extent of Charles's revulsion at the very suggestion of John getting married, is shown by the extraordinary lengths to which he was prepared to go. In order to calm the fears of the couple, Charles placed all the blame on his brother, accusing him in John's words of 'having used my whole Art & Authority to seduce another man's wife' on the grounds that Murray was already committed to Bennet.[54] In crowded meetings of the Newcastle Society, the most important

---

[49] MS diary of John Bennet, 3 October 1749 (MCA: John Bennet/Grace Murray collection).
[50] John Wesley, *Wesley's Last Love*, 90. [51] Ibid. 93. [52] Ibid. 92.
[53] Valentine, *John Bennet*, 216. [54] John Wesley, *Wesley's Last Love*, 94.

outside London and Bristol, Charles and Bennet took turns in attacking their leader:

> The effect of what he & [John Bennet] said...was, that all in the house...were set on fire, filled wth anger and confusion...[Sister] Proctor would leave the house immediately. [John] Whitford would preach with Mr [Wesley] no more...Another dreamer went a step further, and saw Mr [Wesley] in hell-fire. Jane Keith was preremptory 'John [Wesley] is a child of the Devil': Coming pretty near [John Bennet] himself; whose repeated word was, 'If [John Wesley] is not damned, there is no God.'[55]

The brothers finally caught up with each other in Leeds. Charles's initial reaction was to launch a violent verbal assault, and it was only after the intercession of George Whitefield, that the two were reconciled amidst scenes of great emotion. With his brother out of danger, Charles allowed himself to be persuaded that it was all Grace Murray's fault.[56]

Charles Wesley does not emerge with credit from this bizarre affair. What John Wesley's account makes clear is that his brother, the great evangelist and hymn-writer, was prone in moments of stress to hysterical outbursts, characterized by extremes of language and behaviour. In the particular instance of his brother's engagement to Murray, Charles's actions were triggered by a threat to his relationship with John. The reasons that he put forward to justify his opposition, such as the effect of John's marriage on his commitment to Methodism, cannot explain or justify the sheer violence of the reaction. One of the many contradictions of Charles's personality is that even after his own marriage, he remained extremely protective of his relationship with his brother. This is underlined in a series of poems that he wrote in 1751 at the time of John's union with Mary Vazeille. The overriding theme is one of deep personal loss akin to bereavement, very unusual in a man writing about his brother's wedding. Two stanzas from the poem entitled 'Ah woe is me, A man of woe' sum up his mood:

> My other self, but more beloved
> In youth, in manhood tried,
> Faithful for 30 winters prov'd
> Is ravished from my side

[55] Ibid. 95. [56] Ibid. 88.

> O what a mighty loss is mine!
> The anguish who can tell
> The more than anguish, to resign
> A soul, I lov'd so well[57]

Such evidence reinforces the argument that the relationship between the Wesleys was not simply one way; John was the natural leader, but Charles was by no means the unwilling subordinate in their strange yet complementary union. Their mutual dependence existed on such a deep level as to defy rational explanation, which probably explains in part why their relationship has not received the scholarly attention that it deserves. The strength of this bond proved a two-edged sword; a powerful weapon during the 1740s, it became a source of great bitterness in later years.

It is intriguing that the brothers should have decided to embark on marriage at about the same time. On the surface, there are understandable reasons why this should have occurred: they were both in middle age and approaching a time when starting a family might not be a possibility for much longer, but there appear to have been additional underlying factors with specific regard to Charles's brother.

John Wesley dated his decision that he could marry without compromising his ministry to June 1748,[58] despite the fact that he had previously, by his own admission, been very much opposed to marriage.[59] It was just a few months previously that Charles had made the first intimations that he had strong affections for Sarah Gwynne in what amounted to his first serious romantic commitment. In August 1748, just two months after deciding that he could marry as well, John chose Grace Murray for his bride, years after their first meeting.[60] That his attachment was sudden, despite his own subsequent protestations to the contrary,[61] is shown by the fact that Murray herself was

---

[57] Charles Wesley, MS Hymn-book (MCA: MS Richmond), 142–3.

[58] John Wesley, *Wesley's Last Love*, 1.

[59] JW to CW, Published copy letter [25 September 1749]. John Wesley, *The Works of John Wesley*, xxvi. 380–1.

[60] This can be dated with certainty to 1739 or 1740. Rack, *Reasonable Enthusiast*, 259.

[61] 'from a close observation of several years... I am persuaded that she is in in every capacity an help meet for me'. JW to CW, Published copy letter [25 September 1749]. John Wesley, *The Works of John Wesley*, xxvi. 382.

'utterly amazed'.[62] This was at precisely the time that John might have been hearing from other people, as well as his own intuition, that his brother was feeling his way towards matrimony.

The argument could be made that John's abrupt change of heart with regard to marriage was a direct reaction to Charles falling in love with Sarah Gwynne. According to this interpretation, faced with the possible loss of his deepest personal relationship, John was looking for a replacement. Sibling rivalry might also have had a part to play—one is reminded that Charles's Evangelical conversion in 1738 was followed a few days later by John's. Such an interpretation of the psychological background to the Grace Murray affair fits with what we know of the strength of the brothers' attachment, and their mutual fears concerning each others' marriages. Much has been said about the differences in the personalities of the Wesley brothers, with John typically seen as logical and emotionally detached, while Charles was passionate and impulsive; there is truth in this picture, but the Wesleys were more alike than is commonly supposed. Their modes of expression might have been different, but they both exhibited signs of deep emotional insecurity; Charles destroyed his brother's engagement, but John had also been inclined to block Charles's wedding. When one looks at other members of their family, it becomes clear that instability was not the preserve of Charles Wesley's poetic nature, but was in fact a family trait.[63]

The Grace Murray affair left the brothers on the brink of permanent division, despite the apparent reconciliation in Leeds. On 28 October 1749 Charles made the following shorthand entry in his journal; 'Heard that my brother was come. Troubled and burdened yet went to him. No love or joy or comfort in the meeting. No confidence on either side; he did not want to talk with me.'[64] Mutual friends attempted to mediate between the brothers but to no avail.[65]

---

[62] John Wesley, *Wesley's Last Love*, 1.
[63] The stubbornness of their father Samuel bordered at times on the irrational; Charles's son Charles junior was at the very least emotionally immature; his other son Samuel was mentally unstable and Charles's grandson the organist Samuel Sebastian Wesley was regarded as highly eccentric.
[64] CWJ, 28 October 1749.
[65] 'I thank you for speaking to my brother, but in vain do you refer me to him for the result of your conference. I am no longer of his council.' CW to Vincent Perronet, MS copy letter, 13 December 1749. CWJ, 13 December 1749.

Charles adopted what amounted to victim status, which is rather surprising in the circumstances. This is illustrated by a letter that he wrote to Vincent Perronet on 30 October 1749 and subsequently transcribed in shorthand in his journal:

> Yesterday I assisted him [JW] at the Sacrament, but my mouth was stopped all day, my hands hung down, and my heart fainted... Forced by his impatience, I had offered him my account of what has lately happened, though I judged it far better to defer it till his passion should be laid and his eyes opened. It had the effect I expected. He denied the whole. William Shent's account was all lies. Jane Keith's was all lies. His only was altogether true. He had been in no fault at all, in no passion or inordinate affection, but had done all things well, and with the utmost calmness and deliberation. He had been no temptation; the church and work in no danger. That was nothing but my needless panic. As soon as I could recover my astonishment, I told him plainly he was given up to Jewish blindness of heart... I declared I would cover his nakedness as long as I could, and honour him before the people; and if I must at last break with him, would retreat gradually, and hide it from the world. He seemed pleased with the thought of parting, though God knows, as I told him, that I had saved him from a thousand false steps: and still I am persuaded we shall stand or fall together.[66]

Charles refused to accept that he was in any way at fault, neither was he prepared to empathize with, or even acknowledge his brother's pain. This stubbornness and insensitivity, a trait that was again shared with John, was an aspect of his personality that caused considerable tension in his relations with other people.

THE WIDER EFFECTS OF THE GRACE MURRAY AFFAIR

During the unhappy episode of his brother's engagement, Charles displayed another characteristic with important implications. In his attempt to justify his actions, he showed no hesitation in crossing the line between private disagreement and public controversy. When John had been faced with a similar threat to his personal life, and the work of God, namely Charles's own engagement, he had disclosed his doubts, as far as is known, only on a one-to-one basis, but his brother displayed no such restraint, and indeed, by attacking John's character

[66] CW to Vincent Perronet, MS letter, 30 October 1749. CWJ, 30 October 1749.

in Methodist meetings, he called into question his brother's fitness to lead. This inability to be discreet, coupled with his tendency to violent language, was to undermine a number of Charles's relationships in the years to come.

John's sense of betrayal must have been acute. In the ten years from 1739, the brothers had presented a united front to an often hostile world. These years had witnessed the isolation of John from his fellow Anglican ministers and the establishing of a necessary distance from the preachers and Methodist people: given this state of affairs, the close bond with his brother was important on both the personal and professional levels. With two such strong personalities, there would have been private disagreements, but these had never before spilled over into their public ministry. After the Grace Murray affair, the tension between the two men was to become hopelessly entangled with bitter debates over the future of Methodism.

The wider repercussions of the brothers' falling-out took effect almost immediately with the alienation from the Methodist movement of John Wesley's successful rival in love. John Bennet had been one of the most gifted of the preachers, responsible for evangelizing large areas of Lancashire and Cheshire. By the end of 1751, his once close working relationship with the Wesleys lay in ruins and early the following year, he severed his links with them.[67] Various explanations have been put forward for this turn of events; soon after his marriage, Bennet began to exhibit tendencies towards Calvinist theological views and to oppose what he regarded as John Wesley's despotism,[68] but it is probable that the most important single cause of the division was the circumstances leading up to his marriage with Grace Murray. Surviving correspondence between Bennet and John Wesley show that despite mutual expressions of regard and affection, there was in the aftermath of Bennet's nuptials, considerable tension between them, which was hardly surprising in the circumstances. Wesley was convinced that he was the wronged party,[69] a view with which Bennet could not have been expected to agree.

---

[67] Valentine, *John Bennet*, 249–61.   [68] Ibid. 254–7.

[69] 'I was never yet convinced that your (marriage) was according to the will of God... consistent either with justice, mercy or truth. Nevertheless I loved you tenderly both before and since.' JW to John Bennet, MS copy letter, 3 November 1749 (MCA: MS letter book of John Bennet, 76–7).

Charles tried hard to prevent the looming schism but may have helped to provoke it by giving Bennet additional reason to doubt John's sincerity, and his own. Charles's letters to Bennet between 1749 and 1752 display a degree of cloying intimacy that is not reproduced in correspondence with any other preacher. He expresses sentiments of great and unusual affection such as loving Bennet as dearly as his own soul,[70] and he constantly presses for a closer relationship. This desperate reaching out for friendship even extended as far as theological matters—he had heard that Bennet may be flirting with Calvinism, but it made no difference to Charles 'whether you think with Luther or with Calvin'.[71] This was a striking statement from a man who had previously displayed violent antipathy towards Calvinist theology and its champions. He also warned his friend not to allow his wife to meet with John Wesley,[72] which would hardly have assuaged Bennet's fears nearly a year after his marriage.

Charles's wish to cement his close tie with Bennet can be explained by the continued poor relationship with his own brother. He states in one letter that 'it is all over with our friend. Only me he cannot love as before. But I must have patience and suffer all things that the Gospel be not hindered.'[73] Several months later Charles informed Bennet that he 'must make me amends for the loss of my brother whose love I have small hopes of recovering in this world. But I find my heart knit still closer to you and am humbly confident that neither life nor death shall be able to separate us.'[74] Charles was also critical of John's recruitment of certain of the preachers,[75] which was rather indiscreet as Bennet was already beginning to distance himself. It appears that having lost the confidence and affection of John Wesley, Charles was seeking to replace him with John Bennet, and that he felt he was owed as much by a man whose marriage had incurred a heavy cost.

---

[70] CW to John Bennet, MS letter, 23 January [1752] (MCA: DDCW 1/43).
[71] CW to John Bennet, MS letter, 3 September [1750] (MCA: DDCW 1/38).
[72] 'take care not to bring our two friends together again! It was an amazing oversight both in Grace and you: and looked like infatuation. If you regard me as your real friend (and I know you do) follow my Christian advice and never let them meet...' Ibid.
[73] CW to John Bennet, MS letter [15 December 1750] (MCA: DDCW 1/39).
[74] CW to John Bennet, MS letter [15 March 1751] (MCA: DDCW 1/41).
[75] CW to John Bennet, MS letter, 11 August [1751] (MCA: DDCW 1/42).

Given these psychological undercurrents, it is hardly suprising that Bennet began to doubt the sincerity and motivation of his one-time Fathers in the Gospel. In a letter to John Wesley written on 6 March 1750, he complained of the brothers' indiscretion, as a result of which his engagement and marriage was the talk of the societies.[76] His letters to Charles began to display hostility as he gradually withdrew from their relationship, but despite these rebuffs Charles persisted. In January 1752 he gently reminded Bennet of the recent occasion 'when you hastily renounced and would have cast *me* off, but that I clave to you so much the closer and overcame you by love'.[77] As late as March 1752, by which time Bennet had been speaking publicly against the Wesleys for several months,[78] Charles was still expressing his determination to strive for harmony, although Bennet 'may impute my obstinacy of love, to guile, or some selfish design'.[79] Even after the final separation in April 1752, Charles's last surviving letter to Bennet was conciliatory, despite the fact that Bennet had been speaking 'much evil of me'.[80] Such mildness in the face of provocation was most uncharacteristic of Charles Wesley.

Charles's relationship with George Whitefield also became closer at this time. In a letter to the layman Ebenezer Blackwell, written a few days after the fateful Bennet marriage,[81] Charles described accompanying his brother and Whitefield to Newcastle, where Charles 'waited on our friend George...and gave him full possession of our pulpit...He was never more blest, or better satisfied. Whole troops of the dissenters he mowed down.' There is little mention of Charles's brother, other than the wishful comment that the Wesleys and Whitefield formed 'a threefold cord which shall no more be broken'. In a letter to Bennet written in September 1750,[82] Charles referred with apparent equanimity to their 'dear friend' Whitefield speaking of predestination to the Methodists and the subsequent defection of two or three Wesleyan preachers. A more fundamental change in attitude

---

[76] John Bennet to JW, MS copy letter, 6 March 1750 (MCA: MS letter book of John Bennet).
[77] CW to John Bennet, MS letter, 23 January [1752] (MCA: DDCW 1/43).
[78] Valentine, *John Bennet*, 252–3.
[79] CW to John Bennet, MS letter, 3 March [1752] (MCA: DDCW 1/44).
[80] CW to John Bennet, MS letter, 18 May [1752] (MCA: DDCW 1/47).
[81] CW to Ebenezer Blackwell, MS letter, 8 October 1749 (MCA: DDCW 1/24).
[82] CW to John Bennet, MS letter, 3 September [1750] (MCA: DDCW 1/38).

from the days when Charles was violently opposed to Whitefield can hardly be imagined. It is true that their friendship had revived in the late 1740s, but this greater warmth of sentiment can be attributed to Charles's sense of loss and vulnerability in the aftermath of Bennet's marriage.

Regardless of the rights and wrongs of his interference in his brother's personal life, it is evident that Charles, always an emotional man, felt betrayed, angry, and sad. The bitterness of his exchanges with John in later years is in one sense a testimony to how close they had been. The affection no doubt remained, although very rarely expressed, and there are occasional flashes of the pride that Charles felt in his remarkable brother,[83] but the mutual trust and support which both men had taken for granted was largely absent from their lives after 1749. The process had started with Charles's own marriage and was accelerated by the Grace Murray affair.

In February 1751, John Wesley married Mary Vazeille. No doubt concerned that his brother would try to abduct this fiancée as well, John maintained secrecy to the extent that the exact date and location of the wedding ceremony remains unknown to this day. He was wise in his precaution, as shown by the anguish with which Charles greeted John's news of the engagement:

I was thunderstruck, and could only answer, he had given me the first blow, and his marriage would come like the coup de grace. Trusty N. [Edward] Perronet followed...I refused his [Perronet's?] company to the chapel, and retired to mourn with my faithful Sally. [I] groaned all the day, and several following ones, under my own and the people's burden. I could eat no pleasant food, nor preach, nor rest, either by night or by day.[84]

Here again, we see Charles reacting in a way that seems irrational, until one looks at the psychological background to the relationship with his brother. He learned nothing from his involvement with John's romantic relationships and, as far as is known, he never regretted his destructive activities, but rather remained convinced of his rightness. Additional evidence that his worries were based

---

[83] On one occasion he described John's launch of the *Christian Library* as unique and as something that only his brother was capable of achieving. CW to John Bennet, MS letter [15 December 1750] (MCA: DDCW 1/39).

[84] CWJ, 2 February 1751.

on emotion rather than reason is provided by the fact that he was as opposed to John's engagement to the respectable and financially independent Mary Vazeille as he was to the former housekeeper Grace Murray.

The engagements and marriages of the Wesley brothers provide an insight into the fundamental change that took place in their relationship as they entered middle age. In the years to 1749, the bond between them had been unnaturally close; co-workers in a great Evangelical crusade, they had enjoyed a relationship that was deeper than that with any other preacher or Anglican minister. Both appear to have viewed the other's marital intentions as a threat, and each allowed their insecurities to gain the upper hand. This fracture in their personal relationship coincided with and contributed to a parting with regard to their joint ministry as the Methodist movement began to evolve in ways unanticipated in the first heady days of the Revival.

6

Methodism in the Early 1750s

At the same time that the relationship between the Wesley brothers was being tested to the point of destruction, Charles was becoming aware that Methodism was heading in directions that he found rather unsettling. The root causes of the problem were the movement's rapid expansion, and the widening gulf that had appeared between the Methodists and their Anglican point of origin. The Wesleys were in one sense, victims of their own success: by 1748, just nine years after their first venture into open-air evangelism, the brothers found themselves at the head of a sophisticated network of over seventy societies grouped into nine circuits. The geographical spread of the movement was patchy, as one might expect, but a presence had been established in all parts of the United Kingdom, and the way seemed open for continued growth in the years to come.

As Methodism left its pioneer years behind and moved into a period of maturity and growing self-confidence, the brothers faced the challenge of determining what should be the institutional end-result of their efforts? Should Methodists remain part of an Anglican Church that had, at the very least, mixed feelings towards the Evangelicals? Or did the brighter future lie in separation from the parent denomination? The dilemma that this represented was exacerbated by the fact that the movement, by the end of the 1740s, had arrived at a point where the ability of the leadership to maintain effective personal control was threatened. This newly provoked concern over the future of Methodism, and the Wesleys' own authority, combined with the loss of brotherly trust to set the stage for controversies that were to plague the rest of Charles's life.

METHODISM AND THE PREACHERS

One of the essential components of success had been the establishment of a network of lay preachers, responsible for consolidating and often introducing the Revival into many parts of the British Isles. Two categories of preacher evolved: on the one hand were itinerants who were required to abandon their normal occupation and devote themselves entirely to the work of God. Appointed to labour in a specific circuit for periods of one to three years, the itinerants supervised the societies, with the assistance of lay officials such as the class leaders and stewards. The itinerant preacher filled the role of a minister in many respects, except that he was not allowed to administer the Sacraments. Local preachers on the other hand remained in one place and maintained their usual employment, often serving also as class leaders and chapel trustees, providing much-needed continuity. As significant as local preachers were at a local level, it was the full-time itinerants who formed what was effectively a second tier of Methodist leadership. For the sake of simplicity, when reference is made to preachers in the rest of this study, the reader should assume that it is the itinerants who are being referred to. The Wesley brothers were also assisted by a number of ordained Anglican ministers, such as William Grimshaw and John Fletcher, and these were accorded greater status than the preachers. They were, however, only a small handful compared with the itinerants and often had parish responsibilities that limited their effectiveness.

By the early 1750s the itinerants' success and indispensability were becoming major sources of concern to the Wesleyan leadership; in particular, Charles's relationship with certain of these men became a running sore. One of the major issues was that of separation from the Church of England, and that will be examined later in this chapter. First, it is necessary to sketch in the background to the relationship between the brothers and their 'Sons in the Gospel'.

The Wesleys first sanctioned the employment of lay preachers no later than 1741 and their number rose steadily as the work expanded. The early Methodist historian William Myles listed thirty-nine laymen and six Anglican ministers (excluding the Wesley brothers) who commenced itinerant preaching between 1740 and the end of

1744.¹ Myles's list should not be regarded as definitive, but it does reflect the important role that preachers were assuming at an early date.

The inherent danger in elevating members of the laity to positions of responsibility was recognized from the outset. At the 1744 inaugural Conference, John Wesley emphasized that he and his brother were in charge:

Act in all things, not according to your own will, but as a son in the Gospel. As such, it is your part to employ your time, in the manner which we direct... Above all, if you labour with us in our Lord's vineyard, it is needful you should do *that* part of the work which we advise, at *those* times and places, which we judge most for his glory.²

To the end of his life, John insisted that the preachers and people submit to his authority. This was not simply a reflection of his controlling nature but was also an inevitable result of the Methodist situation: the movement consisted of isolated societies administered by men of differing levels of ability and education, and it required a central authority capable of imposing uniformity of doctrine and practice.

The existence of a strong guiding hand does not mean that the Methodists submitted easily, and from the earliest days the brothers discovered that many of their followers were reluctant to fall into line with their commands. Such rebelliousness took several forms, from negligence on the part of two out of three senior preachers³ to general breaches of discipline. The large-scale expulsions that were a feature of the Wesleys' nationwide tours illustrate the difficulties experienced in keeping control, and these problems were magnified when individual itinerants rebelled against the leadership.

One of the earliest divisions occurred in March 1741 when John Cennick parted with the Wesleys on theological grounds. This was at a very early stage in the evolution of a specifically Wesleyan movement, but it does illustrate an interesting point. Cennick, who may have been the first authorized lay preacher, was a man of considerable

---

[1] William Myles, *A List of the Methodist Preachers who have laboured in Connexion with John Wesley* (Bristol: William Myles, 1801), 5.

[2] Wesleyan Methodist Church, *Minutes of the Methodist Conferences from... 1744* (London: Methodist Conference Office, 1812), i. (henceforth *Conference Minutes*), 15.

[3] Ibid. i. 40.

ability; when he withdrew from connexion with the Wesleys, he was joined by ninety of the one hundred and forty-two members of the Kingswood society,[4] despite the fact that one or other of the brothers had been in the vicinity for much of the previous year. The Cennick separation represented a relatively rare occurrence in the first decade of Wesleyan Methodism, but it was one with implications for the future.

The Wesleys and the itinerants forged a strong bond during the 1740s. The brothers were aware of their reliance on lay helpers, while for their part the preachers felt called by God to serve under the Wesleys' direction. There is little evidence to indicate that before the end of the decade Charles's relations with the preachers were unduly troubled. He occasionally expressed doubt concerning individual lack of ability, but personal hostility and mistrust on either side appear to have been lacking, except where there were doctrinal disagreements. Charles expressed appreciation of the talents of several of the lay preachers[5] and was quick to leap to their defence when he felt that they were unjustly criticized.[6] There is virtually no extant correspondence between Charles and the preachers before 1750, but the impression that is given in other primary sources such as the journal is that his relations with the itinerants were harmonious.

It is understandable that Charles's relations with the lay preachers were at their best in this early period as the itinerants were few in number and their influence was limited. Of the nine men who attended the Conference of 1746, four were Anglican ministers;[7] by way of comparison, sixty lay preachers and just three Anglican ministers, including John and Charles Wesley, attended the Conference of 1755.[8] Given such a rapid expansion of the itinerancy, it is hardly surprising that the Wesleys began to experience difficulty in upholding their authority. Another contributory factor to Charles's good relations with the preachers was the fact that his own travelling ministry was second to none. He had personal knowledge of the itinerants

---

[4] Rack, *Reasonable Enthusiast*, 199.
[5] 'Conferred with several who have tasted the love of Christ, mostly under the preaching or prayers of our lay helpers. How can any one dare deny that they are sent of God?' CWJ, 30 April 1746.
[6] Gill, *Charles Wesley*, 233.   [7] *Conference Minutes*, i. 25.
[8] Baker, *John Wesley and the Church of England*, 165.

and shared their triumphs and hardships. The loss of this contact in later years has been cited as a factor in Charles's alienation from men who, unlike himself, remained in the vanguard of the Methodist movement.[9] There is an element of truth in this argument, but it will be made clear that the difficulties between Charles and the preachers after 1750 owed a great deal to causes other than Charles's retirement from the road.

A dramatic turning point came at the beginning of the 1750s prompted by a number of developments. The expansion in the itinerants' numbers, the enhanced standing that they enjoyed in the societies and the increasing sophistication of their duties brought into sharper focus the potential threat that they represented. Some of the preachers had been in the work for a decade and had grown in confidence and stature; a few started to flex their muscles accordingly. Tension began to surface between the Wesleys and men who had hitherto been among their most trusted helpers.

One of the earliest intimations of trouble came on 10 July 1749, when Charles expressed concern about James Wheatley who had gone to the north of England contrary to Charles's advice.[10] This was the beginning of a long-running problem that was not to be resolved until Wheatley's expulsion five years later. Wheatley had joined the itinerancy in 1742 and attended at least one of the Conferences: his origins are obscure, but he possessed charisma and was able to seduce several women in the Norwich and Bristol circuits, which misdemeanours came to light at about the same time as his unauthorized visit to the northern societies. An added cause of concern with Wheatley was his irregular mode of preaching, described by one contemporary as 'unconnected rhapsody of unmeaning words'.[11] Evidently designed to promote a state of high emotion, it belonged to a category of extempore discourse that seemed to justify the fears of the Wesleys' Anglican critics. Wheatley's so-called method became influential in the societies and appears to have attracted other exponents from among his fellow preachers. Despite such scandalous behaviour, John Wesley pardoned Wheatley on at least one occasion, on condition

---

[9] Telford, *Charles Wesley*, 208; Jackson, *Charles Wesley*, ii. 137.
[10] CWJ, 10 July 1749.
[11] Quoted by Heitzenrater, *Wesley and the People Called Methodists*, 185.

that he mend his ways, and Charles played an important role in counselling the miscreant.[12] When he was finally expelled, Wheatley was able to disrupt the Norwich society,[13] and it appears that several of the preachers may already have been lost to the Methodists because of his influence.[14]

At the same time that the Wesleys were trying to curb Wheatley's excess, some of his colleagues were also causing them disciplinary problems. The former pedlar William Darney for example, who had incorporated his societies into the Wesleyan movement in 1747, started to create difficulties with his Calvinist theology and independent ways. On 26 January 1750 John Bennet, who by this time had his own points of grievance with the Wesleys, recorded in his journal:

> In the morning [William Darney] came to meet me. We walked out into the field and he showed me a letter he had received from Mr Wesley wherein he reproves him sharply of many things, particularly of singing his own hymns which he tells him are nonsense. [William] Darney also informed me that a few days ago he saw a letter which Mr Wesley sent to brother [William] Shent... wherein he tells him that 'Brother Darney is not in connexion with him etc'.[15]

Darney appears to have escaped public censure on that occasion, but the following year, he published his own hymn-book, the preface of which contained criticism of the Wesleys' poetic works as being too refined for a northern audience.[16] It is hardly surprising that Darney was subsequently suspended from the itinerancy, although he was eventually readmitted and continued in an uneasy relationship with the brothers until 1768.

A more serious division occurred in April 1752 with the final collapse of the relationship between John Bennet and the Wesleys. The tension arising from the Grace Murray affair has already been discussed, but it is clear that there were unrelated concerns within the societies that Bennet was able to exploit in order to lead a separation. Among his criticisms of John Wesley was the allegation of

---

[12] CWJ, 20 June 1751.   [13] Jackson, *Charles Wesley*, ii. 46.
[14] JWJ, 21 August 1751. John Wesley, *The Works of John Wesley*, xx. 398.
[15] MS diary of John Bennet, 26 January 1750 (MCA: John Bennet/Grace Murray collection).
[16] Laycock, *Methodist Heroes*, 110–11.

popery;[17] this was both in the doctrinal sense, and implied that Wesley conducted himself in a highhanded manner. In support of his contention, Bennet cited the harsh treatment meted out to William Darney and the Wesleys' insistence on having legal title to preaching houses. This latter point represented a direct attack on one of the foundation stones of discipline, as legal title meant that the brothers could dictate doctrine and exclude preachers.[18] That Bennet was not alone in feeling disquiet concerning aspects of the Wesleys' leadership is shown by the fact that parts of several societies left with him.

The preceding examples are only the most prominent and best documented of a rash of disciplinary problems that came to a head between 1750 and 1756. These were revealed in clashes over doctrine, suitability of preachers, and breaches of discipline. Whatever the details of individual cases, the problems as a whole were indicative of a growing feeling within the itinerancy that the preachers should have a voice in determining the character and future of Methodism—something that was anathema to the Wesleys' High Church view of ordained ministry. As early as August 1751, the preacher Charles Skelton was arguing for the itinerants to be given a place in Connexional decision-making,[19] and Charles Wesley reported to his brother that same month that the preachers were complaining all over England that John was ruling with a 'rod of iron'.[20]

The brothers had been aware for some time that storm clouds were gathering. In the summer of 1750 John revealed his growing frustration in a number of letters to the itinerant Edward Perronet, from which these passages are taken:

Charles [Perronet] and you *behave* as I want you to do. But you cannot, or will not preach *where* I desire. Others can, and will, preach *where* I desire, but they do not behave as I want them to do. I have a fine time between one and the other.[21]

[17] 'He told them in the open congregation, that Mr Wesley was a Pope and that he preached nothing but popery...he met the society and said many bitter things of Mr Wesley.' Quoted by Valentine, *John Bennet*, 253.
[18] Ibid. 258–9.
[19] JW to CW, MS copy letter, 17 August 1751. Charles Wesley, MS notebook, [*c*.1750] (MCA: DDCW 8/5).
[20] Baker, *John Wesley and the Church of England*, 160.
[21] JW to Edward Perronet, Published copy letter [19(?) June 1750]. John Wesley, *The Works of John Wesley*, xxvi. 431.

Methodism in the Early 1750s 117

I have not one preacher with me, and not six in England, whose wills are broken enough to serve me as sons in the gospel.[22]

Charles was equally concerned over what he viewed as the related problems of indiscipline and preachers' gifts. His close involvement with the Wheatley affair convinced him of the need for examining the itinerants, and after discussions with his brother he assumed this responsibility on 28 June 1751.[23] Charged with the duty of returning to their normal occupations, individuals who failed to meet the requisite standards, he found much to disturb him during his travels. In Bristol on 5 August, he recorded in his journal:

> [I] went to the Room that I might hear with my own ears one, of whom many strange things had been told me. But such a preacher have I never heard, and hope I never shall again... I cannot say he preached false doctrine; or true; or any doctrine at all, but pure, unmixed nonsense... I could scarce refrain from stopping him... Some begged me to step into the desk and speak a few words to the poor dissatisfied hearers. I did so, taking no notice of Michael Fenwick, late Superintendent of all Ireland![24]

Other sources confirm that there was indeed a problem with the quality and character of some of the preachers. In November 1751, Sarah Perrin complained to Charles that John Hewish had been permitted to preach again despite his drunkenness—John Wesley had been persuaded by the itinerants to give him a second chance. She also mentioned that there had been complaints about Edmund Wells too.[25]

On 11 August 1751, Charles wrote to John Bennet thanking him for the information concerning the unworthiness of Robert Gillespie, whom Charles had consequently relieved of his duties.[26] Charles placed all the responsibility for Gillespie being accepted into the itinerancy onto his brother's shoulders: 'A friend of ours [John Wesley] (without God's consent) made a preacher of a taylor. I with God's help shall make a taylor of him again.'[27] This letter also serves as a reminder of the recent and continuing personal differences between

---

[22] JW to Edward Perronet, Published copy letter [20(?) July 1750]. Ibid. 433.
[23] CWJ, 28 June 1751.   [24] CWJ, 5 August 1751.
[25] Sarah Perrin to CW, MS letter, 4 November 1751 (MCA: 'Letters to CW II'), 57.
[26] CW to John Bennet, MS letter, 11 August [1751] (MCA: DDCW 1/42).
[27] Ibid.

the brothers, as it is inconceivable that Charles would have commented in such a way to a third party just a few years previously. At precisely the time that tension was developing within Methodism, a wall had been erected between the Wesleys.

Several preachers were disciplined as a result of Charles's tour of inspection. Extant in the Methodist Archives is a notebook containing shorthand passages that document the prevailing mood of disquiet.[28] In one of these, Charles records a meeting with his brother on 25 November 1751 in the presence of their friend and adviser Vincent Perronet. After the customary expression of solidarity, the brothers pledged to admit or expel from the itinerancy, only those men whom they both agreed upon and that neither they nor Perronet would restore to the ranks of the itinerants, without the consent of the other two, any preacher who was found wanting. The assistants Michael Fenwick, James Wheatley, William Darney, Eleazer Webster, Robert Gillespie, James Watson, David Trathen, John Madern, and Thomas Webb were consequently relieved of their duties.

This action of expelling no fewer than nine of the approximately forty active itinerant preachers appears to be a firm executive decision designed to reinforce discipline and maintain standards. On closer examination however, an interesting fact emerges—at least four of the nine were subsequently readmitted.[29] Charles may have been scathing in his denunciation of the talents of Fenwick and Gillespie, but it did not prevent them, after an interval, from continuing their Methodist ministry until 1797 and 1764 respectively. John Wesley described James Wheatley in July 1751 as a 'wonderful self-deceiver and hypocrite',[30] yet he was not finally expelled for another three years. Even after Wheatley was thrust out, there was a partial reconciliation in 1758, leading to a cooperation that lasted for a further seven years.[31]

Christian forgiveness and forbearance presumably had a part to play in this acceptance of unworthy assistants back into the fold, but it also reveals just how strong a position the preachers enjoyed: simply put, if Methodism was to prosper, then the itinerants were indispensable and had to be handled accordingly. It was one of John Wesley's

---

[28] Charles Wesley, MS notebook [*c.*1750] (MCA: DDCW 8/5).
[29] Darney, Wheatley, Gillespie, and Fenwick.
[30] JWJ, 8 July 1751. John Wesley, *The Works of John Wesley*, xx. 394.
[31] Baker, *John Wesley and the Church of England*, 129.

gifts that he knew instinctively when to give way to pressure and by how much, yet without seeming to loosen his grip. This balancing act was not something that Charles was temperamentally suited for, but even so, he must have agreed to preachers being readmitted, indicating that either he was not so severe in practice, or that his hands were tied by the necessity of providing for the societies. Charles's position with regard to the preachers was weak at a surprisingly early date. If he was unable to insist that men, deficient in abilities, morals, or doctrinal conformity, were cast out permanently, it should come as no surprise that their more talented colleagues were able to defy him, much to his frustration.

John was certainly worried that Charles would go too far in his enthusiastic purges. On 24 July 1751 he wrote to his brother: 'As to preachers, my counsel is not to check the young ones, without strong necessity. If we lay some aside, we *must* have a supply, and of the two I prefer grace before gifts.'[32] On 8 August, he reminded Charles that they must have forty itinerants or abandon some of the work.[33] Despite his own concern with discipline, it is clear that John wavered between the need for regularity and provision for the societies. The overriding impression is that from 1750 at least, despite the appearance of dictatorial power, John Wesley was in practice a lax disciplinarian, at least where his assistants were concerned, and when his own personal authority was not being called into question.

Within a short space of time between 1750 and 1752, the relationship between the brothers and their preachers altered in step with the changing dynamics of the Wesleyan movement. Charles was to suffer the most from this development: his gradual withdrawal from the itinerancy and short temper fuelled dislike on the part of certain preachers, and the fact that he felt isolated from his brother aggravated the situation. The rising temperature of Methodist affairs can be seen to best effect when looking at the question of separation from the Church of England—yet another fundamental issue that first came to a head in the early 1750s.

---

[32] JW to CW, MS copy letter, 24 July 1751. Charles Wesley, MS notebook [c.1750] (MCA: DDCW 8/5).
[33] JW to CW, MS copy letter, 8 August 1751. Charles Wesley, MS notebook [c.1750] (MCA: DDCW 8/5).

SEPARATION FROM THE CHURCH

The danger that the Methodists would one day divide from the Anglican Church did not escape notice by early observers. Susanna Wesley and Samuel Wesley junior were both concerned about the irregular nature of John and Charles's activities as early as 1739, and in April of that year, Samuel informed John that 'my mother tells me she fears a formal schism is already begun among you, though you and Charles are ignorant of it. For God's sake take care of that, and banish extemporary expositions and extemporary prayers.'[34] Susanna did eventually become reconciled to her sons' Evangelical involvement, but Samuel junior remained deeply suspicious of their infringement of Anglican discipline, and of John's ambition. A few weeks before he died on 6 November 1739, he wrote to their mother that 'they design separation... They are already forbid all the pulpits in London, and to preach in that diocese is actual schism. In all likelihood it will come to the same all over England if the bishops have courage... As I told Jack I am not afraid the church should excommunicate him... but that he should excommunicate the church...'[35] Samuel's concern was reflected in the charge made by other critics that the Wesley brothers, far from revitalizing the Church of England, were potential or actual schismatics.

John took every opportunity to contest the charge of fostering a separation, but there were justifiable grounds to doubt his Anglican loyalty. At the first Conference of 1744, in response to the question 'How far is it our duty to obey the bishops?' Wesley replied, 'In all things indifferent. And on this ground of obeying them, we should observe the Canons, so far as we can with a safe conscience.'[36] He reiterated this principle at the 1747 Conference: 'we will obey the rules and governors of the church whenever we can consistent with our duty to God: whenever we cannot we will quietly obey God.'[37] Such qualifying statements show clearly that his commitment to Anglican–Methodist unity was not to be taken for granted.

---

[34] Samuel Wesley jun. to JW, MS letter, 16 April 1739 (MCA: DDWF 5/15).
[35] Quoted by Baker, *John Wesley and the Church of England*, 58.
[36] *Conference Minutes*, i. 8.
[37] Quoted by Baker, *John Wesley and the Church of England*, 113.

John Wesley's conditional loyalty to the Church of England did not represent a sudden development but was apparent from soon after his Evangelical conversion. In 1739, he responded to Samuel Wesley junior's criticism of his activities with the remark: 'I love the rites and ceremonies of the Church. But I see, well pleased, that our great Lord can work without them.'[38] The roots of this independent thinking can be traced to before the Aldersgate experience of May 1738—the holy club was regarded by some of the Wesleys' contemporaries as a dangerous innovation, while John's pioneering Georgia Hymnal of 1737 ran counter to prevailing Anglican practice. The seeds of Methodist independence from the Church of England may have been planted before the movement was even founded.

Charles Wesley during the 1740s also publicly stated his wish to remain true to the Anglican Church,[39] but in practice this garb of loyalty sat lightly on his shoulders. He attended all the Conferences convened during that decade, with the exception of 1748, but there is no indication in the journal or extant correspondence that he was in any way concerned about his brother's wavering allegiance. Indeed, there are indications that his own defiance would have matched any attempt by the bishops to impede his freedom of action. On 8 July 1743 he wrote that 'John Bray came to persuade me not to preach, till the Bishops should bid me. They have not yet forbid me; but, by the grace of God, I shall preach the word in season, out of season, though they and all men forbade me.'[40] Early the following year, after being told that local Methodists were being repelled from the Sacraments, Charles made the ominous prediction that 'the time, we know, will come, when they shall put us out of their synagogues'.[41] Whether Charles would have ever considered separating from the Church will never be known, but in the first decade of the Revival, he would have hesitated at little else. It was only later in life, beginning with the years between 1750 and 1756 that the foundations of Charles's reputation as the ultimate Church Methodist were laid.

---

[38] JW to Samuel Wesley jun., Published copy letter, 27 October 1739. John Wesley, *The Works of John Wesley* xxv. 695.

[39] 'Expounded the Gospel as usual; and strongly avowed my inviolable attachment to the Church of England.' CWJ, 3 July 1743.

[40] CWJ, 8 July 1743.   [41] CWJ, 11 February 1744.

On 17 July 1751, John complained to Charles that the preachers Charles Skelton and Joseph Cownley were attacking the Church of England. In his annotation, Charles queried if the brothers should not insist on 'invariable attachment to the Church' as a condition of admission to the itinerancy.[42] On 16 January 1752, an agreement was entered into by the brothers stating the conditions governing the acceptance of travelling preachers,[43] and several weeks later the Wesleys signed a statement with eleven itinerants pledging mutual loyalty and support.[44] Later that year on 16 March, a further agreement was made between the Wesleys and four leading preachers stating their intention 'never to leave the communion of the Church of England' without the consent of the other signatories.[45] This document was issued under Charles's name, and it appears that he, not John, was the person primarily responsible.[46] Despite the appearance of harmony, there was underlying tension on this question. After the meeting on 25 November 1751, Charles consulted privately with Vincent Perronet and was advised not to press his brother with regard to signing the articles of agreement, as John might suspect that Charles doubted his word.[47]

The 1752 agreement of mutual trust and loyalty was publicly restated at the Methodist Conferences held between 1754 and 1756,[48] but Charles remained convinced that the itinerants were a potentially destructive force. Even worse, he viewed his brother as a man who could no longer be trusted. As early as August 1751, he had linked these two points in a letter to the Countess of Huntingdon, which is worth quoting at length as an undisguised statement of his views at an important time in Methodist history:

---

[42] JW to CW, MS copy letter, 17 July 1751 (MCA: DDCW 8/5).
[43] These conditions included their examination with regard to 'gifts and grace' and that neither of the brothers should take a preacher from his trade into the full-time ministry without the consent of the other. Ibid.
[44] JW, CW, etc. to the 'Methodist Preachers', Published copy letter, 29 January 1752. John Wesley, *The Works of John Wesley* xxvi. 490.
[45] MS Agreement, 16 March 1752. Ibid. 491.
[46] Baker, *John Wesley and the Church of England*, 160.
[47] Charles Wesley, MS notebook [c.1750] (MCA: DDCW 8/5).
[48] Baker believes that it may have also been reiterated at the 1753 meeting. Baker, *John Wesley and the Church of England*, 161.

Unless a sudden remedy be found; the preachers will destroy the work of God—what has well nigh ruined many of them is their being taken from their trades—most of them was novices without much experience or stability: as fit to command an army as to guide a Christian flock; hence they quickly run themselves out of breath; losing first their grace; then their gifts; then their success; the universal respect they met with turned their heads—the tinner, barber, thatcher forgot himself and set up for a gentleman and looked out for a fortune—having lost the only way of maintaining himself: some have been betrayed by pride into still greater sins...What will become of them...will not each set up for himself and make a new party, sect or religion—or supposing we have authority enough to quash them whilst we live...who can stop them after our death...The most, the only effectual way in my judgement is to set them to work again, to prove them heartily [sic] which has any grace left, and which has not; who is sent of God and who of flesh and blood, sloth, pride and the devil—that man who disdains to work after the apostles' example is no fellow labourer for us...the man who consents to labour at times at his calling proves his obedience and humility, both to us and the Church, he stops the mouths of gainsayers, relieves the poor people of that intolerable burden.[49]

With regard to his brother, Charles confided that he had an additional motive for insisting that the preachers support themselves:

namely it will break his power, their not depending on him for bread, and reduce his authority within due bounds, as well as guard against that rashness and credulity of his, which has kept me in continual awe and bondage for many years, therefore I shall insist on their working as the one point; the single condition of my acting in concert with him, because without this I can neither trust them, nor him—if he refuses I will give both preachers and society to his sole management; for this ruin shall not be under my hands.[50]

Charles was recovering from a fever and had written on 28 July that he had dictated to Sarah Perrin his 'confused thoughts' regarding the state of the Church.[51] It should, however, be questioned just how 'confused' Charles really was, as he was already well on the way to recovery when the Huntingdon letter was written,[52] and any

[49] CW to Selina Hastings, MS letter, 4 August 1752 (MCA: PLP 113.2.5).
[50] Ibid. [51] Baker, *Charles Wesley as Revealed*, 83.
[52] On 4 August, the day that the Huntingdon letter was dated, Charles made the following journal entry: 'found my strength sensibly increase in the fresh air. Spent an hour with the women leaders.' CWJ, 4 August 1752.

suspicion that his strident views were solely the result of feverish ramblings can probably be dismissed. Charles's letter was intercepted and passed to John,[53] not surprisingly evoking a storm of protest. The circumstances in which the letter was copied, and the implications of that particular act, will be examined in the next chapter.

THE SACRAMENTAL CONTROVERSY

The next major incident connected with the separation question occurred in October 1754, with the revelation that the itinerants Charles Perronet and Thomas Walsh had administered Communion in London and Reading, inspiring three others to follow what Charles termed their 'vile example'.[54] This represented a serious infringement of discipline, signifying a de facto separation from a denomination where administration of the Sacraments was the preserve of the ordained ministry.

It is not known how strong or early the call was within the societies for receiving the elements from the hands of lay preachers, but it is interesting that the rebel itinerants administered in London, as the society there was the best placed of any with regard to accessibility to the Lord's Table, either in the capital's many churches or from ordained clergymen in Methodist chapels such as West Street. The argument could therefore be made that this episode is indicative of a separatist trend. Against such an interpretation is evidence from six years later in 1760, when the London society appears to have been solidly against lay administration of the Sacraments. The precise truth is impossible to ascertain as it revolves around the thorny question of the detailed state of Connexional opinion. It may be the case that ordinary Methodists did not equate separation with receiving Communion from a much-loved itinerant and did not particularly care about such details of church order.

The Wesleys discussed the crisis on 19 October 1754 and it became clear to Charles that John himself was on the brink of division: 'I was with my brother, who said nothing of [Charles] Perronet, except, "We

---

[53] Baker, *Charles Wesley as Revealed*, 83.
[54] CW to Walter Sellon, 19th-century copy letter, 1754 (MCA: DDCW 6/92a).

have in effect ordained already". He urged me to sign the preachers' certificates; was inclined to lay on hands; and to let the preachers administer.'[55] This response was in one sense typical of John Wesley, who throughout his Methodist ministry wavered periodically from loyalty to the Established Church, to tacit acceptance of the principle of a distinct Methodist denomination, often professing one while promoting the other. This ambiguity was not new; what was different in the early 1750s was that Charles was no longer his brother's devoted partner.

Charles mustered the support of Anglican Evangelicals such as Walter Sellon and the Countess of Huntingdon. His mistrust of John and the preachers is explicit, together with a hint of jealousy of the relationship enjoyed by some of the itinerants with his brother: 'Pride, cursed pride, has perverted him [John Wesley] and them [the preachers]... In your fidelity to my old honoured mother [the Church of England], you are a man after my own heart... What a pity such spirits should have any influence over my brother! They are continually urging him to a separation... I stand alone, as our preachers imagine.'[56] Charles and others in the pro-Anglican camp went so far as to suspect that John had already ordained in secret.[57] In a letter of 14 December 1754, he complained that he had been excluded from his brother's 'cabinet council', although Charles attributed this to the influence of the preachers rather than to any breakdown in his own relationship with John.[58]

Matters came to a head at the Conference in May 1755, the largest such assembly to date. In attendance were sixty-three itinerants and three Anglican ministers,[59] which statistic is revealing—even allowing for the fact that John retained the decisive voice within Conference until the end of his life, it was inevitable that the views of the preachers would achieve greater prominence. John had already begun to waver from his initial conviction that he should allow the

[55] Quoted by Baker, *John Wesley and the Church of England*, 163.
[56] CW to Walter Sellon, 19th-century copy letter, 1754 (MCA: DDCW 6/92a).
[57] 'Our worthy friend at Clifton [Selina Hastings] could not but believe my brother had *laid on hands*, or they [the rebel preachers] would not have dared to act thus.' CW to Walter Sellon, 19th-century copy letter, 1754 (MCA: DDCW 6/92a).
[58] CW to Walter Sellon, 19th-century copy letter, 14 December 1754 (MCA: DDCW 6/92b).
[59] The Wesleys and William Grimshaw.

Sacraments to be administered and on 4 February 1755, Charles wrote to Sellon with the news that their efforts were having an effect: 'He has spoken as strongly of late on behalf of the Church of England as I could wish; and everywhere declares he never intended to leave her.'[60]

Conference discussed the separation question at length before concluding that regardless of the legality of such a step, it was inexpedient. His purpose achieved, Charles left the meeting to discuss more mundane matters: this may have indicated to the assembled preachers that he felt his primary role was no longer working alongside his brother, but the prevention of separation. Charles was later to acknowledge that this was indeed the case,[61] and towards that end, he engaged in public agitation within the societies. Writing to Sarah a few days after he left Conference, he made the following statement: 'I have delivered my own soul in this society, exhorting them to continue steadfast in fellowship with the Church of England. The same exhortation I hope to have with every society throughout the land.'[62] In the same letter, Charles declared that while the brethren had agreed not to separate, the wound had been only 'slightly' healed. He was obviously unable to relax his guard despite the Conference decision.

Charles Wesley was not alone in fearing that the matter had yet to run its course. William Grimshaw, the Anglican Evangelical and friend of the Wesleys, made this clear in a letter to Mrs Gallatin: 'The design of administering the Ordinances etc by our preachers got seemingly quite quashed at the Leeds Conference. Though since, there appears an intention of reassuming it there. Insomuch that, a rupture is expected in these Societies in a little time.'[63] Charles was characteristically more barbed in his comments—writing to Sellon prior to the Conference, he referred to the separatists as 'delinquents'

---

[60] CW to Walter Sellon, 19th-century copy letter, 4 February 1755 (MCA: DDCW 6/92c).

[61] 'I stay not so much to do good as to prevent evil. I stand in the way of my brother's violent counsellors, the object both of their fear and hate.' CW to Samuel Walker, Typescript copy letter, 21 August 1756 (MCA: DDCW 1/55).

[62] CW to Sarah Wesley, MS letter [9 May 1755] (MCA: DDCW 5/87).

[63] Quoted by Frank Baker, *William Grimshaw 1708–1763* (London: Epworth, 1963), 250.

Methodism in the Early 1750s 127

and 'hypocrites'[64] and victory in the assembly did nothing to moderate his opinions.

How justified was Charles in his suspicion of the preachers? Comparatively few itinerants' personal papers have survived from this period, but for the debate to be taking place at all, there must have been agitation in favour of, if not separation, at least greater freedom with regard to such issues as the Sacraments and registration of chapels as meeting houses. However, Charles was not alone in his support for the Church of England: the legendary Yorkshire itinerant John Nelson wrote in March 1755 that if the Wesleys ever left the Church, he would leave them, and William Shent, the pioneer of Leeds Methodism, was apparently of the same opinion.[65] There was obviously a wide spectrum of opinion within the itinerancy on this important issue. Some men, such as the Perronet brothers, were in favour of formal separation, while others such as John Nelson were vehemently opposed. In between these two extremes were preachers who were content to remain within the Church, but who were at the same time applying for preachers' licences and registering chapels for the legal protection that was afforded.

As for the societies, it is difficult to assess how wide the split had grown with the Church, and the Wesleys appear to have been equally uncertain as to the true picture: John declared in October 1755 that nineteen out of twenty of the preachers 'and an equal majority of the people' were against separation.[66] On the other hand, Charles declared in his sermons and correspondence that he expected to bring only 'the third part through the fire', although this perhaps owes more to the tie-in with the biblical text than any reasoned estimate. As confused as the picture appears to have been, it seems that the Methodist preachers and people were not as inclined towards formal separation as Charles feared.

In the aftermath of the 1755 Conference, John wrote with some exasperation to his brother on 20 June:

---

[64] CW to Walter Sellon, 19th-century copy letter, 4 February 1755 (MCA: DDCW 6/92c).
[65] John Nelson to CW, Xerox copy letter, 4 March 1755 (MCA: PLP 78.53.1a).
[66] JW to Thomas Adam, MS copy letter, 31 October 1755 (MCA: DDCW 8/1).

Do you not understand that they all promised by T. Walsh not to administer even among themselves? I think that a huge point given up: perhaps more than they could give up with a clear conscience.

They showed an 'excellent spirit' in this very thing... when I reflected on their answers I admired *their* spirit and was ashamed of my own.

The practical conclusion was, 'not to separate from the Church'. Did we not all agree in this? Surely either you or I must have been asleep, or we could not differ so widely in a matter of fact!

Here is [Charles Perronet] raving because his friends have given up *all*, and [Charles Wesley] because they 'have given up *nothing*'. And I in the midst, staring and wondering both at one and the other.[67]

The clearest indication of what the future held, was provided by John Wesley in a letter of 24 September 1755 to Samuel Walker:

At present I apprehend those, and those only, to separate from the Church who either renounce her fundamental doctrines, or refuse to join in her public worship. As yet we have done neither, nor have we taken one step further than we were convinced was our bounden duty. It is from a full conviction of this that we have, (1), preached abroad; (2), preached extempore; (3) formed societies; and (4), permitted preachers who were not episcopally ordained. And were we pushed on this side, were there no alternative allowed, we should judge it our bounden duty... to separate from the Church than to give up any of these points.[68]

This letter was written after the 1755 Conference affirmed the link with the Church of England and shows beyond doubt that Charles was correct to suspect his brother on this issue: John never did abandon these points, or ever looked like doing so.

Tension continued in the period between the Conferences of 1755 and 1756. Charles remained on edge, complaining in a letter of 9 June 1755 that 'the preachers are swiftly following the separatists through my brother's dissimulation'.[69] In this letter, and one written two days later, Charles referred to his sense of isolation,[70] which was something that was very much on his mind after the years of close collaboration

---

[67] JW to CW, MS letter, 20 June 1755 (MCA: DDWes 3/8).
[68] JW to Samuel Walker, Published copy letter [24 September 1755]. John Wesley, *The Works of John Wesley* xxvi. 595.
[69] Quoted by Baker, *John Wesley and the Church of England*, 168.
[70] 'My way is plain, to preach everywhere as a supernumerary if not independent. My brother, I foresee will treat me as a deserter.' Ibid.

with his brother. His earlier satisfaction at John's swing back to loyalty to the Church of England was short-lived, and again, he accused John of being untrustworthy.[71]

As for the preachers, Charles regarded them with increasing suspicion and took every opportunity to scrutinize their conduct by enquiry of other people. He was also sharp in his public criticism. In October 1756 he wrote an open letter to the Leeds Society: 'I knew beforehand that the Sanballats and Tobiahs would be grieved when they heard there was a man come to seek the welfare of the Church of England. I expected they would pervert my words... but not let their slanders move you. Continue in the old ship...'[72]

One of the most striking features of Charles's ministry during this period was an almost obsessive concern with loyalty. During his last great preaching tour of 1756, he preached eight times on what he described as his favourite subject: 'I will bring the third part through the fire.'[73] Additionally, there was barely a day when he did not discourse both publicly and privately on the necessity of remaining loyal to the Church of England. This is exemplified by a journal entry written during his visit to Rotherham:

I then advised them to go to Church. The weak and waning were confirmed; 3 out of 4 of the others offended and said 'I made the Church Christ.' After preaching as awakening as I could I plainly told the Society 'that there is no salvation *out of the Church*, that is out of the Mystical Body of Christ or the company of faithful people.' When I had fully explained myself on this head we were all of one mind and heart.[74]

No doubt, most eighteenth-century Christians would have agreed in principle with Charles's observations, but his implied identification of the Church of England as the only true 'Mystical Body of Christ' caused irritation and confusion in places where some preachers were communicating a different message. Charles muddied the waters still further with his own public criticism of the Church, as on 21 October 1756 when he referred to 'the melancholy state of the members of the Established Church, who are the most unprincipled and ignorant of all that are called Protestants'.[75] Charles could presumably have

[71] 'I think it safest not to trust him with my thoughts.' Ibid.
[72] CWJ, 28 October 1756.   [73] CWJ, 17 September–5 November 1756.
[74] CWJ, 24 September 1756.   [75] CWJ, 21 October 1756.

justified such an apparently contradictory statement, but there is no wonder that Methodists, most of whom would have been unacquainted with the twists and turns of theological debate, were somewhat bewildered.

Manchester is a good example of the prevailing uncertainty. Charles arrived on 20 October 1756 to discover that the society membership had halved because of the activities of dissenting preachers. In a meeting with the society, which he described as 'most unsettled and unadvisable',[76] he urged his listeners to attend church and the Sacraments constantly. He subsequently confided in his journal that:

I make more allowance for this poor shattered Society, because they have been sadly neglected, if not abused, by our Preachers. The [class] leaders desired me to not let Joseph Tucker come among them again; for he did more harm than good, by talking in his *witty way* against the Church and clergy. As for poor John Hampson, he *could* not advise them to go to Church, for he never went himself; but some informed me that he advised them *not* to go.[77]

This preaching tour took place after the 1755 Conference ended with the Wesley brothers' 'strong declaration of our resolution to live and die in the communion of the Church of England'.[78] These words when placed against events in Manchester and elsewhere lose some of their force.

Nineteen days before the 1756 Conference opened Charles outlined his emphatic thoughts on what his brother must do:

What I desire of my brother is: 1. That the unsound, unrecoverable preachers should be let depart just now. 2. That the wavering should be confirmed...and established in their calling. 3. That the sound ones should be received into the strictest union and confidence, and...prepared for orders.

To this end my brother ought...to declare and avow, in the strongest and most explicit manner, his resolution to live and die in the communion of the Church of England. 1. To take all proper pains to instruct and ground, both his preachers and his flock in the same...2. To wait with me upon the Archbishop, who has desired to see him, and tell him our whole design.

---

[76] CWJ, 21 October 1756.   [77] Ibid.
[78] Quoted by Heitzenrater, *Wesley and the People Called Methodists*, 195.

3. To advise...with such of our brethren the clergy as know the truth, and do nothing without their approbation.[79]

The final Conference decisions would have satisfied Charles on few of these points. There was for example no wholesale expulsion of 'dissident' preachers and while it was determined that Methodism would remain in the Church, it would only be for so long as it was 'lawful and possible to continue in it'.[80] Within a few months of the 1756 gathering, Charles had withdrawn from the itinerant ministry, an act symbolic of the brothers' divergent paths.

CONCLUSION

The first half of the 1750s represented a fundamental turning point in Charles Wesley's life and ministry. The sharp definition of the dividing line between his pre-1750 place in Methodism and the years that followed, particularly after 1756, will become explicit in the remainder of this study. Having introduced the themes of private disagreement and public discord, it is necessary to conclude with a statement of what these years tell us of Charles's personality, and the way that his Methodist role evolved.

One could argue that John Wesley's ambiguous actions with regard to the separation question justified his brother's suspicions, but this does not explain Charles's failure to react until after 1749, despite explicit warnings from family members and fellow Anglicans. There were occasions during the 1740s when Charles felt the need to remind his brother that Methodism was a part of the Anglican Church, as in March 1744 when he advised that the words of a loyal address to King George II could be construed as presenting Methodism as an independent sect, but the warning is mild and lacks the undertone of mistrust that coloured later communications on the separation question. A foretaste of his later attitude was revealed on 17 October

---

[79] CW to Samuel Walker, Published copy letter, 7 August 1756. Transcribed by Luke Tyerman, *The Life and Times of the Rev. John Wesley, M.A., founder of the Methodists*, 3 vols. (London: Hodder and Stoughton, 1871–2), ii. 245.

[80] Quoted by Rack, *Reasonable Enthusiast*, 299–300.

1748, when Charles came across the licence registering the New Room as a Dissenters' meeting house. He scribbled his opinion on the document in no uncertain manner: 'I protest against this needless, useless, senseless license—Charles Wesley.'[81] However, this was an isolated incident compared with the bitter confrontations of just a few years later.

It is difficult to identify anything in the early 1750s so radically different in John Wesley's public views on Methodism and the Church as to justify his brother's suspicion of his motives; and it must always be remembered that Charles himself had been a prime mover in leading the Methodists down a separate path with statements and actions that were no less radical than those of his brother. As for the preachers, their growing numbers and increasing confidence would eventually have given rise to disciplinary problems, but here again, there were underlying factors that provoked particularly sharp differences with Charles Wesley. Attacks by preachers on the Church were not unknown in the 1740s, but this did not result in Charles regarding the body of preachers with innate suspicion, unlike the post-1750 period.

What had changed was the brothers' relationship. Their engagements and marriages destroyed their trust in one another and Charles was not the kind of person who could divorce his ministry from his personal anxieties. This seismic shift occurred over the course of just a few months in 1749, and was compounded by John's marriage a year later. Charles's sense of betrayal was so deep that it literally altered the course of his life and ministry, and it is against this background that his constant preoccupation with keeping faith should be viewed. For the rest of his life, he exhibited deep mistrust of his brother and the preachers. His regular exhortations to the societies to remain true to the 'Old Ship' were no accident and so emphatic did this aspect of his character become that a close family member remarked that 'he could not replace his confidence where he had experienced treachery'.[82] The twist in the tale was that it was not the itinerants'

---

[81] Bristol Quarter Sessions, MS licence of the New Room as a Dissenters' meeting house, 17 October 1748 (MCA: DDCW 6/48).

[82] Charles Wesley, *Sermons by the late Rev. Charles Wesley, A.M. Student of Christ-Church, Oxford. With a memoir of the author by the editor* (London: Baldwin, Cradock, & Joy, 1816), p. xxxiii.

alleged rejection of the Church that was at the root of Charles's bitterness, but his conviction that having betrayed their relationship, John could no longer be trusted on any important question. This is not to argue that issues such as the Church and the preachers were unimportant, but they were the results of the brothers' alienation, not the cause. Charles's deep resentment of John altered his contribution to Methodism in ways that will become clear in the rest of this work.

7

Continuing Family Quarrels and the Methodist Opinion of Charles Wesley

The last two chapters highlighted a crucial phase in the development of Charles Wesley's relations with his brother and his changing views of the Methodist movement. After ten years of intense collaboration, the lives of the Wesley brothers parted in dramatic fashion. The special nature of their bond meant that acrimony and a strong sense of betrayal accompanied this division and Charles's peculiar character ensured that his resentment spilled over into the public work at precisely the time that Methodism itself began to change. As the years passed it became impossible to disentangle private conflict from differences in opinion over the Anglican–Methodist question and this set the pattern for the rest of Charles's life. To gain a deeper understanding of these events, it is necessary to take the discussion one stage further by looking at what happened to further divide the brothers on a personal level between 1751 and 1756, and how these various upheavals impacted on Charles's standing within the Methodist movement.

CHARLES WESLEY AND MARY VAZEILLE

In February 1751, Charles reacted to his brother's engagement to Mary Vazeille with a hysterical display of public grieving.[1] This would have done little for his relationship with his future sister-in-law,

---

[1] For example, CWJ, 2–3 February and 17 February 1751.

which had been amicable to that point. Vazeille's reputation in Methodist circles has been appalling since her own day; as early as November 1752, Vincent Perronet remarked on her 'angry, bitter spirit',[2] while Rack states that 'she seems to have been a woman of a naturally jealous and possessive temperament which easily spilled over into a state of mental instability'.[3] There is no doubt that John made a terrible mistake in marrying Vazeille, but it is difficult not to feel some measure of sympathy for his wife. John declared just weeks after his marriage that he could not understand a preacher travelling less as a married man than he did as a bachelor;[4] if Mary had assumed this to be an exaggeration, she would have soon realized her mistake. She had also entered an arena where every action and word was subject to misinterpretation by Methodists who regarded her as they had done Grace Murray, with jealousy and resentment.[5] Like Caesar's wife, she had to be beyond criticism[6] and this pressure contributed to the problems created by her own instability.

After the wedding, Charles made a genuine attempt to welcome Mary into the family and when the marriage showed early signs of stress, he offered a sympathetic ear.[7] This positive attitude during the summer of 1751 was part of a general thaw in relations between the brothers. John wrote with some surprise to Ebenezer Blackwell in July that his brother's 'mind seemed to be altogether changed... He was quite free and open to us, and pressed us to make use of his house in his absence.'[8] This spirit of reconciliation did not last long and cracks

---

[2] Quoted by Tyerman, *John Wesley*, ii. 108.
[3] Rack, *Reasonable Enthusiast*, 267.
[4] JWJ, 27 March 1751. John Wesley, *The Works of John Wesley*, xx. 380.
[5] 'Now my dear, is the time for you to overcome evil with good. Conquer Sally Clay and Sister Aspernall altogether, with as many more as come in your way.' JW to Mary Wesley, Published copy letter, 30 March 1751. John Wesley, *The Works of John Wesley* xxvi. 455–6.
[6] 'Your name is precious among this people. They talk of you much, and know not how to commend you enough, even for those little things, your plainness of dress, your sitting among the poor at the preaching...' JW to Mary Wesley, MS letter, 22 May 1752 (MCA: MAM JW 5.54).
[7] 'Found my sister in tears; professed my love, pity and desire to help her. Heard her complaints of my brother, carried her to my house, where after supper, she resumed the subject, and went away comforted.' CWJ, 21 June 1751.
[8] JW to Ebenezer Blackwell, Published copy letter, 3 July 1751. John Wesley, *The Works of John Wesley* xxvi. 469.

soon started to appear in relations between the couples, with money representing an early source of friction.

Charles's marriage settlement had always been a concern for his brother, and at a time when the financial demands of Methodism were an increasing drain on his resources, he was presented with the expenses attendant on his own marriage. To make matters worse, John had to resign his Lincoln College Fellowship and thereby lost a valuable source of income.[9] During the spring and summer of 1752 there was an attempt to renegotiate the terms of the 1749 agreement. Charles, perhaps surprisingly, seemed content for this to happen: he was irritated by John's complaints and may have suspected his brother of using money as a means of control—this was certainly his suspicion just a few years later.[10]

The issue of money and the establishment of family harmony were tied together in two letters of January 1753 written to Charles by Ebenezer Blackwell, one of the trustees of the 1749 agreement. There is a clear note of desperation as Blackwell tries to bring the warring parties together:

> I hardly know how to write more to the purpose than my last and I am vastly discouraged in attempting anything further since I have received your letter... You seem to take the intentions of my letter far different from what I meant, for I only mean this. In the first place to have that true Christian love and friendship established between you all which is absolutely necessary for your carrying on the great work you seem to be called to and in the 2nd place to have any agreement between your brother and you with regard to your marriage settlement to be in the most strongful and effectual manner complied with...[11]

Blackwell asked Charles and Sarah to come to London to discuss the matter, but evidently did not expect a positive response, and sent a second letter just two days after the first:

> It is not my present design to enter into any arguing about the cause of the unhappy difference which now exists between you and your wife and

---

[9] Rack, *Reasonable Enthusiast*, 76.

[10] 'perhaps he means to starve me into compliance: yet I think he knows me better'. CW to Samuel Lloyd, MS letter, 27 July [1755] (MCA: DDCW 1/54).

[11] Ebenezer Blackwell to CW, Xerox copy letter, 20 January 1753 (MCA: PLP 9.23.2).

Mr John Wesley and his wife... if you and Mrs Wesley will but come to town... I am persuaded with the assistance of a friend or two we shall be able under the directions of our God to put all things in such a situation as will make you all perfectly easy and perfectly happy, that from henceforth you may go on with that love and harmony which is and must be expected of any persons so engaged and united as you two are.[12]

The precise conclusion to the talks is unknown, but it is most unlikely that the settlement was adjusted in John's favour, as Blackwell had already precluded the possibility.[13] In any case, the Gwynne family would have certainly resisted any attempt to reduce their daughter's guaranteed income and, as Charles was quick to point out in his reply to Blackwell, it was Sarah's family that had the final say in the matter.[14]

By late 1753, Charles was avoiding contact with his sister-in-law and in December that year when John was seriously ill, he asked his wife and brother to be reconciled: both agreed, only for Charles to voice considerable doubts about her sincerity.[15] By the spring of 1755, John was again trying to bring his wife and brother together, but with no success. His letter of 9 April to the faithful Blackwell indicates the extent of the alienation: 'Being very fully persuaded that my brother would gladly embrace any overture of peace, I told him almost as soon as we met what my wife had agreed to. He answered not one word. After a day or two I spoke to him again. It had the same success... From the whole I learn that there is no prospect of peace. When one is willing, then the other flies off.'[16] For his part too, in that spring and summer of 1755, Charles was convinced that relations with his brother and his wife had irretrievably broken down. The shocking extent of the collapse is revealed in a letter that he sent to the Countess of Huntingdon in the aftermath of the death of Charles

---

[12] Ebenezer Blackwell to CW, Xerox copy letter, 22 January 1753 (MCA: PLP 9.23.3).

[13] 'Sir, it is neither in yours or the trustees' power to give up anything that is settled on Mrs [Sarah] Wesley, therefore I beg of you not esteem me such a fool as to ask it.' Ebenezer Blackwell to CW, Xerox copy letter, 20 January 1753 (MCA: PLP 9.23.2).

[14] 'my wife will do nothing without consulting her relations, and I have neither power nor inclination to force her'. CW to Ebenezer Blackwell, MS letter, 24 January 1753 (MCA: DDCW 1/48).

[15] CWJ, 2 December 1753.

[16] JW to Ebenezer Blackwell, Published copy letter, 9 April 1755. John Wesley, *The Works of John Wesley* xxvi. 553–4.

and Sarah's infant daughter Martha Maria: 'He [John Wesley] cannot *feel* my reasons for staying with my wife. I sent him word, as soon as she was delivered. He has never since taken the least notice of her, or her child. I did not particularly mention the child because I would not give him, or his wife, pain. I do not inform him of her death, because I would not give them pleasure.'[17]

While observing the expected codes of public behaviour,[18] Charles, as usual, found it difficult to disguise his true feelings. Among the people outside the family who were aware of the prevailing hostility, were Ebenezer Blackwell, William Briggs,[19] and Edward Perronet.[20] This exposure of private quarrels would have done nothing to improve an already emotionally charged situation.

By 1755 Mary was also accusing John of adultery with several of his followers, and in later years even with Sarah Wesley,[21] which would have done little to improve Charles's disposition. There is no doubt that Mary had emotional and perhaps mental problems exacerbated by marriage to a man who had no intention of compromising his ministry. Charles too contributed to the situation with a nature that was quick to suspect the worst and slow to forget.

FINANCIAL TROUBLES

The domestic tension between the brothers and their wives formed a backdrop to other concerns that combined to widen the gulf as the 1750s passed their course. Again, money was a key area of discord and requires detailed examination against the general background of Methodist finance. The marriage settlement of 1749 guaranteed Sarah an income in her own right, amounting to £100 per annum from the

---

[17] CW to Selina Hastings, Typescript copy letter, 28 July 1755 (MCA: DDCW 1/95).
[18] 'I have done her honour before the people, and behaved (though I say it) very much like a gentleman.' CW to Sarah Wesley, MS letter [9 May 1755] (MCA: DDCW 5/88).
[19] JW to CW, Published copy letter, 31 October 1753. John Wesley, *The Works of John Wesley* xxvi. 529.
[20] CW to Sarah Wesley, MS letter, 30 September [1753] (MCA: DDCW 7/98).
[21] Tyerman, *John Wesley*, ii. 109–10.

sale of Methodist publications.[22] In addition, Charles continued to draw an allowance of £50 from the societies, although he may have waived this after 1751 because of his brother's complaints.[23] Sarah also had access to the proceeds from an additional sum of £1,000 invested for her by the Gwynne family.[24]

Charles's personal accounts survive for the period 1752–8.[25] This records his average annual income as just over £227, which did not apparently include his preacher's allowance of £50. The exact total varied considerably from year to year but rarely dropped below £200: this was made up of the sums of money outlined above, together with 'presents', which consisted of gifts from admirers,[26] bequests,[27] and miscellaneous items.[28] The money coming in from 'presents' could be surprisingly large—for example, £69 17s. 0d. in 1755, and a very impressive £152, 2s. 0d. in 1756. Unfortunately, Charles and Sarah's household expenses have not survived for this specific period so it is impossible to assess how much was given up for Connexional use or to charity. However, his income and expenditure account is extant between 1772 and 1781,[29] and this reveals that in one sample year (1772), out of a total household income of just over £322, about £22 was given to the poor; the only other item of expenditure that could be classed as Connexional was travelling expenses. In addition, Charles joined with John in providing financial assistance of £10 per annum to their sister Martha Hall during the early 1750s, and he probably helped his other sisters as well.[30]

---

[22] MS settlement upon the marriage of CW to Sarah Gwynne, 9 August 1749 (MCA: DDCW 6/87).

[23] It does not appear as an entry in Charles's personal accounts for 1752. Charles Wesley, MS accounts, 1752–8 (MCA: DDCW 4/10).

[24] 'Whereas the said Sarah now wife of the said Charles Wesley was before the said marriage possessed of and entitled unto the said sum of £1000...the interest or produce whereof is hereby also intended to be settled as a further provision for the said Sarah and the issue of the said marriage.' MS settlement upon the marriage of CW to Sarah Gwynne, 9 August 1749 (MCA: DDCW 6/87).

[25] Charles Wesley, MS accounts, 1752–8 (MCA: DDCW 4/10).

[26] For example, the £50 given to Charles by Lady Robert Manners in 1756 after he officiated at her wedding. Ibid.

[27] For example, the £30 legacy left by Mr Thomas in 1752. Ibid.

[28] For example, the proceeds from selling Charles's horse in 1755. Ibid.

[29] Charles Wesley, MS accounts, 1772–81 (MCA: DDCW 8/8).

[30] CW to Martha Hall, MS letter, 17 June [1753/4?] (MCA: DDWes 4/15).

It has been argued, or at least assumed, that the Wesley brothers lived according to the same rules concerning money that they imposed on their preachers, summed up by the injunction to 'Take no money of anyone. If they give you food when you are hungry, or clothes when you need them, it is good. But not silver or gold. Let there be no pretence to say we grow rich by the gospel.'[31] John certainly lived according to this rule, but Charles as a married man appears to have regarded all available sources of income as his, or at least his family's, to use.

Charles and Sarah's standard of living compared very favourably with that enjoyed by the majority of parish clergy. It has been estimated that at the beginning of the eighteenth century, 3,826 livings of the total 9,180 had an income of less than £50 per annum.[32] In some parishes little changed in over a hundred years: Robert Jarratt, Vicar of Wellington in Somerset between 1791 and 1843 survived on just £15 per year.[33] Few livings were as poor as Wellington, but in 1835 one-quarter of the Anglican clergy in Wales still received less than £100.[34] There is an even starker comparison that can be made between Charles's income and that of the itinerants. It was only in 1752 that Conference introduced payment for their services and that was set at just £12 per annum, augmented at the discretion of individual societies: some of the poorer circuits experienced difficulty in providing any assistance well into the nineteenth century.[35]

His brother's finances made John Wesley acutely uncomfortable. It was not that he believed that the preachers should be paid to the same level, or even paid at all, but rather that Charles was not remaining strictly true to Christian principles in accepting such a high level of domestic income. This is clarified by examining John's views on wealth: he defined a rich man as someone who 'has the necessaries and conveniences of life for himself and his family, and a little to

---

[31] Quoted by Kingsley Lloyd, *The Labourers's Hire: The Payment and Deployment of the Early Methodist Preachers (1744–1813)* (Bunbury: Wesley Historical Society Lecture 34, 1968), 5.

[32] William Gibson, *Church, State and Society 1760–1850* (New York: St Martin's, 1994), 29.

[33] Donald Lewis (ed.), *Dictionary of Evangelical Biography*, 2 vols. (Oxford: Blackwell, 1995), i. 605.

[34] Gibson, *Church, State and Society*, 31.

[35] Lloyd, *The Labourers's Hire*, 13–15.

spare for them that have not...'[36] He made this principle the foundation stone of Methodist social doctrine. The accounts of the London Society reveal that during the 1770s, one-third of society expenditure in an average year was dedicated to direct relief of the poor.[37] John lived up to his own standards by giving away a considerable part of his personal income, amounting to an estimated £30,000 during his lifetime.[38]

John's most emphatic statement to his brother on this subject came in a letter of 4 December 1751:

> There is another tender point, which I would just touch on. The quarterly contribution of the classes...is to keep the preachers, and to defray all the expenses of the house, but for this it never did yet suffice. For you therefore (who have a hundred and fifty pounds a year, to maintain only two persons), to take any part of this, seems to me utterly unreasonable. *I could not* do it, if it were my own case—I should account it robbery...I have often wondered how either your conscience or your sense of honour could bear it, especially as you know I am almost continually distressed for money; who am expected to make up the deficiencies of this, as well as all the other funds.[39]

How justified was John's criticism? Charles's personal habits could not be termed extravagant and he had considerable family obligations, something that John, with his peculiar views on marital responsibilities, did not appear to understand. Charles gave his marriage a high priority and this did not come cheap: the largest items of expenditure in the Wesley household in 1772 were £154 on general housekeeping and £85 on the children[40]—a total that was almost equivalent to the combined financial allowances of twenty itinerant preachers. Sarah's friends were drawn from the gentry and aristocracy and certain standards had to be maintained. Such was Charles's love for his 'dearest Sally' that he would have found it difficult to deny her anything in his power. In this sense, his brother's attack was harsh in its failure to take into account the change in Charles's circumstances. It should also be acknowledged that John was something of

---

[36] Quoted by Theodore Jennings, *Good News to the Poor: John Wesley's Evangelical Economics* (Nashville: Abingdon, 1990), 106.
[37] MS steward's Book of the London Society, 1766–1802 (MCA).
[38] Rack, *Reasonable Enthusiast*, 361.
[39] JW to CW, MS letter, 4 December 1751 (MCA: MAM JW 5.50).
[40] Charles Wesley, MS Accounts, 1772–81 (MCA: DDCW 8/8).

an ascetic—in a letter to Blackwell in June 1753, he admitted: 'you do well to warn me against "popularity, a thirst of power and of applause; against envy, producing a seeming contempt for the conveniences or grandeur of this life; against an affected humility; against sparing from myself to give to others from no other motive than ostentation".'[41] It is valuable sometimes to consider just how unreasonable John Wesley could be: totally single-minded, he demanded the same level of commitment from everyone else, and the fact that Charles was his brother added to the expectation.

Over the question of money, both men had cause to feel aggrieved. John made extreme demands on his followers and co-workers, but he was no hypocrite—his refusal to compromise his principles contributed to the breakdown of his own marriage. On the other hand, after 1749, Charles's priority lay more with his family than with falling into line with his brother's rigid expectations. In this and other respects, he was a deep disappointment to John who was only too aware that the poor Methodists were supporting his brother's family in their genteel lifestyle.[42] Connected with this subject of money and respectability was yet another bone of contention, namely Charles's friends.

CHARLES WESLEY AND THE SOCIAL AND CALVINIST ELITE

The Wesleys had always shown great ease in crossing social barriers. Of a respectable family themselves, they had experienced comparative poverty in their youth and this gave them empathy with the poor. In their ministry, the brothers made a point of reaching out to people abandoned by society, such as the notorious Kingswood colliers, and John made his views clear when he told his fellow clergymen: 'The rich, the honourable, the great, we...leave to you. Only let us alone with the poor.'[43] Charles's ministry shows that he was equally

---

[41] JW to [Ebenezer Blackwell?], MS letter, 27 June 1753 (MCA: Colman 44).

[42] 'I have never done so much for any of our preachers (except my brother) as for William Prior.' JW to Robert Gillespie, MS letter, 9 November 1753 (MCA: MAM JW 3.28).

[43] Quoted by Jennings, *Good News to the Poor*, 49.

concerned with the poor on a pastoral level and felt that there was spiritual corruption associated with wealth. He told Thomas Hardwick in December 1747 that he should not be saddened by God's instruction to sell all, for he would receive his reward in heaven[44] and this theme was reflected in Charles's sermons.[45]

However, there was a difference between the brothers that surfaced after Charles's marriage. John had an unusually strong suspicion of high society exemplified by his dislike for the practice of paying deference to the rich and respectable in public worship.[46] While remaining conservative in his views on secular authority, he was radical in his social attitudes. This is not to say that he lacked wealthy supporters: it is a measure of his charisma that he attracted followers from across the social spectrum. Charles, on the other hand, does not appear to have been as concerned with the condition of the poor. This is very much a question of extent; he was certainly responsive to their spiritual needs and by the standards of most people, was generous in his own giving. In his poetic work, he deals occasionally with the theme of those in need, such as his hymn for 'The Fatherless and Widows',[47] but the fact that only a handful of poems were specifically devoted to this aspect of his ministry indicates that his personal interest was not as strong. This should not be seen as a critical reflection of Charles's faith, but rather as testimony to John's exceptionally keen awareness of issues surrounding material wealth and its spiritual implications.

This subtle difference became apparent after 1749 as Charles began to mix with the gentry and nobility on a more intimate basis. His circle of friends and acquaintances began to reflect his wife's privileged background and within a few years the couple's closest friends included members of the gentry and aristocracy. These included the

---

[44] CW to Thomas Hardwick, MS letter, 22 December [1747] (MCA: DDCW 1/16a).

[45] 'preached to the fine folk of selling all to buy the pearl. They took it marvellously well.' CW to Sarah Gwynne jun., MS letter, 2 November [1748] (MCA: DDCW 5/7).

[46] 'In every congregation in England... there was undeniably a faulty respect of persons. In our chapel there is a place kept for Lady [Huntingdon] till the Creed; if she does not come before then, anyone takes it that is next... I doubt whether this respect to her be not too great. But I yield this point to my brother's judgement.' JW to Elizabeth Hutton, Published copy letter, 22 August 1744. John Wesley, *The Works of John Wesley* xxvi. 114.

[47] Charles Wesley, *Unpublished Poetry*, iii. 313–14.

merchant Samuel Lloyd, Mary Degge (who married a son of the Duke of Rutland in 1756), Colonel and Mrs Samuel Gumley and Lady Gertrude Hotham. In many cases, John mixed with the same people, but their relationship with Charles was more relaxed, existing on a social as well as a pastoral level. Charles and Sarah were able to entertain in the fashion of respectable society, unlike his brother, whose constant itinerancy and unstable wife would have discouraged similar intimacy, even if John had been inclined to indulge in what he would have probably regarded as frivolous intercourse.

Charles and Sarah's friends were almost all supporters of the Evangelical cause and did not therefore represent an entirely negative distraction. At a time when persecution was still going on, it was advantageous to have a friendly ear in important circles, and rich sympathizers were a significant source of income. Nor did the couple neglect other sections of the Methodist family; preachers in Bristol for example were periodically entertained at the Wesleys' home,[48] but it is clear from Charles's letters that his closest friends were increasingly from the upper strata of society, something that John would have regarded with innate suspicion.[49] The seeds of this development bore particular fruit after Charles's adoption of a settled ministry in 1756. His loyalty to the Church of England was reinforced by his friendly relationship with important lay people, for whom respectability and the link with the Church went hand in hand. The importance of this emerging Church Methodist faction will become clear.

The 1750s also saw the strengthening of ties between Charles and the leadership of the Calvinist wing of the Revival represented by Whitefield and the Countess of Huntingdon. In spite of the theological differences that had once provoked hostility, the three established very warm relations during this decade. The Countess was regarded as an intimate family friend and nursed Sarah through an attack of smallpox at significant risk to her own health,[50] while Charles lauded Whitefield as a model for the preachers and his own children.[51] John

---

[48] Brailsford, *A Tale of Two Brothers*, 173.
[49] 'I gave all our brethren a solemn warning not to love the world, or the things of the world. This is one way whereby Satan will surely endeavour to overthrow the present work of God.' Quoted by Jennings, *Good News to the Poor*, 132.
[50] Gill, *Charles Wesley*, 156.
[51] CW to Sarah Wesley, MS letter [22 December 1755] (MCA: DDWes 4/89).

reacted to this development with concern tinged with a little jealousy. In October 1753, he urged Charles to follow his directions with regard to the itinerancy, as he was a better judge than the Countess.[52] It was even whispered by some of the preachers that Charles was leaning towards Calvinist doctrine,[53] and while this charge was untrue, he was certainly more relaxed than formerly in his dealings with its advocates. Again, part of the reason for this change in attitude can be attributed to the effects of his marriage into the Gwynne family. Sarah's father Marmaduke was a Calvinist, and while Sarah's own theological opinions are unclear, she certainly worshipped at Whitefield's Tabernacle Chapel in Bristol years after her marriage—she was eventually warned by her husband that for the sake of keeping '*some* terms with my brother' it would be politic to stay away, at least for a while.[54]

Other tensions surfaced in the five years before Charles's withdrawal from the itinerant ministry in 1756. His extended periods relaxing with his wife and her family provoked his brother to sharp criticism: on 20 July 1752, John sent a letter to Ebenezer Blackwell containing the following cryptic passage: 'I am afraid you was not forwarded by one who was in town [London] lately; neither was that journey of any service to his own soul. He has not brought back less indolence and gentle inactivity than he carried to London. O how far from the spirit of a good soldier of Jesus Christ.'[55] In the footnote to this letter in the most recent edition of John Wesley's works, Baker tentatively identifies the lazy visitor as one of the Perronet brothers, but it could equally have been Charles Wesley, who was in London from at least January[56] until the middle of April 1752.[57] Certainly, the criticism fits perfectly with John's opinion of his brother at this time—in May 1753 he expressed the hope that Blackwell could persuade 'our friend' to share the travelling with him as John could not

---

[52] JW to CW, Published copy letter, 20 October 1753. John Wesley, *The Works of John Wesley* xxvi. 527.
[53] Brailsford, *A Tale of Two Brothers*, 252.
[54] CW to Sarah Wesley, MS letter, 24/25 December [1750s?] (MCA: DDCW 7/95).
[55] JW to Ebenezer Blackwell, Published copy letter, 20 July 1752. John Wesley, *The Works of John Wesley* xxvi. 497.
[56] CW to John Bennet, MS letter, 23 January [1752] (MCA: DDCW 1/43).
[57] 'I cannot set out hence till Monday April 13.' CW to John Bennet, MS letter, 3 March [1752] (MCA: DDCW 1/44).

visit both the north of England and Ireland in the same year.[58] Five months later, he issued a direct challenge to his errant sibling: 'Take one side or the other. Either act really in connexion with me: or never pretend to it...I mean, take counsel with me...as to the places where you will labour...At present you are so far from this I do not even *know* when and where you intend to go.'[59] John's closing salutation contained another sting in the tail as he unusually wished his brother 'zeal' as well as peace and love.

Charles of course had no intention of falling into line with his brother's commands. He had discovered the delights of a domestic existence with a wife whom he doted upon and a circle of family and friends whose company and support he enjoyed. His visits to his wife's family, and to Margate, a resort patronized by fashionable society, provoked John to further outbursts.[60] Charles's excuse that sea bathing was good for his health[61] would not have impressed an older brother who believed that exercise and a Spartan diet were quite enough for the maintenance of strength.

It is interesting that just as Charles had once transferred his loyalties from Samuel junior to John, now the bond shifted to Sarah. This was noticed by Brailsford, who described how 'the overpowering influence which John...had wielded over his brother was swiftly passing into the hands of his wife...the relation between Charles Wesley and his wife was one in which he played the feminine role.'[62] In 1746 Charles had complained to his brother that '[I] have so little success in my remonstrances that I have many times resolved never to contradict your judgement...'[63] In the early 1750s, Charles was still voicing that complaint, and in almost identical terms, but this time it was his young wife who was the overbearing partner.[64] Other letters

[58] JW to Ebenezer Blackwell, MS letter, 28 May 1753 (MCA: MAM JW 1.59).
[59] JW to CW, Published copy letter, 20 October 1753. John Wesley, *The Works of John Wesley* xxvi. 527.
[60] 'I should wonder if Wales or Margate...did not hinder your taking any step which I desire.' JW to CW, MS letter, 16 July 1755 (MCA: DDWes 3/110).
[61] For example, CW to Sarah Wesley, MS letter, 22 September [1755] (MCA: DDCW 5/73).
[62] Brailsford, *A Tale of Two Brothers*, 231.
[63] CW to JW, MS letter [15 July 1746] (MCA: DDCW 6/12).
[64] 'You give me no opportunity to make objections, for you ask my mind *after* the thing is done. Yet I cannot find fault as you pretty well know.' CW to Sarah Wesley, MS letter, 24/25 December [1750s?] (MCA: DDCW 7/95).

The Methodist Opinion of Charles Wesley 147

reveal the extent to which Charles was willing to defer to Sarah, his junior by nineteen years—he regularly told her that he was leaving decisions in her hands, which was rather unusual for an eighteenth-century husband, and he was at pains to stress the paramount place that she occupied. It is an unacknowledged facet of Charles's character that he seemed to be capable of forging close relationships only by distancing himself from old ones. This can be seen in the way that he had once given offence to Samuel Wesley junior by switching his loyalty to their brother; this pattern repeated itself after 1749 but with John as the aggrieved party.[65]

The 1750s saw the opening skirmishes in a battle between the Wesleys that was to last for nearly forty years as Charles asserted himself against a man for whom control was part of his character and upbringing. Like his mother, John believed in the necessity of breaking the wills of the people alongside him, and the fact that his own brother was rebelling against his hold would have been particularly galling. Charles's sudden emergence as the champion of the Church and his refusal to submit to John's authority should be seen as products of his reaction against their former relationship. In one sense, Methodism after 1749 became the battleground over which the Wesleys waged their own personal conflict, rooted in character rather than issue.

CHARLES WESLEY'S RELATIONS WITH THE PREACHERS

We have seen that by the middle of the 1750s, Charles's opinion of the preachers was largely negative. His biographers have experienced difficulty in addressing this subject: some, such as Jackson and Telford, acknowledge or imply that Charles's personality was a source of friction,[66] yet moderate this by reference to his admirable qualities, sometimes within the same passage of text. The impression is thereby

---

[65] 'The note delivered to me...convinces me that I must not expect to see the writer [CW] of it at our approaching Conference. This is indeed deserting me at my utmost need.' JW to Ebenezer Blackwell, MS letter, 5 March 1751 (MCA: MAM JW 1.57).
[66] Jackson, *Charles Wesley*, ii. 446; Telford, *Charles Wesley*, p. xiii.

given that Charles was not necessarily unpopular or misunderstood. Their delicate handling of this important area of Charles's ministry necessitates a new examination of the question in order to gain an insight into his standing with his fellow Methodists.

Comparatively little of Charles's correspondence with the itinerants has survived, although extant letters do indicate that at various times after 1750, he was on good terms with such individuals as Christopher Hopper,[67] John Jones,[68] and Joseph Cownley.[69] The tone of their communications to him is respectful but with sufficient personal comment to suggest that relations were genuinely cordial. It is noticeable that the few surviving letters written by preachers to Charles during the last twenty years of his life tend to be from men who had known him during the 1740s and early 1750s, and with a few exceptions,[70] he does not appear to have been on close terms with the second generation of his brother's helpers. Nevertheless it is rare to find direct criticism of Charles by an itinerant, which can perhaps be explained by the kinship between the Wesleys and the fact that Charles continued to exercise a measure of personal authority—the preachers would have been careful not to overstep the mark, but it is possible to discern troubled undertones: Charles referred in August 1756 to the efforts of 'bad men' to drive him from the movement and to the fact that he was hated and feared by the more radical of his brother's advisers.[71] Such extreme sentiments may be attributed to his emotional nature and mode of expression, but it is apparent from other sources that there was a hardening in attitudes.

The preacher Michael Fenwick wrote one of the few extant manuscripts that is directly critical of Charles Wesley. Only an undated extract survives and the internal evidence is so ambiguous that it could have been written at any time from the 1750s to the 1770s. Regardless of the exact date, this letter, which was addressed to Charles, is invaluable for what it reveals of the impression that Charles Wesley made on some of his contemporaries:

[67] Christopher Hopper to CW, MS letter, 11 September 1763 (MCA: DDPr 2/24).
[68] John Jones to CW, MS letter, 10 April 1762 (MCA: DDPr 2/27).
[69] Joseph Cownley to CW, MS letter, 26 April 1760 (MCA: DDPr 2/16).
[70] For example, Samuel Bradburn and Joseph Benson.
[71] CW to Samuel Walker, Typescript copy letter, 21 August 1756 (MCA: DDCW 1/55).

[John Wesley] I know has a mind bent to help his preachers, but he says that you have done them more hurt than ever you will be able do them good while you live. This I think is true. For some years I have looked upon Mr CW [Charles Wesley] amongst his brother's preachers just like one that had catched the plague and while God was increasing their number Mr Charles I could only compare to a wild bull in a net. For these ten years I have lain under a hedge permitting you to drive your chariot Jehu like raising a very great dust... as for evil speaking together with tittle tattle this nation Sir cannot compare with you—No, it really seems as if God had permitted Satan to devote you to this very thing...[72]

Even allowing for Fenwick's eccentric nature, which was common knowledge within Methodism, this letter throws up some interesting points. Charles's frantic efforts to thwart the activities of potential or actual separatists were obviously arousing anger, while his inability to disguise his sentiments added to the irritation. It should be remembered that until the end of his life, John Wesley was also publicly opposed to separation, yet his popularity was not undermined.

In searching for reasons for Charles's troubled relationship with the preachers, one can again discern money as a factor. As has already been noted, he enjoyed a very good income compared with the itinerants; it is a sobering thought that lay preachers who were pressed into the armed forces by their persecutors were financially better off as a result.[73] There is no direct evidence that Charles Wesley's income was a source of grievance, but it is reasonable to assume that some preachers would have noted the high standard of living that he and his family enjoyed. Any resentment would have been aggravated by Charles's lack of sensitivity: one of his charges against the preachers was that they represented a financial burden, apparently unaware of or unconcerned with the incongruity of such comments from a man whose family life was heavily subsidized by the Methodist movement.

Charles was also scathing in his comments about the ability of certain preachers and was obviously unwilling to tolerate anything

---

[72] Michael Fenwick to CW, MS letter, undated (MCA: DDPr 2/22).

[73] In 1760, according to contemporary statistics provided by Joseph Massie, a sailor was paid £20 per annum and a soldier received £14. By way of comparison, a Methodist itinerant received just £12. Geoffrey Holmes, and Daniel Szechi, *The Age of Oligarchy 1722–83* (London: Longman, 1993), 353.

less than both grace and gifts. This was in contrast to his brother, who appears to have been appreciative of well-meaning effort. Any resentment that Charles's sharp tongue provoked would have been exacerbated by a characteristic of his personal ministry, namely his shortcomings. Charles's public worship and preaching frequently reached heights of eloquence and power, but on occasion he also plumbed the depths, as illustrated by this letter written to Charles in March 1749 by his good friend Ebenezer Blackwell:

> You did indeed read the prayers but alas! it was more like a Priest of the world who had been up all night and was now half asleep in the desk, Sir, I say that neither myself nor many that were about me could understand one half of what you said...And as for the 1st lesson in particular you read it so very low that I dare say not one in ten throughout the chapel could hear or perfectly understand...I must own that your discourse had very little effect on me and I am afraid not much more on many others.[74]

No minister, regardless of ability, can inspire all the time, especially when preaching and praying extempore, but Charles's attacks on others would have seemed unduly harsh if his own labours were not always of the highest quality. It is also interesting to compare Blackwell's account of that Sunday morning service with Charles's own recollection: 'An extraordinary blessing attended the Word preached both at the chapel and every other place. In the Sacrament I was constrained to pray again and again with strong cryings and tears.'[75] This should stand as a warning for scholars not to accept first-hand testimony at face value, even that of the Wesleys.

By the early 1750s, hostility towards Charles Wesley was mounting in certain quarters of the itinerancy. This is revealed not merely through the invective of men such as Fenwick or Charles's own suspicions of what the preachers were saying behind his back, but in more subtle ways as well. Criticisms of Charles Wesley and complaints about his behaviour began to be whispered in his brother's ear, where they found a sympathetic response. In August 1752, John confronted his sibling with statements by some of their preachers that he was lax with regard to the rules of the bands and that he agreed with

---

[74] Ebenezer Blackwell to CW, Xerox copy letter, 18 March 1749 (MCA: PLP 9.23.1).
[75] CWJ, 19 March 1749.

The Methodist Opinion of Charles Wesley 151

Whitefield concerning perseverance and possibly predestination.[76] Also, in the autumn of 1752, Charles's letter to the Countess of Huntingdon, declaring the need to check John's power,[77] was intercepted and handed to the Methodist leader. It is possible that concern about Charles's theology was a result of genuine confusion, but intercepting a private letter can only be regarded as an act of provocation.

An argument can be made that Charles's enemies were seeking to damage a power base that had always to some degree depended on his special relationship with John. Charles certainly believed this to be the case, referring to efforts to exclude him from his brother's 'cabinet council'.[78] Charles's earliest biographer John Whitehead confirmed that tales were circulating within the movement that Charles was 'an enemy to all the lay-preachers and no friend to Methodism itself'.[79] This traffic in whispers was not simply a one-way street: correspondence by itinerants criticizing John Wesley is very rare but examples do survive. In April 1760, the veteran preacher Joseph Cownley wrote a letter to Charles that was sharply critical of his brother, accusing him of disloyalty to men such as himself who had been at his side since the early days.[80] Charles's annotation on this letter is in itself illuminating, as he describes Cownley as 'sensible, loving'. This pattern of covert tale-telling became a particular feature of Methodism as tension over the future of the movement mounted and the brothers came to represent radically different perspectives.

Part of the problem was that the Wesleys were increasingly predisposed to believe the worst of one another. Their disagreements had been well known since the time of the Grace Murray affair and

---

[76] JW to CW, Published copy letter, 8 August 1752. John Wesley, *The Works of John Wesley* xxvi. 498.

[77] CW to Selina Hastings, MS letter, 4 August 1752 (MCA: PLP 113.2.5).

[78] CW to Walter Sellon, 19th-century copy letter, 14 December 1754 (MCA: DDCW 6/92B).

[79] John Whitehead, *Some Account of the Life of the Rev. Charles Wesley, A.M. Late Student of Christ-Church Oxford, collected from his Private Journal* (London: printed by Stephen Couchman, 1793), 270.

[80] 'His [John Wesley's] behaviour to me since I became an invalid though I obeyed him as long as I was able and longer than I was well able... has been such that if I did not love and honour him, out of principle, I should have taken my leave of him long since and in no very friendly manner... There are several of my brethren who might make the like complaint with me.' Joseph Cownley to CW, MS letter, 26 April 1760 (MCA: DDPr 2/16).

caused their friends considerable anxiety. Charles's quick temper and lack of discretion contributed to the situation; his complaints concerning his brother were freely voiced to Anglican ministers and lay people and could certainly have been considered unwise—several of his correspondents differed from the Wesleys on theological grounds, and could, if they had wished, have used Charles's comments to stir up trouble. There is at least a strong possibility that individuals or groups may have used the differences between the brothers to push particular agendas. A divided leadership is vulnerable to such manipulation and Blackwell's strongly expressed sentiments on the need for fraternal unity suggests that such fears were apparent as early as 1752.[81] This undercurrent of rivalry and party feeling will become increasingly clear. We will now turn to look at opinion at the grassroots of Methodism concerning Charles Wesley and his pro-Anglican viewpoint.

CHARLES WESLEY AND THE METHODIST PEOPLE

There can be no doubt that Charles was respected and liked by the majority of people with whom he came into contact. His early Evangelical tours were greatly valued and for many years after he withdrew from the travelling ministry his correspondents were urging him to reconsider.[82] His criticism of individuals was largely confined to his brother and certain itinerants and while he was a firm upholder of discipline, there was another, much warmer side to his nature. In commenting on Charles's ministry in his closing years, Jackson drew on the memories of surviving members of the London society. Their experience of Charles Wesley was of someone who was 'singularly tender and affectionate in his manner, when addressing those that were "afflicted in mind, body, or estate"'.[83] Despite an occasional abruptness Charles possessed a strong pastoral sense and his letters

---

[81] Ebenezer Blackwell to CW, Xerox copy letter, 20 January 1753 (MCA: PLP 9.23.2).

[82] For example, Joseph Cownley to CW, MS letter, 26 April 1760 (MCA: DDPr 2/16).

[83] Jackson, *Charles Wesley*, ii. 433.

and journal regularly refer to the positive response that he received from congregations and individuals.

It is enlightening to consider the different ways in which people responded to the Wesleys on a personal level. John was of course held in tremendous regard and his influence was such that his followers considered their 'sovereign pastor as a sovereign good'.[84] However, he paid a personal price for this central place, experiencing difficulty in relating to the lives of ordinary people; John Wesley always had to be the dominant partner in any relationship, and his sense of personal mission seems at times inhuman in its intensity. Charles's relationship with lay people was different in at least one important respect. His letters are deeply spiritual but they are also very human: he wrote of his wife and children, using his own domestic experience to empathize with the sufferings of others. For example, in 1785, he comforted Thomas Marriott on the death of his son: 'Jesus wept—to see his creatures weeping: therefore he does not disapprove your feeling your loss; neither do you offer God a sacrifice which costs you naught... My partner sympathizes with yours. We lost our only son by the smallpox.'[85]

It is hardly surprising that some Methodists felt that Charles was more accessible and understanding. In August 1776, Ann Chapman wrote of the people's concern about the quality of the Bristol preachers. She asked Charles to approach his brother on their behalf for 'the people here are discouraged and say its of no use for them to speak: I believe they think of Mr W. [John Wesley] as some do of our K. [King] that he will not hearken to any remonstrance.'[86] Charles was regularly made aware of people's fears about aspects of Methodism, which was in part a response to his own requests for information, but was also a reflection of his approachability compared with a supreme leader who did not like to be contradicted.[87] The preacher John Pawson remarked that even at the age of 85, John Wesley 'loves to have his

---

[84] Charles Wesley, *Sermons*, p. xxxi.
[85] CW to Thomas Marriott, MS letter, 24 September 1785 (MCA: DDCW 7/116).
[86] Ann Chapman to CW, MS letter, 21 August 1776 (MCA: DDCW 2/13).
[87] 'I have often heard you do not take those persons to be real friends who reprove you or tell you what they think wrong: but cleave to those who give you praise and respect.' Sarah Ryan to JW, March 1764. Quoted by Rupp, *Religion in England*, 397.

own way and he must have it.'[88] For people such as Ann Chapman and Joseph Cownley,[89] Charles provided a sympathetic ear and a channel through which they could express their hopes and fears.

LAY ATTACHMENT TO THE CHURCH OF ENGLAND

Nineteenth-century historians gave the impression that Charles and his sympathizers were in the minority with regard to separation from the Church of England. This is implied by remarks like that of Jackson dismissing Charles's supporters as 'croakers and busy-bodies.'[90] The failure to examine the state of general Methodist opinion has the effect of portraying Charles Wesley as being isolated, particularly after 1756, and it is somewhat ironic that his own comments reinforce this viewpoint.[91] Yet the large collection of letters written to him by lay Methodists contain no expressions of disloyalty to the Church despite the occasional persecution that people suffered. This may be attributed to prior knowledge of his views, but the same applies equally to John's extant correspondence. There is occasional criticism of the lack of spiritual vitality within the Church of England,[92] but Charles was equally scathing on that subject.[93] Instead, it is clear from these letters that many and perhaps even the majority of early Methodists regarded the Church of England as their spiritual home. In March 1760, the London layman John Parry wrote of his love of the Church in the following words: 'As for my part Sir, I cannot see any cause, or excuse that man can make, why he should forsake her communion because (as far as I can see) her doctrine, discipline and

---

[88] John Pawson to Charles Atmore, MS letter, 19 March 1789 (MCA: PLP 82.5.2).

[89] Joseph Cownley to CW, MS letter, 26 April 1760 (MCA: DDPr 2/16).

[90] Jackson, *Charles Wesley*, ii. 137.

[91] For example, CW to Walter Sellon, 19th-century copy letter, 14 December 1754, (MCA: DDCW 6/92B); CW to Walter Sellon, 19th-century copy letter, 1754 (MCA: DDCW 6/92a).

[92] 'I being of the Church of England, I was at a great loss to find a spiritual friend that could give me any spiritual comfort. What ministers I liked in the Church, I found their lives was so contrary to their doctrine.' Samuel Flewit to CW, MS letter, November 1741 (MCA: EMV 14).

[93] 'Incouraged a poor girl...daily threatened to be turned out of doors by her master, a great swearer and strict churchman; a constant communicant and habitual drunkard.' CWJ, 2 December 1750.

liturgy is such (if properly attended to) as leads to holiness of life ... I do desire to be more and more thankful that I was brought up by so tender a mother.'[94]

Over time even non-Anglican members of the societies, such as Sarah Perrin, came to regard themselves as both Methodist and Anglican, although in Perrin's case it was initially with reluctance.[95] There was, of course, a wide diversity of opinion within the Wesleyan movement and more research needs to be done on how this was affected by such factors as social class and geographical location. Charles himself testified in his journal to the existence of Methodists who felt little attachment to the Anglican Church,[96] but on the other hand, individual societies were centres of loyalty well into the nineteenth century, London being the best-known example. It has recently been argued that such pro-Church feelings were more widespread than previously supposed,[97] and certainly the traditional view that 'many of the early Methodists ... had only slight connexions with the Established Church; others had none at all; some were hostile'[98] needs fresh evaluation.

There appears to have been contemporary agreement with Charles Wesley over the unsuitability of some of the itinerants and there is no doubt that a number of the early preachers did not bring credit to the movement. In addition to the well-known cases from the early 1750s of itinerants falling short of expectation, there were other more obscure examples. In 1756, the Evangelical John Newton wrote of the Methodist preachers in Liverpool: 'I have been quite pained & ashamed to see what empty ignorant pretenders have undertaken to speak to the people in the name of God at that place.'[99] It appears also that Charles was justified in his complaints that some itinerants were using their quasi-ministerial status to develop ideas beyond their

---

[94] John Parry to CW, MS letter, 29 March 1760 (MCA: EMV 118).
[95] Sarah Perrin to CW, MS letter, October 1743 (MCA: Folio volume entitled 'Letters Chiefly to the Wesleys', vol. 2), 31.
[96] CWJ, 24 September 1756.
[97] For example, Mark Smith, *Religion in Industrial Society: Oldham and Saddleworth 1740–1865* (Oxford: Clarendon, 1994), 169–70.
[98] Bowmer, *The Sacrament of the Lord's Supper in Early Methodism*, 70.
[99] Quoted by Bruce Hindmarsh, *John Newton and the English Evangelical Tradition between the Conversions of Wesley and Wilberforce* (Oxford: Clarendon, 1996), 126.

original function.[100] In 1760, the preacher Joseph Cownley complained that:

> the door to preaching with us *is as wide* as our societies, so that any ignorant or designing man...may preach without any more ado unless to procure somebody or other to inform your brother, which is not always needful, that he is well enough qualified for it. And there is no man that takes this work upon him though never so unfit for it but may find at least some old woman who will abide by it that he is the finest man they ever heard in all their life.[101]

From a later period, a Newcastle man described two of the preachers as 'arrant coxcombs'[102] while a third was 'wholly unacquainted with that humble mind that was in Christ'.[103] Even John Wesley felt the occasional need to put a preacher in his place for adopting airs and graces.[104]

During his tours of the first half of the 1750s, Charles found little difficulty in finding people willing to report itinerants for wrongful behaviour. Some of the best examples date from his visit to Manchester in October 1756: 'the [class] leaders desired me not to let [Joseph Tucker] come among them again; for he did them more harm than good, by talking in his *witty way* against the Church and clergy...When we set the wolf to keep the sheep, no wonder that the sheep are scattered.'[105] It may be suspected that Charles was told what people thought he wanted to hear, but while this may have been true in some cases, there were individuals who took it upon themselves to curb separatist tendencies. In 1755, Brother Norton of the London society attacked the itinerant Enoch Williams for his 'profane wickedness' in saying prayers at the graveside of a dead child contrary to Anglican practice.[106] Ironically, Williams himself was opposed to separation[107] and was so upset that he sought the advice of the Wesley

---

[100] 'the universal respect they met with turned their heads—the tinner, barber, thatcher forgot himself and set up for a gentleman and looked out for a fortune'. CW to Selina Hastings, MS letter, 4 August 1752 (MCA: PLP 113.2.5).
[101] Joseph Cownley to CW, MS letter, 26 April 1760 (MCA: DDPr 2/16).
[102] Quoted by Henry Abelove, *Evangelist of Desire: John Wesley and the Methodists* (Stanford: Stanford University Press, 1990), 17.
[103] Ibid. 17–18.   [104] Ibid. 13–14.   [105] CWJ, 21 October 1756.
[106] Enoch Williams to CW, MS letter, 21 June 1755 (MCA: EMV 137).
[107] 'You know my sentiments concerning those things...it is not my duty to perform any of those sacred offices which are peculiar to you and those who are Established ministers except preaching.' Ibid.

brothers and was vindicated by both.[108] It is a tendency of human nature to feel resentment or jealousy of individuals in a position of spiritual leadership, especially when no distinct qualifications of education or social status are involved. Many itinerants were regarded with love and respect, but that would not have been true in every case and there was certainly genuine concern that some preachers were leading people away from the Church of England. This fear even extended to John Wesley, who was barred by Ebenezer Blackwell from visiting his home in 1755 when it appeared that he was in favour of separation.[109]

Scholarship has only in recent years begun to look closely at the strong attachment felt for the Church of England by early Methodists.[110] The vast majority of people in eighteenth-century England and Wales were members of the Established Church, and while many would not have attended worship regularly, there was considerable sentimental attachment.[111] Anglicanism pervaded all areas of public life and was regarded as an important asset in the maintenance of national cohesion and sense of identity. The Wesleys by virtue of their orders and often-professed loyalty were able to draw into the Methodist movement people who had no wish to be Dissenters. The brothers were not the only ordained Evangelicals to derive benefit from their association with the Church; George Whitefield was alleged to have remarked that 'being a minister of the Church of England, and preaching its Articles, is a means under God, of drawing so many after me'.[112] At the same time, the Evangelicals' radical approach and acceptance of members from other

---

[108] Charles Wesley's detailed response does not survive, but his annotation on Williams's letter refers only to Norton's 'roughness', implying that he considered Williams's treatment to have been unnecessarily harsh.

[109] Baker, *John Wesley and the Church of England*, 167.

[110] For example, John Walsh, 'Methodism and the Origins of English-Speaking Evangelicalism', in David Bebbington, Mark Noll, and George Rawlyk (eds.), *Evangelicalism: Comparative Studies of Popular Protestantism in North America, the British Isles and beyond, 1700–1990* (Oxford: Oxford University Press, 1994), 27–8.

[111] 'The church could attract the kind of tribal loyalty given to kin or to parent; powerful feelings were drawn to it by the presence of ancestors in its graveyard. It was Mother Church.' Walsh and Taylor, 'Introduction: The Church and Anglicanism', 27.

[112] Quoted by James Bate, *Methodism Displayed or Remarks upon Mr Whitefield's answer to the Bishop of London's last Pastoral Letter* (London: printed for John Carter [1739]), 20.

denominations provided them with an appeal that other more conventional clergymen could not hope to match. Many of the brothers' followers would have feared life outside the Establishment and one of the keys to understanding why Methodism and the Church of England remained so long in what appears in some ways to have been an unhappy marriage was this fear of division. Aversion to schism and lingering fears about the renewal of sectarian conflict was not simply a feature of the universities, Church, and government, but was encountered at every level of English society. Here again, the institutional tolerance of the Church of England was vital, enabling Anglican-Methodists to explore their spirituality in innovative and sometimes controversial ways, but without leaving the familiar bosom of the Church. The reluctance to sever the link with the Church of England and the conviction that such a move was unnecessary would have been even more pronounced in the thousands who attended Evangelical worship but without seeking formal membership of a Methodist society.[113] John Wesley himself was only too aware of this complication. In his published *Reasons against Separation* of 1758, he emphasized the offence and alienation that a division would cause: '[separation] would occasion many hundreds if not some thousands of those who are now united with us, to separate from us'.[114] It appears that Charles Wesley was more in tune with Methodist opinion than is commonly realized.

CHARLES WESLEY'S RETIREMENT FROM THE ITINERANCY

One of the central events in Charles Wesley's ministry was his abandonment of the itinerancy in 1756. This seemingly abrupt and unannounced step followed seven years of worsening tension, and it is appropriate to end the survey of the second phase of Charles's

---

[113] 'A proportion often suggested is two adherents to every one member, though some would say three or more.' Rack, *Reasonable Enthusiast*, 437.

[114] John Wesley, *Reasons against a Separation from the Church of England* (London: printed by W. Strahan, 1758), 4.

Evangelical involvement by examining the reasons why he decided to withdraw permanently from the forefront of Methodism. Undoubtedly, an important factor in the retirement was his family commitments and personal needs. Sarah provided him with the emotional and domestic stability that he had lacked since leaving Epworth at the age of 9. Charles's extreme reluctance to be absent from her side was deeply felt, and was to become more pronounced over the years. He was absent during some of the crises of their early married life, such as the death of their firstborn son and Sarah's own life-threatening illness. Such distressing incidents would have caused him to rethink his priorities.

Historians have also cited declining health as a certain factor in his decision.[115] It is true that Charles complained, particularly in his later years, of a range of physical ailments from bowel complaints[116] to chest problems[117] and it is noticeable that after his marriage he was at pains to stress to his wife that he was not overdoing things.[118] He seems in fact to have changed during the 1750s from a physically fit and energetic man, to one who was conscious of the need to preserve declining strength. In the preface to a collection of hymns published in 1762, Charles stated that his poor health had 'disabled me for the principal work of the ministry'.[119] However, this is a subject that warrants closer examination. In the several years before 1756, Charles does not in reality appear to have been unduly fragile; he did suffer from periodic illness and was apparently plagued by rheumatism, but on other occasions he revelled in a punishing regime of travel and hard work.[120] There are many instances of his energy and enthusiasm at an age when he would have been regarded as an old man. Charles certainly gave the impression that he was becoming worn out, but one should ask if this stemmed from a desire to spend time with his family, and his futile search for an excuse that would be acceptable

---

[115] For example, Gill, *Charles Wesley*, 163.
[116] CW to Sarah Wesley, MS letter [1 September 1773] (MCA: DDCW 7/32).
[117] CW to Sarah Wesley, MS letter, 21 March 1771 (MCA: DDCW 7/59).
[118] For example, CW to Sarah Wesley, MS letter, 29 July [1759?] (MCA: DDCW 5/93).
[119] Charles Wesley, *Short Hymns on Select Passages of the Holy Scriptures*, 2 vols. (Bristol: printed by E. Farley, 1762), preface to vol. i, unnumbered page).
[120] For example, CW to Sarah Wesley, MS letter, 30 September [1753] (MCA: DDCW 7/98).

to his demanding brother. Even after 1756, his settled ministry was characterized by hard work, and he was still preaching until a short time before his death at the age of 81. The Anglican Evangelical John Berridge commented that 'matrimony has quite maimed poor Charles'[121] and there is an element of truth in his remark. This is not to say that he consciously malingered, but it undoubtedly suited him to give due regard to his advancing years.

This question of Charles's health and apparent slowing down illustrates an important point about the study of the Wesleys. Their lives ran in tandem from their days at Oxford and Charles's labours, with the exception of his poetry, have never been examined in isolation. A few of John's biographers have had a tendency to draw unflattering comparisons between their subject's later ministry and that of Charles;[122] this is unfair, for John was exceptional in his energy and longevity. By any normal standards, Charles was effective, diligent, and hard-working throughout his long life.

A third reason that is often cited for Charles settling down was his desire to avoid controversy.[123] This theory may have originated with the Wesley family—in two letters of 1826, his daughter Sally wrote that her father had said that he withdrew from the forefront of the movement principally to avoid contention.[124] Yet this contradicts what we know of Charles's nature. He was no stranger to dispute and his aggressive personality is apparent from as far back as his schooldays;[125] itinerant preachers, Anglican prelates, and Calvinist Evangelicals had ample experience of Charles's uncompromising character. In this, the Wesley brothers were very much alike; John was more restrained in his reactions, but in both men there was the same iron resolve, and in Charles's case, a temper and a tongue to match. The fact that Charles occasionally regretted his impetuosity, or that his family sought to obscure it with noble motives,[126] does not make

---

[121] Quoted by Nigel Pibworth, *The Gospel Pedlar: The Story of John Berridge and the Eighteenth-Century Revival* (Welwyn: Evangelical Press, 1987), 121.
[122] For example, Tyerman, *John Wesley*, ii. 358.
[123] For example, Jackson, *Charles Wesley*, ii. 135–6.
[124] Sally Wesley to [Henry] Moore, MS letter, c.1818 (MCA: DDWes 6/15); Sally Wesley to anon., MS letter, 7 June 1826 (MCA: DDWes 6/14).
[125] Gill, *Charles Wesley*, 32.
[126] 'he would bemoan his natural warmth, which to us appeared in affection only, or zeal for good'. Sally Wesley to anon, MS letter, 7 June 1826 (MCA: DDWes 6/14).

it any the less true. Jackson suggested that Charles withdrew from the itinerancy out of deference to his brother,[127] but this should be dismissed as a pious platitude. After 1756 he showed every inclination to take issue with John whenever he saw the need, which was frequent. In conclusion, it would appear that Charles's decision to adopt a more settled lifestyle was a direct result of family responsibilities. It may be the case that health and an increasingly fraught relationship with the preachers had a bearing on the matter, but it is unlikely that they would have provoked such a decision in themselves. If Charles did genuinely feel that he was withdrawing for the sake of Methodist peace, it was certainly not a commitment that he kept to in the years that followed.

[127] Jackson, *Charles Wesley*, ii. 136.

8

A New Phase of Charles Wesley's Ministry

After withdrawing from the itinerancy in 1756 Charles Wesley appeared to slip into the background of the Methodist movement, restricting his labours to Bristol, and in later years London. This can be seen as a move into comparative obscurity, as Charles left the centre of the Methodist stage to concentrate on raising a family and writing verse. While there is no doubting the significance of such areas of his life, it would be a mistake to assume that these years were devoid of other interest, and indeed, a strong argument can be made that Charles's behind-the-scenes activities in the years between 1756 and 1788 represent one of the most fascinating aspects of his contribution to the development of early Methodism.

It is important to emphasize that Charles did not abandon his public ministry entirely but continued to preach extensively and lead worship in two of the premier societies in the country. He and Sarah had made their home in Bristol shortly after their marriage and he always had great affection for the city and its people. After his retirement from the road, Charles frequently officiated at the New Room and neighbouring societies, but by the 1760s Bristol's importance in Methodist terms was beginning to give way to other centres such as Newcastle and Leeds, and increasingly, Charles's own ministry had London as its primary focus. He spent long periods in the capital and he finally moved his family there in 1771. In concentrating his ministry in London, Charles was located at the centre of British Methodism. The London society had the largest membership in the country and was the hub of such Connexional activities as printing and book distribution. London Methodism did not have a monopoly on rich lay members, but it did have a higher concentration by virtue of the city's place at the centre of national life. Prominent figures in commerce such as William Marriott, Samuel Lloyd, and John Horton worshipped at the Foundery and at West Street Chapel, while Evangelicals within the Houses of Parliament such as William Wilberforce and Lord Dartmouth were often resident in the city. London was in fact the one society through which Charles could have hoped to exercise an important influence over Methodist affairs nationally. One of the reasons why he was the object of such dislike in certain quarters, even in his years of comparative retirement, was because he was still a figure to be reckoned with.

Charles's withdrawal from the itinerancy underlined his changing role within the Methodist movement. His chief priority now was to thwart the activities of separatist preachers. In a letter written to his brother on 23 October 1756, Charles made this intention very clear: 'The short remains of my life are devoted to this very thing, to follow your sons... with buckets of water, and quench the flame of strife and division which they have, or may kindle.'[1] It is worth noting Charles's effective denial of any personal responsibility for establishing and encouraging an itinerant lay ministry, but placed all the blame on John's shoulders; it is hardly suprising that he tried his brother's patience. In August 1756, Charles confided to the Evangelical clergyman Samuel Walker that he remained within the movement 'not so much to do good, as to prevent evil'.[2] Charles Wesley was no longer a revivalist itinerant but a self-appointed guardian of the Church-Methodist gate. He was to find in both London and Bristol a circle of friends and supporters who reinforced his convictions, and whose pro-Anglican leanings were bolstered by his formidable presence. Charles's activities in this, the third phase of his Evangelical ministry, should not be seen in isolation from the emergence of this strong body of opinion.

Charles's ministry in Bristol and London was exercised against a background of continued Methodist expansion. The number of circuits in Britain and Ireland rose from thirty-nine in 1765 to sixty-four

---

[1] Quoted by Baker, *Charles Wesley as Revealed*, 97.
[2] CW to Samuel Walker, 19th-century copy letter, 21 August 1756 (MCA: DDCW 1/55).

by 1780.[3] During the same period, the number of lay itinerants increased from ninety-four to one hundred and sixty-eight.[4] There were also the first stirrings of overseas activity, as the movement was introduced into the West Indies in 1759 and North America shortly after.

The single most important issue that dominated polity in the second half of the century remained the link with the Church of England. The continuing success of Methodism at home and overseas forced into greater prominence the question of the relationship with the Church. As pressure to separate mounted in certain quarters, a pro-Anglican Methodist opposition emerged as a counterweight and battle-lines were drawn that were to last until the early nineteenth century. The Victorian Wesleyan Methodist Church was in part at least a product of the compromise that brought this conflict to a close. This chapter will examine one of the major controversies of the period, namely the Norwich dispute of 1760. By looking in detail at one episode rather than embarking on a wider but inevitably less detailed survey, it is possible to gain a sharp insight into the grassroots reality of early Methodism as the movement approached an important crossroads.

A STORM IN EAST ANGLIA

There was an uneasy public peace with regard to separation between 1756 and 1760, but there were developments behind the scenes that made a renewal of conflict inevitable. One of these was the increasing incidence of Dissenters' licences being applied for by preachers and on behalf of preaching houses. These granted a measure of legal protection from persecution, but raised inevitable questions about the link with the Church of England.

The powder keg exploded in February 1760 with the revelation that three itinerants of the Norwich circuit were administering Communion. The men concerned, John Murlin, Paul Greenwood, and Thomas Mitchell, were well-regarded preachers of long standing, and their actions represented a significant threat to the connection with

[3] *Conference Minutes*, i. 47–8 and 143–5.   [4] Ibid.

the Anglican Church. The Wesley brothers were in London when the news broke. In a letter to his wife written on 2 March, Charles described how in leading that morning's worship, he felt 'constrained to pray for these poor sheep, that they may be kept after our departure from the grievous wolves and sectarian teachers: and never leave the Church till Christ left it'.[5] Having made his initial stand in a typically public and forthright manner, Charles attended Spitalfields Chapel and handed his brother a letter in response to John's request that Charles travel to Norwich to deal with the situation. Charles transcribed this letter for Sarah's benefit:

> I have thought and prayed about going to Norwich, and am ready to go; but not on a fool's errand. Your want of resolution yesterday saved you the reading of a long letter. Did you give Murlin and his fellows the least check? Did you blame them in the slightest word? What must be the consequence? The rest [of the preachers] secure in your weakness will do what they wish... If your weak conscience will not let you touch them, what signifies my going to [Norwich]? You will not stand by me. Your fear and dissimulation will throw all the blame upon me and perhaps disown me. Write a letter by me to the preachers, what you would have them and me to do. Blame them as strongly as your conscience will let you. Otherwise you betray them and all the preachers; you betray your own authority, and our children and our Church; and are the AUTHOR OF THE SEPARATION.[6]

Stung into action, John exhorted the Spitalfields congregation to remain steadfast in the Church of England. The generally poor opinion that Charles entertained of his brother at this time is illustrated by his observation to Sarah that 'nothing else which he said was worth remembering'.[7]

The following day, Charles informed his wife of the outcome of John's deliberations, namely that no action would be taken until Conference assembled in five months' time.[8] This decision could be construed as evidence of John's statesmanlike qualities, although some might also agree with Charles that his brother was simply irresolute. A third possibility is that John Wesley wanted to gauge the wider Methodist reaction to events in Norwich before making his

---

[5] CW to Sarah Wesley, MS letter, 2/3 March 1760 (MCA: DDCW 7/57).
[6] CW to John Wesley, MS copy letter, 2 March 1760 (MCA: DDCW 7/57).
[7] CW to Sarah Wesley, MS letter, 2/3 March 1760 (MCA: DDCW 7/57).
[8] Ibid.

decision. Charles certainly felt that it suited John to have the Conference vote in favour of allowing preachers to administer and that the delay of five months would favour its advocates.[9] While Charles was always inclined to believe the worst, it is nevertheless certain that his brother's mind was not resolved on a particular course of action, despite his strong words to the Spitalfields congregation. In a letter to Charles written on 23 June 1760, he referred to the 'bad dilemma, leave preaching, or leave the Church. We have reason to thank God, it is not come to this yet. Perhaps it never may.'[10] The fact that John did not rule out the possibility if circumstances compelled justified his brother's fears.

Historians of early Methodism have long accepted that there was inherent contradiction in John Wesley's profession of loyalty to one denomination while laying the foundations of another,[11] but have been reluctant to believe that this sprang from anything other than the purest of motives.[12] Yet it has already been shown that John possessed an unusually dominant and ambitious personality, and his life's record with regard to this issue shows that he was only brought back from the brink of separation several times by a combination of circumstances and pressure from other people. John's burning sense of mission coupled with his egotism would not allow him to rule out the possibility of cutting the ties with his Mother Church. Charles knew his brother better than anyone and he certainly felt that John was capable of underhand dealings in pursuit of what he perceived to be a higher good. The brothers' friend William Grimshaw also expressed doubts about John's sincerity during the Norwich

---

[9] 'At the Conference, I presume, he will put it to the vote whether they have a right to administer. Then by a large majority they consent to a separation.' Ibid.

[10] JW to CW, MS letter, 23 June 1760 (MCA: DDWes 3/12).

[11] Summed up by the 19th-century Wesleyan minister Joseph Beaumont: 'Mr Wesley, like a strong and skilful rower, looked one way, while every stroke of his oar took him in the opposite direction.' Benjamin Gregory, *Sidelights on the Conflicts of Methodism during the Second Quarter of the Nineteenth Century* (London: Cassell, 1898), 161.

[12] 'The story of the separation of Methodism from the Church of England is one of the humble apothecary prescribing homely remedies for spiritual ills...Methodism was the result, not of the fulfilling of an ambitious dream, but of the constant frustration of hopes which we now see as fruitless.' Baker, *John Wesley and the Church of England*, 4.

A New Phase of Charles's Ministry

dispute,[13] although his reservations might be at least partly explained by the fact that he was responding to a complaint from Charles.

Why did the preachers of that particular society take this radical step and how representative were the Norwich Methodists of the movement at large? It has been persuasively argued that the itinerants acted in response to local pressure;[14] the controversy would therefore appear to represent strong evidence of a wish at grassroots level for a break with the Church of England. However, the situation is not so clear-cut when one looks in detail at the local picture and compares it with the Methodist situation elsewhere.

East Anglia was a stronghold of traditional Dissent. John Wesley observed during his visit to Norwich in March 1759 that the majority of the Methodist communicants were from a Nonconformist background,[15] and it is reasonable to assume therefore that the bond with the Church was not as strong as in other parts of the country. The picture is rendered more complicated still by the fact that the Wesleyans formed a joint society with worshippers at the Calvinist Tabernacle Chapel,[16] a result of the rapprochement with the disgraced itinerant James Wheatley who had pioneered the cause in the city.[17] John Wesley divided the combined society in March 1759 into classes, 'without any distinction between them who had belonged to the Foundery or the Tabernacle'.[18] This example of evangelical cooperation was at the root of the trouble that occurred less than a year later. The Tabernacle people were accustomed to receive Communion from their preacher William Cudworth and had held services during Anglican church hours. Baker is probably correct to argue that it was their influence that proved decisive in persuading the itinerants to administer.[19]

---

[13] 'I little thought that your brother approved or connived at these things, especially at the preachers' doings at Norwich. If it be so...it's time for me to shift for myself. To disown all connection with the Methodists.' William Grimshaw to CW, MS letter, 31 March 1760 (MCA: DDPr 2/63).
[14] Baker, *John Wesley and the Church of England*, 129.
[15] JWJ, 18 March 1759. John Wesley, *The Works of John Wesley*, xxi. 179.
[16] Opened by George Whitefield in August 1755. Cyril Jolly, *The Spreading Flame: The Coming of Methodism to Norfolk 1751–1811* ([Dereham]: published by Cyril Jolly, n.d.), 12.
[17] Ibid. 3–6.
[18] JWJ, 29 March 1759. John Wesley, *The Works of John Wesley*, xxi. 181.
[19] Baker, *John Wesley and the Church of England*, 129.

There was animosity towards the Wesleys within the Calvinist part of the Norwich society[20] and John Wesley had suspected early in 1759 that there would be reluctance to fall into line with his leadership.[21] Cudworth was vehemently opposed to Arminian doctrine and had engaged in pamphlet warfare on the subject. It is difficult in fact to see how such collaboration could have worked; certainly, John was to have cause to regret his typically confident assertion that he could bring the people to order as 'hitherto there has been no King in Israel'.[22] He visited the city in August 1759 and preached at the Tabernacle to a 'large, rude, noisy congregation. I took knowledge what manner of teachers they had been accustomed to, and determined to *mend* them or *end* them.'[23] The following week, he told the assembled society that 'they were the most ignorant, self-conceited, self-willed, fickle, untractable, disorderly, disjointed society that I knew in the three kingdoms'.[24] It should come as no surprise therefore that this same congregation was at the centre of trouble less than six months later.

The situation in Norwich posed particular difficulties, the combination of which according to John Wesley's own testimony was unique in British Methodism. Hostility or indifference towards the Church of England may have been an element of this explosive mix, but it was by no means the most important. The administration of Communion appears to have been a by-product of a tense local situation, rather than a defiant symbol of impending separation on a wider scale.

THE WIDER METHODIST REACTION

There is no evidence in the primary sources that the example of the Norwich preachers was followed elsewhere, despite the five-month hiatus. This is not to say that such a possibility does not exist, as the

---

[20] 'I rode to Forncett, twelve miles from Norwich... We found William Cudworth had preached there in the morning... The people looked as direful upon me as if it had been Satan in person.' JWJ, 25 March 1759. John Wesley, *The Works of John Wesley*, xxi. 180.
[21] JWJ, 1 April 1759. Ibid. 181. [22] JWJ, 25 March 1759. Ibid.
[23] JWJ, 30 August 1759. Ibid. 226. [24] JWJ, 9 September 1759. Ibid. 227.

Wesleys would not necessarily have discovered what local Methodists were doing behind their backs; the Norwich itinerants had apparently been administering the Sacrament for many months before the leadership found out. It is, however, unlikely that such a controversial action would have escaped attention, if it had occurred over any length of time or to an appreciable extent.

We know of the detailed reaction of ordinary Methodists to the controversy in only two places, namely London and the 'Great Haworth Round', which straddled the border of Lancashire and Yorkshire.[25] Both these circuits occupied important positions; London for reasons that have been outlined and Haworth because it was at the centre of a region where Methodism enjoyed tremendous success and which was to remain a stronghold well into the nineteenth century. It is interesting that these circuits apparently represented very different viewpoints.

On 17 March 1760, Charles attended the capital's Spitalfields Chapel and reported to Sarah as follows:

I read the Reasons against leaving the Church...A spirit of unanimity breathed in all, or most of our hearts. Great confidence I felt that they will be none otherwise minded than myself, that they are determined to live and die in their calling.

I told them my brother and I had agreed that I should warn them after this manner...I did not speak a disrespectful word of the Lay preachers. Our [class] leaders (J. Jones informs me) are sufficiently scandalized at their licensing themselves, that is coming to the people *with a lie in their pocket*. I shall see how this matter is. God is plainly at work...I met the select band, where all seemed satisfied with our last night's assembly. Several seconded my word...Bestowed another hour on the preachers who *seem* (for I see not their hearts) likeminded. J. Murlin, I cannot but believe sincere. I have sent up for Paul Greenwood.[26]

---

[25] The Haworth Circuit in 1760 stretched over a large area from Birstal and Bradford to the south, Nidderdale in the east, Burnley in the west and the Cumbrian coast to the north. The village of Haworth was at the centre of the circuit by virtue of the presence of the Anglican minister William Grimshaw. Colin Dews, *A History of Methodism in Haworth from 1744: Comprised for the One Hundred and Fiftieth Anniversary of the Sunday School, 3 May 1981* (Keighley: Bronte Print, 1981), 10.

[26] CW to Sarah Wesley, MS letter, 17 March [1760] (MCA: DDCW 5/108).

Charles may have avoided speaking disrespectfully of the lay preachers on that occasion, but he was unable or unwilling to curb his tongue for long. He reported to Sarah with satisfaction on 11 April that in a society meeting he had 'asked a preacher how he reconciled it with sincerity, his licensing himself as a Protestant Dissenter while he continued a member of the Church of England? He frankly owned himself a Dissenting minister. The Communion of Saints was immediately up in arms. I could not stay to appease or govern their zeal.'[27] The reaction of the preacher to being put on the spot in such a way and then being left to fend for himself can well be imagined. Two days later, Charles again stirred up popular feeling by reading out William Grimshaw's spirited condemnation of events in Norwich:[28]

> All cried out against the licensed preachers: many demanded that they should be silenced immediately: many, that they should give up their licenses; some protested against ever hearing them more... The lay preachers pleaded my B's [brother's] authority. I took occasion from thence to moderate the others... and desired the [class] leaders to have patience till we had our Conference... 'My chief concern upon earth', I said, 'was the prosperity of the Church of E. [England]. My next, that of the Methodists, my 3rd, that of the preachers...' They all cried out they would answer for 99 out of 100 in London if [sic] they would live and die in the Church.[29]

Public opinion in London appears to have been solidly in favour of remaining within the Church of England. The evidence is admittedly reported from a particular viewpoint, but it is in accord with what we know of the conservative nature of Methodism in the capital. It is also valuable to point out that the attachment to the Church appears to have crossed social boundaries. The prominent role played by wealthy Church-Methodists in fighting against separation can give the impression that such opinions were the preserve of the social elite, but it will become clear that this was not the case and that Charles and his friends were more representative of British Methodism than is commonly supposed.

If Charles had good reason to be satisfied with the reaction in his immediate vicinity, he would have been disturbed by William

---

[27] CW to Sarah Wesley, MS letter, 11 April 1760 (MCA: DDCW 7/3).
[28] William Grimshaw to CW, MS letter, 31 March 1760 (MCA: DDPr 2/63).
[29] CW to Sarah Wesley, MS letter [13 April 1760] (MCA: DDWes 9/13).

A New Phase of Charles's Ministry

Grimshaw's summary on 31 March 1760 of feeling within the Haworth circuit:

> The licensing of preachers and Preaching Houses is a matter that *I never expected to have seen* or heard of among the Methodists. If I had, I dare say, I had never entered into connection with them. I am in connection with them, and desire to continue so. But how can I do it consistently with my relation to the Church of England? For as it is with you, so it is with us... many of *the preachers in these parts* have got licensed at the Quarter Sessions. Several of the preaching houses and other houses are got licensed. To be sure the *Methodists are no longer members of the Church* of England; They are as real a body of dissenters from her, as the [Presbyterians], [Baptists] and [Quakers]...
>
> Nor is this spirit merely in the preachers, it is in the people also. There are so many inconveniences attend the people, that in most places they all plead strenuously for a settled ministry. They cannot, they say in conscience receive the Sacraments as administered in our Church. They cannot attend preaching at 8, 12, and 4 o'clock on Lord's Days and go to Church etc. They reason these things with the preachers and urge them upon ordination... for my part, though I do not approve of every thing in our liturgy, yet I see nothing so material amiss in it or our Church or constitution... as to justify my separation from her.[30]

This pessimistic assessment of public opinion in the Methodist heartland is plausible. The hold of the Church of England in the villages and farms around Haworth was traditionally weak:[31] parishes encompassed large, thinly populated areas, and to attend worship it was often necessary to travel long distances in harsh upland country.[32] It is hardly surprising that there should have been a general wish for a 'settled ministry' and complex theological debate would have had little meaning in isolated communities with a 90 per cent illiteracy rate.[33]

[30] William Grimshaw to CW, MS letter, 31 March 1760 (MCA: DDPr 2/63).
[31] Dews, *A History of Methodism in Haworth*, 10.
[32] John Newton described the area around Haworth at the time of Grimshaw's appointment as 'bleak and barren' and the inhabitants as possessed of 'little more sense of religion than their cattle, and were wild and uncultivated like the mountains and rocks which surrounded them'. Quoted by Faith Cook, *William Grimshaw of Haworth* (Edinburgh: Banner of Truth Trust, 1997), 45.
[33] Revealed by reference to the Nidderdale Anglican marriage register between 1740 and 1790. Joanna Dawson, 'Methodism at the Grassroots within the Great Haworth Round', *Proceedings of the Wesley Historical Society*, Yorkshire Branch Occasional Paper, 3 (1978), 6.

As in Norwich, parts of the Haworth circuit were strongholds of Dissent. The Archbishop's Visitation in 1743 recorded the existence of Quaker meetings in settlements that were to be susceptible to the work of itinerant preachers in the decade that followed.[34] This aspect should not, however, be overstated, for while many local Methodists would have come from a Nonconformist background, it would not have been the case throughout the circuit—the Visitation listed the number of dissenting families in the chapelry of Haworth itself as just 3 out of a total of 326.[35]

It is possible to present an alternative to Grimshaw's gloomy prognosis. Five years previously, he had implied that lay administration of the Sacraments was not an issue of local concern,[36] and there do not appear in the interim to have been worrying developments. In his letter of 31 March 1760, he confessed that he rarely wrote to Charles because he seldom had anything to write about,[37] and there is some suggestion that Grimshaw, like Charles, had a tendency to worry unnecessarily.[38] This may have been fuelled by embarrassment that two of the Norwich preachers, Greenwood and Mitchell, were products of his ministry.[39] A strong argument can in fact be made that far from weakening the Church of England, Grimshaw and his lay helpers revived Anglican fortunes in Haworth and adjacent parishes. In 1742, when he was appointed to the curacy, Grimshaw recorded the number of communicants as twelve;[40] within a year, this had risen to between fifty and sixty,[41] and in May 1748, he reported to the Archbishop of York that in the summer, he administered to as many as twelve hundred;[42] this in a town that had a population of about 2,200.[43] Services became so popular that nine months after his arrival Grimshaw drafted a proposal to enlarge the church.[44] Many people

---

[34] Dawson, 'Methodism at the Grassroots', 13.
[35] Cook, *William Grimshaw*, 66.
[36] 'As to the Lay Preachers new scheme, I've no relish for it, nor is it expedient...because few of the clergy deny this sacrament [Communion] to our people. Nor is the reception of it from a carnal minister's hand any objection thereto, or any obstruction to the communicant's blessing, provided he receives in faith.' William Grimshaw to Mrs Gallatin, 2 May 1755. Transcribed by Laycock, *Methodist Heroes*, 149.
[37] William Grimshaw to CW, MS letter, 31 March 1760 (MCA: DDPr 2/63).
[38] Cook, *William Grimshaw*, 226.   [39] Ibid. 225.   [40] Ibid. 57.
[41] Ibid. 66.   [42] Ibid. 125.   [43] Ibid. 52.   [44] Ibid. 62.

were obviously travelling in from other parishes to attend services in Haworth, and while this might be seen as testimony to the poor quality of Anglican provision elsewhere in the region, it should be noted that people walked and rode long distances to hear a Church of England minister in an Anglican setting.

By the late 1740s, the small isolated country town of Haworth was an unlikely centre of mass evangelism. The Wesleys[45] and Whitefield[46] made it a regular stop on their itineraries and their visits attracted huge interest, but it was Grimshaw who was the driving force. His ministry left an indelible impression[47] and while he was irregular in his Evangelical activities, his own loyalty to the Church was without question. Much has been written about the persecution that Grimshaw experienced from some of his fellow clergy, most notably George White of Colne,[48] but this was not always the Anglican reaction. After hearing Grimshaw preach, Archbishop Gilbert of York took him by the hand and said 'I would to God that all the clergy in my diocese were like this good man.'[49] Grimshaw's own view of separation was unequivocal and in keeping with the fear of discord that was current in contemporary society: 'By these means, Satan stirs up disputes, contentions and controversies...and then divides the Church of Christ into sects and parties.'[50]

The argument could be put forward that it was Grimshaw's personal and spiritual qualities that were paramount and that his Anglican orders were incidental. No doubt this was the case with some of his listeners, but there were others who would have agreed with their fellow Evangelicals elsewhere that there was no bar to being both Methodist and Anglican. The Nidderdale parish records reveal that Thomas Green, who entertained John Wesley eight times, was

---

[45] Charles Wesley's journal records that his first visit to Haworth was on 22 October 1746 and his last was on 17 October 1756. John made at least eighteen visits between May 1747 and April 1790. Dews, *A History of Methodism in Haworth*, 7.
[46] Baker estimated in his doctoral thesis on Grimshaw that Whitefield visited Haworth about seventeen times. Cook, *William Grimshaw of Haworth*, 196.
[47] When preparing a biography of Grimshaw that was never subsequently published, James Everett visited Haworth in 1826 and found that 'though 60 years had elapsed...his presence was still visible...stop an aged person, utter the name of Grimshaw—it operates like a charm'. Ibid. 144.
[48] Baker, *William Grimshaw*, 130–43.
[49] Quoted by Cook, *William Grimshaw*, 198.   [50] Ibid. 230.

an office holder of the parish church, as was the local preacher and class leader Thomas Pullen, while Moses Rayner was in charge of the orchestra at Middlesmoor Church in addition to leading three classes.[51]

It should be questioned whether a wish for what Grimshaw referred to as a 'settled ministry' under the supervision of Methodist preachers was incompatible in people's minds with continued loyalty to the Church of England. To Charles Wesley and William Grimshaw, steps such as lay administration of Communion amounted to separation, and that was a matter of supreme importance. In those places where the issue was brought to public notice, emotions would obviously be stirred up, yet it is unlikely that the majority of lay Methodists accorded it the same significance. Throughout the eighteenth century, most of the Wesleys' followers obeyed, apparently without objection, their instructions to attend both Methodist and Anglican worship. Lacking the theological training of the Wesleys, their priority was spiritual solace whether that was to be found in a Methodist or an Anglican setting, or both. Bishop Samuel Horsley wrote in 1790 that 'The bulk of the people submit with much complacency to the religion of the state; and, where no undue arts are employed to perplex their understandings, do not usually trouble themselves or their neighbours with theological niceties.'[52]

Where people found it difficult to attend their parish church they would have naturally gravitated towards the Methodist meeting, and over a period of time this would inevitably have weakened the bond with the Church, but this should not necessarily be seen as evidence of a wish to separate. Nor was this a one-way process, for in response to the ebb and flow of local conditions people drifted quite happily between preaching house and parish. In 1786 the Vicar of Eastchurch in Kent noted that a Methodist meeting that had started during the tenure of an unpopular curate disappeared in response to his replacement.[53] When viewed in this context, it appears that John Wesley

---

[51] Dawson, 'Methodism at the Grassroots', 12.
[52] [Samuel Horsley], *An Apology for the Liturgy and Clergy of the Church of England* (London: printed for J. F. and C. Rivington, 1790), 9.
[53] Jeremy Gregory, *Restoration, Reformation and Reform, 1660–1828: Archbishops of Canterbury and their Diocese* (Oxford: Clarendon, 2000), 229.

was correct to argue that his brother was extreme in his fears.[54] The Methodist people had minds of their own and to consider them as 'poor sheep' corrupted by 'grievous wolves and sectarian teachers'[55] was an oversimplification of a complex issue. This brings us back to the important point that Charles was reacting not simply to concerns for the future of the movement, but to his own deeply rooted personal anxieties. He apparently failed to see that the Methodist people were not as far down the separatist path as he feared.

THE METHODIST PEOPLE AND THE LATE EIGHTEENTH-CENTURY CHURCH OF ENGLAND

When one looks closely at the place of the Church of England in national life during the second half of the eighteenth century, it becomes clear that the ties between Methodism and the Church remained strong at a local level even after fear of sectarian conflict started to fade. This was not simply a question of sentiment: until 1837, all marriages, other than those of Quakers and Jews, had by law to take place according to Anglican rites and even after that date not all Methodist chapels sought registration as a place where marriages could be legally performed.[56] With regard to baptism, the Wesleys frequently officiated at the Foundery and in private homes,[57] although its celebration was officially restricted to Anglican ministers working in association with the societies. Some preachers baptized any way[58] and Methodist registers begin to appear from 1772,[59] but for most people having a child christened in a Methodist chapel was not an option even if they felt strongly on the issue. Chapel burials in the eighteenth century were also rare because, with the exception of London's City Road which opened its own burial ground in 1779,

---

[54] For example, 'Your gross bigotry lies here, in putting a man on a level with an adulterer because he differs from you as to church government.' JW to CW, MS letter, 16 July 1755 (MCA: DDWes 3/11).
[55] CW to Sarah Wesley, MS letter, 2 March 1760 (MCA: DCW 7/57).
[56] William Leary, *My Ancestors were Methodists*, 2nd edn. (London: Society of Genealogists, 1990), 8.
[57] Bernard Holland, *Baptism in Early Methodism* (London: Epworth, 1970), 90–2.
[58] Ibid. 107–8.
[59] See Holland's list of baptism registers begun before 1791. Ibid. 170–2.

very few Methodist places of worship could offer this service. It was not until 1803 that the Wesleyan Conference directed circuits to keep registers of burials, and that instruction seems to have been widely ignored.[60] The inability to offer certain vital functions until very late in the century contributed to keeping people both Methodist and Anglican.

Some of the Wesleys' followers would have attended Anglican services and received its Sacraments under duress, but this does not appear to have been the case for the majority. William Leary discovered that it was not uncommon in the nineteenth century for Methodist children to be baptized in both chapel and parish church.[61] In the Canterbury Diocesan Visitation of 1806, the Rector of Dover remarked that the Methodists 'are not only punctual in their attendance at church, and at the sacrament, but in the course of twenty-three years I have often been called to visit them in sickness'.[62] As late as 1851, the Vicar of Treswell in Nottinghamshire remarked on his returns for the Ecclesiastical Census that attendance at morning service on Census Sunday was below average because the Methodists were holding a large meeting.[63]

The separation question was rendered complicated by this ingrained loyalty towards the Church of England. This was not something that many people could have easily articulated as it was grounded in centuries of community and family life. When people attended services in their local parish church, they were often worshipping in the same building where multiple generations of their family had been baptized, married, and buried; it was their church in a way that transcended any definition of legal establishment. It is true that during the eighteenth century the traditional structure of English society was starting to break down as people migrated from rural areas to emerging towns and cities such as Leeds, Birmingham, and Manchester.[64] The argument has often been made that the Anglican

---

[60] Leary, *My Ancestors were Methodists*, 8. [61] Ibid. 7.
[62] Quoted by Gregory, *Restoration, Reformation and Reform*, 229.
[63] *Religion in Victorian Nottinghamshire: The Religious Census of 1851*, 2 vols., Centre for Local History Record Series 7, ed. Michael Watts (Nottingham: University of Nottingham Department of Adult Education, 1988), i. 36.
[64] The population of Manchester increased from about 10,000 in 1717 to over 70,000 by 1801. W. H. Chaloner, 'Manchester in the Latter Half of the Eighteenth Century', *Bulletin of the John Rylands Library*, 42 (1959–60), 41–2.

Church failed to respond effectively to this radical demographic change, particularly with regard to the construction of new churches and the modification of existing buildings. This view certainly has some merit as will be shown by our later examination of the situation in the town of Devonport, but recent scholarship does indicate a more positive Anglican response in some areas to rapid urbanization.[65] Certainly there is considerable evidence that despite the fracture of local communities, many Methodists continued, well into the next century, to regard themselves as part of the Church of England. The prominent Methodist historian Abel Stevens, writing in the 1870s, mused on the glorious future that Methodism would have enjoyed if formal separation had occurred in the 1750s when the 'popular mind [had] so little ground of sympathy with the clergy'.[66] In the light of the above evidence and additional material that will be presented later, it must be seriously doubted whether Methodist public opinion in Britain would have countenanced formal separation at any time during the eighteenth century.

The dual loyalty exhibited by members of the societies applied to some of the itinerants, despite Charles Wesley's unfortunate tendency to tar them all with the same brush. Francis Gilbert, one of the pioneers of West Indian Methodism, writing to Charles at the time of the Norwich dispute, declared himself opposed to the actions of his colleagues on the grounds of the confusion that would result, but he did make an important qualification: 'Were I to preach the Gospel in any distant part of the world, where there was no plan of a church yet laid, and where the Sacrament was not given more than once or twice in the year in the Church after the English Establishment [Church of England], I am now apt to think that it might then be my duty to give the Sacrament as well as to preach.'[67] Gilbert went on to say that he was prepared to take Anglican orders if a bishop willing to ordain him could be found. In this letter, Gilbert epitomizes the pragmatism that characterized both the Church of England and the Methodist movement. The prominent Irish itinerant John Johnson was similarly opposed to the action of his Norwich colleagues; he told Charles in

---

[65] For example, Smith, *Religion in Industrial Society*, 33–46.
[66] Stevens, *History of Methodism*, i. 314.
[67] Francis Gilbert to CW, MS letter, 15 March 1760 (MCA: DDWes 2/54).

1763 that he had 'often thought that desire in the hearts of some of the preachers to give the Sacrament, would be the means of destroying the work'.[68] As late as 1826, Adam Clarke, the first itinerant to be three times President of the Wesleyan Conference, described the Anglican Church as the 'purest national Church in the world' and himself as possessing not 'a particle of a dissenter in me'. He also acknowledged that even after holding such high office in the Wesleyan Connexion, he would be prepared to seek Anglican ordination if he was allowed to preach wherever he pleased.[69]

It is evident that old habits and loyalties died hard. Given the level of duality that was inherent in Methodism, it is not surprising that even the Wesleys and their close colleagues were confused as to where people's loyalties and intentions truly lay. In the decades after 1750, there were many shades of Methodist opinion over the separation question, and as many interpretations as to what constituted loyalty to the Church of England. Charles's self-appointed role as the champion of the 'Church-Methodist' interest, and the privileged if stormy access that he enjoyed to his brother would be extremely important in shaping the future of the Wesleyan movement.

In the event, the Methodists did not separate from the Anglicans in 1760 or for many years thereafter. In the months before Conference debated the Norwich affair, Charles gathered support from itinerants and ordained Evangelicals. His language was typically forceful; he told the preacher John Nelson that he would rather see him dead than a dissenting minister.[70] Based on such comments it is easy to dismiss Charles as a hysteric and this certainly formed part of his nature, as exemplified by his reaction to his brother's marriage. However, he was also a gifted and subtle disputant and it is this character trait that is illustrated by the remark to Nelson, a blunt-speaking Yorkshireman with little patience for sophisticated debate.[71] Charles was aware of his friend's straight-talking ways and adapted his style accordingly.

[68] John Johnson to CW, MS letter, 2 June 1763 (MCA: EMV, 92).
[69] Adam Clarke to George Wilkinson, MS letter, 27 January 1826 (MCA: PLP 25.7.8).
[70] CW to John Nelson, MS letter, 27 March 1760 (MCA: DDWes 4/92B).
[71] 'no other preaching will do in Yorkshire but the old sort that comes like thunder claps upon the conscience for fine preaching doth more harm than good here'. John Nelson to CW, MS letter, 4 March 1755 (MCA: PLP 78.53.1).

It is noticeable that when he wrote on the same day to the more educated Christopher Hopper,[72] his comments regarding the controversy are rationally stated and the tone is moderate.[73] When considering Charles, it is important to remember this formidable intellect and insight.

At the Bristol Conference in August 1760, the Welsh preacher and Anglican loyalist Howell Harris reported the debate on separation.[74] John Wesley's loyalty to the Church had strengthened in the preceding months, possibly after considering the lack of enthusiasm among his followers for following the Norwich example, and he killed the opposition's chance of success by threatening to leave the Methodists if they abandoned the Church. Harris also reported that John was quite meek in his reaction, whereas Harris and Charles Wesley were the 'rough workers'. The Conference decision ended the Norwich dispute. As in earlier controversies, the preachers were not disciplined for their act of defiance.[75]

The Norwich dispute exemplified Charles's new place within the Methodist movement and underlined his role as the champion of the Church of England. This episode is also significant for the insight that it provides into the shadowy world of the grassroots of the Methodist societies. The opinions of ordinary people with regard to issues such as separation were of fundamental importance for the future of the Wesleyan arm of the Revival. Methodism was not simply the Wesleys or the preachers, it was also the rank and file of the membership. Such men and women had their own view on the movement that they wished to be part of, and their opinions form the backdrop to any examination of the evolution of Methodist identity and Charles Wesley's controversial input. This is of particular significance when looking at events leading up to the landmark year of 1784.

[72] Hopper was a self-educated man, fluent in Hebrew and Greek, and had worked as a schoolmaster prior to entering the itinerancy.
[73] CW to Christopher Hopper, MS letter, 27 March 1760 (MCA: DDWes 4/92D).
[74] Baker, *John Wesley and the Church of England*, 178.   [75] Ibid.

9

Methodism at the Crossroads

The year 1784 was described by John Whitehead, biographer and intimate of the Wesleys, as the 'grand climacterical year of Methodism'.[1] Whitehead was referring to two events that impacted on the movement on each side of the Atlantic. In Britain, John Wesley appointed the annual Conference of preachers as his successor and by registering this Deed of Declaration in the courts he ensured that the Methodist movement could survive its leader's death. A few months later in September 1784, he ordained two preachers for the United States formally establishing for the first time a distinctive Methodist ministry and thereby a de facto denomination independent of the parent Anglican Church. Taken together these events represented the culmination of the movement's early institutional development. They also appear, on the surface at least, to have dealt a fatal blow to Charles Wesley's hopes that Methodism would remain a part of the Church of England. Before analysing the events of the year in detail, it is necessary briefly to sketch in the background with regard to Charles Wesley's continuing involvement in Methodism and the trends within the movement that reached a climax in 1784.

In the years since the Norwich dispute of 1760, Charles had maintained his retirement from the itinerancy, much to the disappointment of John, who periodically attempted to rouse his sibling from

---

[1] John Whitehead, *The Life of the Rev. John Wesley, M.A. some time Fellow of Lincoln College, Oxford. Collected from his private papers and printed works; and written at the request of his executors. To which is prefixed, some account of his ancestors and relations; with the life of the Rev. Charles Wesley, A.M. collected from his private journal and never before published. The whole forming a History of Methodism, in which the principles and economy of the Methodists are unfolded*, 2 vols. (London: printed by Stephen Couchman, 1796), ii. 404.

what he regarded as incomprehensible inactivity. All such efforts were resisted and domestically these years were the happiest of Charles Wesley's life. In 1771 the family settled in London; a decision prompted by the need to provide specialist musical training for Charles's talented sons and the realization that his ministry would be more effective in the capital. It also suited John Wesley to have his brother close at hand to keep an eye on the important London society.[2]

The pace of Methodist expansion was accelerating both at home and abroad. Membership in Britain and Ireland increased from 25,911 in 1767[3] to 49,167 in 1784,[4] by which time there were hundreds of preaching houses, many of them purpose-built. Advances at home were matched by events overseas: West Indian Methodism was born in 1759 with the return of the lay convert Nathaniel Gilbert to his native Antigua, and by 1785 Methodist membership in the region stood at 1,100.[5] In North America, efforts commenced in the 1760s, and by 1789 membership in the United States had reached 43,265.[6] One of the striking characteristics of this early overseas activity was the lack of official support from Britain, indicating a level of energy that not even the Wesleys could anticipate or dictate. The first formally appointed missionary did not arrive in the Caribbean until 1785, while North America did not receive British itinerants until 1769. This tradition of 'unplanned voluntary evangelism'[7] contributed to the establishment of an independent Church in the United States at an early date and this in turn helped to pave the way for events in Britain.

By 1784 Methodism was clearly outgrowing its original purpose of revitalizing the Church of England and was forcing its way onto a much wider stage. This is not to say that the majority of British Methodists were in favour of formal separation from the Anglicans, as will be made clear. In seeking to explain how de facto separation

[2] John Telford, *The Life of John Wesley* (London: Hodder & Stoughton, 1886), 292.
[3] *Conference Minutes*, i. 71.
[4] The figure of 64,155 recorded in 1784 included an American membership of 14,988. Ibid. i. 172.
[5] Rack, *Reasonable Enthusiast*, 476–7.
[6] Wesleyan Methodist Conference, MS journal, 1789 (MCA: Wesleyan Conference collection).
[7] Rack, *Reasonable Enthusiast*, 483.

did occur, despite Methodist opinion being against it, it is necessary to describe in some detail the sequence of events whereby John Wesley took what is commonly regarded as the definitive step in establishing a Methodist Church.[8] The other side to this question is the role played by Charles and his supporters, who appear to have been more representative of the views of the Connexion, and yet were the losers in this crucial battle. What has never been revealed is the extent of the underlying animosity and the unsavoury tactics indulged in by the contesting parties with the full knowledge and implied cooperation of the Wesleys. This gap in our knowledge of Methodism's inner workings is nowhere more apparent than in the coverage of the 'climacterical year'. An analysis of two connected episodes from the 1770s will help to set the scene by providing a glimpse into Methodist party politics as the struggle for control of the future of the movement gathered pace.

THE MARK DAVIS AFFAIR

One of the central questions from the 1750s onwards was the leadership succession. John Wesley's extraordinary vigour was the occasion of much amazement, yet there could be no denying the fact that one day his guiding hand would be removed. Their leader's periodic bouts of ill health served to concentrate the minds of his followers on this thorny question. Charles Wesley, who in the early years had been the obvious candidate to replace his brother, expressly ruled himself out of consideration, even before his retirement from the itinerancy,[9] although stepping aside from the succession did not mean that he abandoned any of his interest in the future shape of Methodist government.

Charles and John were in agreement that the leader of the Methodists had ideally to be an Evangelical clergyman. The two

---

[8] 'If ever there was a year when Wesley could be said to have irrevocably severed himself and Methodism from the Church of England it was 1784.' Baker, *John Wesley and the Church of England*, 218.

[9] At the time of his brother's illness in 1753, Charles publicly declared to the London society that he 'neither could nor would stand in my brother's place'. Quoted by Heitzenrater, *Wesley and the People Called Methodists*, 188.

Methodism at the Crossroads 183

favoured candidates at different times were William Grimshaw and John Fletcher, both of whom were reluctant to commit themselves to full-time itinerancy, and who in any case predeceased the Methodist leader. A third option was the Irish clergyman and onetime Methodist preacher Mark Davis. His time under consideration was short-lived and has merited only a brief mention in the secondary literature,[10] but the events surrounding his candidature are interesting, both for the fact that they are well-documented in Charles's papers, and also for the picture that they give of the pro-Anglican section of Methodist opinion.

A native of Dublin, Davis served as a Wesleyan itinerant for fourteen years before taking Anglican orders in about 1770.[11] His Methodist ministry had been well regarded[12] and in 1772 Davis and the Wesleys engaged in conversations with a view to his rejoining the movement as an ordained clergyman. It appears likely from the extant correspondence that it was John Wesley who made the first approach and he also seems to have been the more enthusiastic of the brothers.[13] In a letter to Davis written on 10 December 1772, Charles outlined the situation with regard to the leadership question:

All which we would or can do for keeping them [preachers and societies] together after our departure is to commend them to the most solid and established of our preachers... whom we advise to keep close together and regulate the Society as near as may be, according to their old rules. Now this is impossible without a clergyman or two at their head. Wherefore my brother has so often and so warmly invited you to come and help.[14]

Having raised the tantalizing possibility that Davis could be the next leader of the Methodists, Charles assured him that he would not be subject to the authority of the itinerants: 'both they and the Society *must* be under your government. It is not in my brother's or my power

---

[10] See e.g. Baker, *Charles Wesley as Revealed*, 129–30; Heitzenrater, *Wesley and the People Called Methodists*, 254.
[11] Baker, *John Wesley and the Church of England*, 207.
[12] In 1762, Davis was described by the Dublin society as 'a choice servant, wonderfully endowed with uncommon talent, which he used with unwearied application for his Master's glory, and their spiritual advantage'. Quoted by Charles Crookshank, *History of Methodism in Ireland*, 3 vols. (Belfast: R. S. Allen, 1885–8), i. 154.
[13] John Horton to CW, MS letter, 4 December 1773 (MCA: DDPr 1/43).
[14] CW to Mark Davis, MS letter, 10 December 1772 (MCA: DDCW 7/60).

to order it otherwise after our death ... the people after us will choose for themselves; and the major part of them prefer a clergyman to a lay preacher.'[15] Charles invited Davis to accompany him to London to commence a trial period at the Foundery, and if things worked out, then the people would 'all look upon you as their future father and guardian'.[16] Davis spent about a year in the capital, but his ministry was not a success. His demands for a salary of £80 were grudgingly accepted,[17] but his insistence on compensation for alleged expenses tried the patience of London Methodists.[18] Davis's ministerial labours were unimpressive,[19] and to add insult to injury, he was strongly suspected of cheating Charles Wesley in the matter of a horse.[20] His connection with the Methodists was severed by mutual consent in March 1774.[21]

Much of what we know concerning the Mark Davis affair comes through the medium of letters written to Charles Wesley by his friend John Horton and these also provide valuable information concerning the leadership of the important London society. Horton was a wealthy merchant, prominent in the capital's civic and business affairs and a member of the Common Council of the city.[22] He was on close terms with both Wesley brothers and served as an executor of John Wesley's will, as well as attending Conferences in London and Bristol.[23] Horton was, in short, one of a select group of Methodist laymen who exercised considerable influence behind the scenes: other examples include William Marriott and Edward Allen in London, Henry Durbin and William Pine in Bristol, William Hey in Leeds and James Walker in Sheffield. It was such men, rarely mentioned in the pages of Methodist history, whose financial generosity facilitated the

[15] CW to Mark Davis, MS letter, 10 December 1772 (MCA: DDCW 7/60).
[16] Ibid.
[17] John Horton to CW, MS letter, 30 July 1773 (MCA: DDPr 1/41).
[18] John Horton to CW, MS letter, 28 February 1774 (MCA: DDPr 1/47).
[19] 'He [Davis] is very quiet, but not very useful.' JW to CW, MS letter, 13 January 1774 (MCA: MAM.JW.5.51). See also, John Horton to CW, MS letter, 4 December 1773 (MCA: DDPr 1/43).
[20] Charles Wesley, MS entitled 'The Conscientious and Xtian behaviour of the Revd. Charles Wesley, when shamefully treated by a hypocritical clergyman [Mark Davis] and cheated in a horse' [1773] (MCA: DDCW 7/111).
[21] John Horton to CW, MS letter, 28 February 1774 (MCA: DDPr 1/47).
[22] Joseph Benson, 'Character and Death of John Horton', *Methodist Magazine*, 1:26 (1803), 211.
[23] Ibid. 211–15.

building of chapels[24] and the work among the poor for which the Methodists were famous.[25] This is not to say that the Wesleys did not also value the widow's mite; it was one of the strengths of the movement that everyone contributed according to their means, but a reliance on wealthier members was inevitable. This was the case in provincial towns as well as large cities and it would be fair to say that most societies had at least one benefactor.[26]

Early Methodists were well aware of the need to attract rich recruits; the itinerant Samuel Bardsley wrote in June 1773 of keeping the best seats in the newly built Nottingham chapel for the 'strangers: gentle folks' who sometimes 'drop in'.[27] John Wesley, who had a marked suspicion of wealth and gentility, would have felt uncomfortable with Bardsley's sentiment, but such insights into the reality of early Methodism are valuable. It is hardly surprising that the wealthy and respectable tended to occupy prominent administrative positions as circuit stewards and chapel trustees—they were the major contributors to chapel building projects and possessed the necessary financial and management expertise to run Methodism at the local level. The fact that many were conservative with regard to Anglican-Methodist relations was a major factor in the movement's internal wrangling.

The link with the Church of England was of particular importance for the wealthy and socially prominent of the Wesleyan movement. In addition to the spiritual comfort that many genuinely derived from attendance at the parish church, there were other more secular considerations. The late eighteenth century was a time of increasing religious toleration, but there remained advantages to be gained

---

[24] For example, the wealthy merchant Edward Allen 'was one of those friends who came forward when the New Chapel [London's City Road] was erected, and to enable Mr Wesley...to place the chapel quite out of debt, advanced several hundred pounds...In other ways he aided Mr Wesley and the London Society with his means, as well as with his personal services.' Stevenson, *City Road Chapel*, 524.

[25] It is estimated that William Marriott gave away as much as £10,000 per year, and while not all his philanthropy was Methodist-related or publicized, his membership of the society would have reflected credit on the movement. Stevenson, *City Road Chapel*, 183.

[26] The annals of local Methodism frequently record the generosity of men such as the banker Thomas Doncaster, who in 1776 gave £50 towards the erection of the first chapel in the Lancashire town of Wigan. Marjorie Swindlehurst, *John Wesley and Wigan* (Wigan: Owl Books, 1991), 19.

[27] Samuel Bardsley to John Shaw, MS copy letter, 16 June 1773 (MCA: BRD 1/4).

by membership of the Established Church. In England and Wales, Dissenters remained subject to certain restrictions—they were not allowed to graduate from the universities, act as the executor of a will, hold commissioned rank in the military, or be appointed to many civil offices.[28] Many of these restraints were theoretical rather than real,[29] but there were still instances of religious discrimination as well as social and political stigma attached to the label 'Dissenter'.[30] Such a consideration would have meant little to the poverty-stricken Methodists who formed the majority, but for men such as Horton, to leave the Church of England would have been to step away from the Establishment in more than just the religious sphere, which would have been no small matter in an acutely class-conscious society.

Horton's letters reveal that he was a member of a committee that met with Davis and advised John Wesley with regard to how matters should proceed.[31] Little is known about this group although it appears to have been a standing body connected with the Foundery and was not specially created to handle the Davis affair.[32] The fact that the committee was deeply involved in delicate negotiations that had a possible bearing on the future national leadership of the Wesleyan movement indicates its importance. The exact membership is unclear, although it included Richard Kemp[33] and John Folgham,[34] two prosperous tradesmen[35] who subsequently became trustees of City Road Chapel (a body that became well known for its conservative inclinations), and the Anglican minister William Ley was also on

---

[28] Michael Watts, *The Dissenters: The Expansion of Evangelical Nonconformity 1791–1859* (Oxford: Clarendon, 1995), ii. 417–18; Paul Langford, *Public Life and the Propertied Englishman 1689–1798* (Oxford: Clarendon, 1991), 72–3.

[29] 'The penalties were those attending conviction under the law, and conviction was virtually unknown.' Langford, *Public Life*, 73.

[30] Ibid. 90.

[31] For example, John Horton to CW, MS letter, 11 December 1773 (MCA: DDPr 1/44).

[32] Horton refers to a committee secretary and to the fact that Davis was only one of the items on the agenda. Ibid.

[33] Kemp attended meetings with Horton and others with regard to the Davis situation a about 30 July 1773 (DDPr 1/41), 24 January 1774 (DDPr 1/46), and about 28 February 1774 (DDPr 1/47).

[34] Folgham attended the meeting held about 30 July 1773. John Horton to CW, MS letter, 30 July 1773 (MCA: DDPr 1/41).

[35] Kemp was a framework-knitter and Folgham was a cabinet-case maker. Stevenson, *City Road Chapel*, 530, 569.

Methodism at the Crossroads 187

hand during part of the negotiations.[36] The pro-Anglican viewpoint was obviously well represented, although the itinerant Alexander Mather also attended at least one of the meetings.[37]

Horton and his associates wielded considerable influence and were not backward in expressing their opinions. During the deliberations held in July 1773, John Wesley began to read out a letter that referred to the opposition to Davis's appointment of the preachers Thomas Olivers and Alexander Mather: Horton interrupted and asked him to desist because of Mather's presence.[38] Concern was expressed at several points in the correspondence that John Wesley was weak and that he was taken in by Davis's 'smooth tongue'.[39] Horton even expressed satisfaction that the committee could take on much of the responsibility for direct negotiations,[40] and it was the committee rather than Wesley himself that appears to have taken the final decision with regard to Davis's severance payment.[41]

Horton's correspondence with Charles Wesley underlines the fact that John's brother still enjoyed considerable influence, even if that was exercised away from public gaze. He expected to be kept informed of developments and his alignment with prominent laymen added weight to the powerful Church-Methodist faction. The issue of Methodism and the Church was never far from Horton's mind, or that of Charles Wesley. The comment was made in the letter of 30 July 1773 that Davis's faults would damage the standing of Anglican clergy within the societies and that this was worsened by John Wesley's inability to see that his recruitment was a mistake.[42] Horton's own view of separatist preachers was made plain in his letter of 6 August 1773:

Your Brother is drawing up a plan for settling all the preaching houses in one general trust, if he can accomplish this, there may be a possibility

---

[36] For example, John Horton to CW, MS letter, 24 January 1774 (MCA: DDPr 1/46).
[37] John Horton to CW, MS letter, 30 July 1773 (MCA: DDPr 1/41).
[38] Ibid.
[39] For example, John Horton to CW, MS letter, 11 December 1773 (MCA: DDPr 1/44).
[40] Ibid.
[41] John Horton to CW, MS letter, 28 February 1774 (MCA: DDPr 1/47).
[42] John Horton to CW, MS letter, 30 July 1773 (MCA: DDPr 1/41).

of keeping the preachers in some tolerable order, but if something is not done...I should not wonder if many shake off his authority and if *he* is unable to govern, what can be expected from those who may succeed him in the management of these headstrong gentlemen [?][43]

On another occasion, Horton reported to Charles that someone had complained to John Wesley of the hatred felt by the preachers Olivers and Mather towards Anglican clergymen in general.[44] He recorded with satisfaction that John 'listened to it with attention as a matter of consequence in its aspect on the future'. In fact, John could not have been too concerned, as both Olivers and Mather remained high in his estimation.

The fact that John Wesley leaned on a group of lay advisers, some of whom had their own agendas, should not be seen as evidence that he was abdicating any aspect of his authority. He made similar use of a cabinet council of senior itinerants, but remained until the end of his life possessed of the final word in policy matters. It was an important element of John's gift for leadership that he used the talents of the people around him, while appeasing and satisfying conflicting viewpoints. Not least among such entrenched interests was that represented by the people who to a large degree funded Methodism and lent respectability to the movement.[45] There have been many debates concerning the reasons for John Wesley's aversion to formal separation, but little has been said concerning the obstacle represented by pro-Church Methodists of wealth and influence. To put it simply, the Methodist leadership in Britain could not afford to alienate such people.

CHARLES WESLEY AND CITY ROAD CHAPEL

With the opening of London's City Road Chapel on 1 November 1778, the animosity between Charles and the preachers surfaced again over the issue of pulpit control. City Road was a visible sign

[43] John Horton to CW, MS letter, 6 August 1773 (MCA: DDPr 1/42).
[44] John Horton to CW, MS letter, 30 July 1773 (MCA: DDPr 1/41).
[45] In London ordinary collections proved insufficient to cover expenditure, with the result that extra giving by wealthy Methodists was required on an annual basis. John Horton to CW, MS letter, 11 December 1773 (MCA: DDPr 1/44).

of burgeoning Methodist confidence and stature after forty years of struggle. The new chapel at the heart of the world's greatest city was both an elegant place of worship and a centre of administration,[46] and to officiate in what the veteran itinerant Joseph Sutcliffe called the 'temple of Methodism'[47] would have been a source of considerable pride to itinerants. Unfortunately for their ambitions, Charles Wesley was determined to exclude them from both the pulpit and the altar. To his mind, preaching at the new chapel and celebration of the Sacraments was the preserve of Anglican clergymen, of which there were several officiating at Methodist chapels in London. The reaction to this stand was predictable: in a letter to his brother written on 16 June 1779, Charles related that the London preachers John Pawson, Thomas Rankin, and Peter Jaco, had written to their brethren elsewhere 'of their ill usage by the clergy here; not, I should suppose by quiet John Richardson,—not by passive Dr Coke, for he, they say, is gone to Bristol, that he may not be a witness of their cruel persecution. The persecuting clergy, therefore, are neither more nor less than your own brother.'[48]

The preachers' complaints were voiced two months after John Wesley had tried to ease tension by allowing the itinerants to preach at the new chapel whenever his brother was absent.[49] That Charles was proving obstructive is made clear by his admission in the letter of June 1779 that he refused to be absent, continuing to officiate at City Road twice each Sunday,[50] despite advancing age and supposedly fragile health. He defended his stand on the grounds that he had the best right after John himself, and that it was where he could do the most good. Charles acknowledged that the itinerants disagreed and were claiming that his poor performance in the pulpit was affecting attendance. After assuring his brother that this was not the case, Charles denied that he had any quarrel with the preachers, whom he accused of being led astray by pride. In this letter, Charles was at

---

[46] John Wesley underlined its significance by mounting a national appeal for help with the building costs. Stevenson, *City Road Chapel*, 65.
[47] Joseph Sutcliffe, MS history of Methodism in 4 volumes, 1853 (MCA: Wesley collection), ii. 917.
[48] Quoted by Tyerman, *John Wesley*, iii. 299–300.
[49] Sutcliffe, MS history of Methodism, ii. 917.
[50] CW to JW, Published copy letter, 16 June 1779. Tyerman, *John Wesley*, iii. 299–300.

pains to be seen as a model of reason and tolerance and even offered to vacate the capital in favour of Bristol, if John decided that was the best course. He went so far as to claim that far from being an enemy of the preachers, he was in fact their true friend for if there was no 'man above them, what would become of them? How would they tear one another in pieces? Convince them if you can, that they want a clergyman over them, to keep them and the flock together.'[51]

This accusation that Charles's ministry reduced attendance at the premier chapel in the country needs to be considered, as it lends weight to the impression of Charles as an isolated figure, devoid of contemporary relevance. Tyerman, in one of the most influential Methodist biographical works, quotes from a manuscript written by the itinerant John Pawson that 'the [City Road] congregation fell off exceedingly; and that the society was brought into great disorder'.[52] Tyerman goes on to state that: 'though in years past, Charles Wesley's ministry had been exceedingly attractive and powerful, what shall we say now? John Pawson writes: "When he was favoured with freedom of mind, which was but seldom, then his preaching was truly profitable; but in general it was exceedingly dry and profitless."'[53]

It is true that Charles's preaching could be disappointing, as testified to thirty years previously by Ebenezer Blackwell, but this was not always the case. The following eyewitness account from 1786 illustrates both the positive and negative aspects of his pulpit ministry:

On arriving in Bristol (says J.S.) I heard singing and joined the congregation just before the text was read... The preacher was an aged gentleman in a plain coat and white wig. His voice was clear, his aspect venerable and his manner devout. In his introductory sentences, he was very deliberate and presently made a pause of some moments. This I attributed to his age and infirmities, but in a while he made a second pause twice as long... This to me was painful but the people took no notice of it. However, he helped himself out by three verses of the hymn 'Five bloody wounds he bears...' And when I was most *affected* with sympathy for his infirmities, as I then thought, he quoted his text in Greek with remarkable fluency... Coming then to the great Salvation, he was on his high horse, age and infirmities were left behind. It was a torrent of doctrine, exhortation and compulsive eloquence bearing down all before him... I said at last... the preacher must be Mr Charles.[54]

---

[51] Tyerman, *John Wesley*, iii. 299–300.   [52] Ibid.   [53] Ibid. iii. 301.
[54] Thomas Marriott, MS memoranda book, *c*.1800 (MCA: Diaries collection).

In any case, the effectiveness or otherwise of Charles's sermons should not be regarded as the only measure of his ministry—such was the quality of his pastoral work that it was still remembered fifty years after his death.[55]

There certainly appears to have been a measure of disruption within London Methodism. In October 1779, John Wesley reported a considerable membership decrease, which he attributed to jealousy between the preachers,[56] but there was in fact no serious damage. The membership of the society fell by just 114 from 2,550 recorded at the Conference of 1779 to 2,436 a year later, after which it gradually recovered. As for City Road itself, the Sacramental collections recorded in the accounts do not indicate a long-term pattern of poor attendance.[57] The connection that has been made between Charles Wesley's failing ministerial efforts and shrinking numbers in the London society should probably be viewed as exaggeration.

The preachers were certainly angry over Charles Wesley's treatment of their London colleagues. Sutcliffe, writing decades later in his manuscript history of Methodism, displays a very palpable outrage even after the passage of sixty years:

What would the fifty superintendents... think, who had denied themselves of bread, by not making the yearly collections and solicited aids from every member, and every friend to build this temple of Methodism, and now to be totally excluded from the pulpit, and be branded with epithets of laymen, ambition and pride etc—laymen? How can we call them laymen, who had been...twenty or thirty years in the work, had formed circuits, built chapels...[58]

The existence of such hostility, nursed long after Charles Wesley died, had an inevitable effect on the writing of Methodist history. This is particularly the case when one considers that nineteenth-century Wesleyan scholarship was almost exclusively a preserve of the ministry.

[55] Jackson, *Charles Wesley*, ii. 433.
[56] Quoted by Stevenson, *City Road Chapel*, 76.
[57] In 1779, the first full year that the chapel was open, Sacramental collections amounted to £193 16s. 7d. This dropped to £176 a year later but increased to £192 9s. 10d. in 1781 and remained stable during the rest of the decade. London Society, MS steward's accounts, 1766–1802 (MCA: Wesley collection).
[58] Sutcliffe, MS history of Methodism, ii. 918.

It would be a mistake to assume that Charles Wesley was the only obstacle to preachers officiating at City Road Chapel. The twenty-four original lay trustees were men of means and pro-Anglican sentiment;[59] they included Ebenezer Blackwell, John Horton, John Folgham, and Richard Kemp. As trustees, they enjoyed considerable authority under the terms of the Model Deed of 1763, and they and their successors were able to prevent itinerants from administering the Sacraments at City Road until 1826,[60] nearly forty years after Charles Wesley died. Nor was London the only society where trustees acted as a brake on separation: in other centres such as Newcastle and Bristol, their counterparts were equally staunch in support of the Church of England. The involvement of the trustees is not documented in the historic reporting of the City Road affair, but their presence behind the scenes is unmistakable. The children and grandchildren of early trustees often preserved a link with the movement,[61] and Victorian Methodism would have been careful to avoid criticism of families whose generosity had made possible the construction of chapels across the country.

Charles was very aware of the importance of the financial consideration. Writing to his brother on 2 April 1779,[62] he slyly observed that with regard to the chapel's building costs, 'many of our subscribers you know, were not of our society, but of the Church: out of goodwill to them... I wished the Church service continued there'.[63] It was not just the opinions of men such as Horton and Kemp that had to be taken into consideration, but those sympathizers who attended worship and helped the movement financially, yet never sought formal membership.

---

[59] They included one banker, one silk-broker, three merchants, and one gentleman. Stevenson, *City Road Chapel*, 250.

[60] Ibid. 153.

[61] For example, the family of the City Road trustee Charles Greenwood maintained a link with Methodism until the death in 1811 of his son Thomas (also a trustee). Ibid. 361–2; John Buttress, the grandson of the trustee William Cowland was himself a trustee of City Road and a treasurer of the Methodist Missionary Society until his death in 1861. Ibid. 577–8.

[62] Sutcliffe, Ms history of Methodism, ii. 917.

[63] Quoted by Baker, *Charles Wesley as Revealed*, 132.

THE DEED OF DECLARATION

The issues that have been highlighted in the examination of the Davis and City Road affairs came to a head in 1784. The first was that connected with the leadership succession. With John Wesley in his eighties, it was obvious that something needed to be done if Methodism was to survive. The great worry was that his followers would divide and scatter in the event of his death: as early as 1763 the Irish itinerant John Johnson summed up the situation in a letter to Charles Wesley: 'I dread the day when *your brother and you shall* be taken from us... sometimes I think the *Lord will stand by us*... at other times I think we shall be suffered to *divide: and be destroyed*.'[64]

For some years, the Methodists had taken gradual steps towards establishing a legal position with regard to the status of chapels and the right of itinerants to preach. Now the time had arrived to take that process one stage further by appointing a legally acceptable hierarchy that would eventually form the government of the Connexion. During the 1770s various avenues had been explored, ranging from the itinerant Joseph Benson's suggestion that the best of the preachers should be ordained by the Wesleys and their clerical colleagues, to John Fletcher's proposal that Methodism be formed into a 'general society' of the Church of England.[65] By this time, it was clear that there would have to be a form of collective leadership after John Wesley's removal, although this was not incompatible with the idea of a Church of England minister as the titular head of the movement; in addition to preserving a link with the Church, such an arrangement would have helped to prevent a dogfight between ambitious preachers eager to step into Wesley's shoes. There was also of course, another scenario and one that certain itinerants were no doubt considering, namely collective power in the hands of preachers independent of any Anglican connection.

In 1777, an important player arrived on the scene in the person of the clergyman Thomas Coke. A graduate of Oxford, Coke had been ejected earlier in the year from his curacy at South Petherton

---

[64] John Johnson to CW, MS letter, 2 June 1763 (MCA: EMV), 92.
[65] Rack, *Reasonable Enthusiast*, 466.

in Somerset for attempting to incorporate Methodist practices into his ministry.[66] In the face of this undeniably rough treatment, he reacted against his Anglican background: he did not go so far as to repudiate his orders or speak openly against the Church, but his actions after joining the Methodists suggests that he was driven in part by anger against the Church establishment. Coke later claimed that he turned against the Anglicans only in about 1782 or 1783,[67] but there is little to indicate that he possessed much loyalty in the earlier years of his Methodist involvement. He allied himself with pro-separation itinerants such as John Pawson and, in 1779, distanced himself from attempts to bar preachers from the City Road pulpit. These were hardly the actions of a man who was later to describe his attitude at this time as that of a pro-Anglican bigot;[68] certainly Charles Wesley was quick to point out to his brother that his latest recruit was siding with dissident preachers.[69]

Young and ambitious, Coke swiftly achieved a position of prominence in John Wesley's inner circle and within a few years was suspected, probably correctly, of regarding himself as the heir apparent to the Methodist throne.[70] Coke's recruitment represented a radical departure from the earlier pattern of ordained helpers such as John Richardson and Mark Davis. Unlike them, he felt little or no loyalty to the Church of which he was a minister, but at the same time, he was willing to use his clerical status to enhance his personal standing within Methodism. This is not to say that Coke's ambition was incompatible with spirituality or administrative gifts, but it does explain why there was mutual animosity in his relationship with Charles Wesley. By his own admission, Coke, as early as 1779, regarded John's brother as an enemy of Methodism and was

---

[66] Coke was publicly dismissed in the presence of the congregation. His replacement as curate was waiting to step into the pulpit where he preached a sermon directed against his predecessor. Vickers, *Thomas Coke*, 35.

[67] 'For five or six years after my union with Mr Wesley, I remained fixed in my attachments to the Church of England, but afterwards...I changed my sentiments and promoted a separation from it.' Thomas Coke to Samuel Seabury, Typescript copy letter, 14 May 1791 (MCA: PLP 28/7/17).

[68] Ibid.

[69] CW to JW, Published copy letter, 16 June 1779. Quoted by Tyerman, *John Wesley*, iii. 299.

[70] Rack, *Reasonable Enthusiast*, 496.

influenced by working alongside individuals who felt the same.[71] The introduction of such a man into an already volatile situation was a major factor in the events of the 'climacterical year'.

Coke was one of the prime movers behind the 1784 Deed of Declaration, the legal document that established Conference as the successor to the Wesleys. The Deed was a product of the realization that there was no institution that could exercise legally sanctioned Connexional control over the Methodist movement. Fears were expressed on this point by the preachers at the Conference of 1782 whereupon Coke sought the advice of the lawyers William Clulow and John Maddocks; their opinion was that Wesley needed to clarify the situation.[72] A deed was accordingly drawn up on John Wesley's instructions, with Coke's assistance, and enrolled in Chancery on 9 March 1784.[73] The deed appointed one hundred named itinerants to form the legal Conference, which after the death of the Wesleys, would guide the affairs of the Connexion and be presided over by a President, elected for one year. Other aspects of organization were also outlined, but it is unnecessary to enter into detail concerning them. It is sufficient to say that the deed ensured that Methodism had a legal constitution and could survive the deaths of its founders.

One might assume in retrospect that the Deed of Declaration was a crucial stepping-stone on the way to an independent Church and this is true in certain respects. However, the question of whether or not Methodism would continue to exist in association with the Anglicans was left unresolved. In fact, it was important for both separatists and Church Methodists that the deed was executed, as otherwise the future of the movement would have been dependent on the lives of two elderly men.

Charles Wesley's reaction has not been recorded in the primary material, but it is unlikely to have been negative for the reasons outlined above. He attended the Conferences of 1782[74] and 1783[75]

---

[71] Thomas Coke to JW, Typescript copy letter, 15 December 1779 (MCA: PLP 28.3.10).
[72] Vickers, *Thomas Coke*, 62–3.
[73] John Wesley, MS Declaration and Appointment of the Conference of the People called Methodists, 28 February 1784 (MCA: Accession 1977/075).
[74] This Conference was held in London so it is most unlikely that Charles was absent.
[75] CW to Sarah Wesley, MS letter [July/August 1783] (MCA: DDCW 7/86).

at which the issue was debated, and the decisions with regard to the necessity of the deed were described as unanimous.[76] He was also personally involved, to the extent that his own 'life-estate' in Methodist chapels was preserved intact, which meant that Conference could not take control until after the Wesleys had both died—a sobering thought for certain of the preachers. The 1784 Deed may not in itself have represented a certain break with the Church of England, but taken in conjunction with the other event of that year, namely the North American ordinations, it did increase the likelihood of separation becoming a reality.

AN ORDAINED MINISTRY FOR THE UNITED STATES

The ordinations were a direct result of the establishment of an independent United States. The position of the Anglican Church in the American colonies had never been as dominant as in the mother country, and was further damaged by the upheavals associated with the independence struggle. According to one contemporary account of the situation in Virginia: 'a large number of the churches were destroyed or irreparably damaged; 23 of her 95 parishes were extinct or forsaken; and of the remaining 72, 34 were destitute of ministerial services; while of her 98 clergymen, only 28 remained'.[77] In such a chaotic situation it was virtually impossible for Methodists to have easy Sacramental access and this had been the case even before the war as the Church struggled to cope with an expanding frontier society.

John Wesley's dilemma was that ordination of itinerants was the only viable solution to the American problem. Yet this would signify formal separation by allowing preachers to become ministers, qualified to perform the Sacraments. His brother Charles underlined this fact in the immediate aftermath of the ordinations when he obtained the opinion of his old school friend Lord Chief Justice Mansfield to the effect that 'Ordination was Separation'.[78] Typically, John refused to accept even this unequivocal statement by one of

[76] Vickers, *Thomas Coke*, 63. [77] Quoted by Tyerman, *John Wesley*, ii. 427.
[78] Ibid. 273.

Britain's most eminent judges and continued to deny to his dying day that he had broken with the Church.[79]

The suggestion has been made that John was manipulated into taking this step; Charles for example blamed his brother's senility and Thomas Coke's ambition, while Whitehead attributed the ordinations to the ambitions of a party of the preachers.[80] However, it is widely accepted by modern authorities that John Wesley acted in this matter, as in most others, in accordance with his own will.[81] The timing was forced on him by circumstances beyond his control but ultimately it was his decision.

There were conversations between John Wesley and Coke concerning the American problem in October 1783 and again the following February, during which Wesley broached the possibility of ordinations;[82] Coke was initially hesitant but came round to Wesley's point of view.[83] At the Leeds Conference of 1784, Wesley informed the assembled itinerants of his intention to send Coke to America, but said nothing about ordaining;[84] he did however reveal the full details to his cabinet council of senior preachers. According to John Pawson, who was present, their reaction was hostile: 'the preachers were astonished... and to a man opposed it. But I plainly saw that it would be done, as Mr Wesley's mind appeared to be quite made up.'[85] Wesley also consulted several Evangelical clergymen during his visit to Leeds; they pointed out that it 'seemed inconsistent with... former professions regarding the Church'.[86] Wesley walked out of the meeting in a fit of pique, which suggests that he was interested only in their approval, not their opinion. Despite this ringing lack of endorsement, Wesley remained fixed in his intention. On 1 September 1784, with the assistance of the Anglican ministers James Creighton and Thomas Coke, he ordained the preachers Richard Whatcoat and Thomas Vasey as deacons. A day later, they were ordained as presbyters, on

---

[79] Ibid. 320–2.   [80] Whitehead, *John Wesley*, 404.
[81] For example, Baker, *John Wesley and the Church of England*, 266; Vickers, *Thomas Coke*, 76–8.
[82] Baker, *John Wesley and the Church of England*, 263.
[83] Thomas Coke to JW, Published copy letter, 9 August 1784. Quoted by Vickers, *Thomas Coke*, 77–8.
[84] Baker, *John Wesley and the Church of England*, 264.
[85] Quoted by Rack, *Reasonable Enthusiast*, 512.
[86] Quoted by Baker, *John Wesley and the Church of England*, 265.

which occasion Coke was appointed Superintendent.[87] The level of secrecy was such that the ordinations took place at four in the morning in a private house.[88]

The preceding brief narration of the circumstances attendant on the ordinations covers well-known ground. What has not been fully examined is the reaction of the various parties within Methodism and this will be the focus next.

If one accepts that Methodist opinion by the 1780s was tending towards separation, which is the impression that has often been given,[89] then the response of the itinerants is surprising. We have already seen that the cabinet of senior preachers was unanimously opposed and their colleagues appear to have been equally aghast as shown by the following reaction from an unnamed preacher: 'Ordination among Methodists! Amazing indeed!... Who is the father of this monster, so long dreaded by the father of his people and by most of his sons... Years to come will speak in groans the opprobrious anniversary of our religious madness for gowns and bands.'[90] This comment provides a valuable sidelight on the complex nature of feelings about separation, as it suggests that there was feeling within Methodism that the preachers, unlike Anglican ministers, simply did not need 'gowns and bands' to validate their divine calling. Another anonymous itinerant wrote: 'I wish they had been asleep when they began this business of ordination: it is neither *episcopal* nor *presbyterian*; but a mere hodge-podge of inconsistencies.'[91] Later in the decade as ordinations were carried out for first the Scottish and then the English work, opinion was similarly lukewarm if not negative. In 1786 for example, when Wesley was urged to ordain a preacher for Yorkshire, a majority of Conference was against.[92]

It is difficult to draw firm conclusions concerning this lack of enthusiasm, although some explanations can be put forward. Separation had long been a distinct possibility, but the decisive break with

---

[87] Rack, *Reasonable Enthusiast*, 513.
[88] Harrison, *The Separation of Methodism from the Church of England*, 7.
[89] For example, ibid. 12–13; Church, *More about the Early Methodist People*, 255–6; Rack, *Reasonable Enthusiast*, 525; Jackson, *Charles Wesley*, ii. 377.
[90] Quoted by Tyerman, *John Wesley*, iii. 439.   [91] Ibid.
[92] Rack, *Reasonable Enthusiast*, 519–20.

the Church had been avoided. The preachers could have been excused for feeling uncomfortable at this radical step, especially when a man who professed himself a strong churchman presented them with a fait accompli. Their discomfiture would have been aggravated by the fact that the ordinations followed soon after the Deed of Declaration: in appointing just one hundred named preachers to form the voting body, Wesley had given offence to many of their colleagues.[93] Men such as John Hampson, who had been a preacher since the 1750s, discovered that he was not in the so-called Legal Hundred, unlike Charles Atmore, a travelling preacher for just three years. The fact that it was a matter of common sense to make the Legal Hundred representative of the cross-section of itinerants, rather than based simply on seniority, did not prevent anger with Wesley's selection. Now the preachers discovered that not only would a small number of their colleagues be given additional status, but that Thomas Coke was appointed 'Superintendent'—his ambition and special place in Wesley's counsel was already causing hostile comment and eyebrows would have been raised even further at this unprecedented mark of favour.[94] It is true that these first ordinations applied only to the United States, but their significance would have been lost on few observers.

The preachers may also have been nervous of reaction within the societies. Lay opinion will be considered later, but at this juncture it is appropriate to point out that during the first half-century of the movement's history, the majority of itinerants had shown themselves to be pragmatic in their approach to church order. Where there had been pressing local circumstances that justified a breach, as at Norwich in 1760, then the itinerants had been ready to act, but not otherwise, despite grumbling by individuals. In this they demonstrated themselves to be true gospel sons of John Wesley, and of course of his brother, who had shown a similar approach before his reinvention as the champion of the church.

A final possibility should also be considered, namely that there was more attachment to the Church of England among the body of preachers than is commonly supposed. Fervent expressions of loyalty

---

[93] Baker, *John Wesley and the Church of England*, 231–2.
[94] Vickers, *Thomas Coke*, 64.

to the Establishment are virtually non-existent, but if separatist views were standard, than one would expect the ordinations to have been greeted with enthusiasm or anticipation, even if accompanied by nerves. Yet this was not the case. There were certainly preachers who wished to separate; John Pawson makes this clear when writing about the Conference of 1785: 'It was generally expected that something effectual would have been done... respecting our separating from the Church of England, which it was thought by many of the preachers and people also, would be much for the glory of God: But this happy time is not yet come.'[95] But there were others who did not see a need to break with the parent body; the book steward John Atlay was an Anglican loyalist and was outspoken on the issue at the 1785 Conference,[96] while his fellow itinerant James Watson was also against separation, despite his own dissenting background.[97] Some well-respected ministers of the younger generation such as Joseph Benson and Adam Clarke, both of whom served as President of Conference, retained affection for the Church until the end of their lives. Consideration should also be given to the following statement by Joseph Sutcliffe: 'Having known many of the preachers of that day [1778], I think they were sincerely attached to the Book of Common Prayer. Most of them, anterior to their conversion, had attended the Church and Sacrament and in their principles they had long defended themselves against the charge of dissent.'[98] Sutcliffe goes on to criticize the Church for not 'taking them [the preachers] by the hand', but this is not the statement of an enemy, but of a man who felt let down by his parent denomination.

The state of the majority opinion is difficult to estimate. On the one side, there were itinerants such as Pawson, who exhibited such personal antipathy towards Anglican clergymen that it perhaps flavoured his view of what his colleagues were thinking:[99] on the other side of the fence were loyalists such as John Atlay and Joseph Benson.

---

[95] Joseph Entwisle, MS account of the life of John Pawson, c.1820 (MCA: Diaries collection), 32.

[96] Moore, *John Wesley*, ii. 329.

[97] Marion Banks, 'Diary of a Birmingham Methodist', *Proceedings of the Wesley Historical Society*, 39 (February 1974), 102.

[98] Sutcliffe, MS history of Methodism, ii. 919.

[99] 'What miserable readers are nine in ten, not to say ninety-nine in an hundred of the clergy, with all their learning?... I do really believe that to separate from the

In the middle was Sutcliffe and others of a like mind, who felt that the itinerants were part of an Anglican family that had spurned their efforts, leaving separation as the only way that their ministry could be completely fulfilled. This is not to say that they felt pleased at the prospect of schism—even Pawson was convinced that separation could only be achieved by stages,[100] which may account for his initial hostility towards John Wesley's dramatic announcement that he would ordain for North America.

There was of course no such ambivalence in the reaction of Charles and his supporters. John had kept him completely in the dark concerning his plans—Thomas Coke, senior preachers, and select Evangelical clergymen were all informed in advance about the ordinations, but not John Wesley's brother. It is interesting that even men whom Charles would have regarded as friends and allies maintained secrecy; Anglican clerics such as John Fletcher and Walter Sellon,[101] despite their own reservations, all respected John Wesley's confidence. One suspects that they were only too aware of how John's impetuous brother would react and did not wish to provoke the storm that would surely break.

On 4 November 1784, the wealthy lay Methodist Henry Durbin wrote to Charles from Bristol with the news that his brother had issued a printed letter announcing the ordinations.[102] John's letter was dated 10 September,[103] but was not released to the public for nearly two months after that date, probably to coincide with the anticipated arrival of Coke's party in New York. Durbin, who was very much of Charles's own persuasion with regard to the separation issue, declared that henceforth John 'should not preach in the churches, or read the prayers, as he has renounced [the Church of England]'. Durbin reported that such was the horror felt within parts of the Bristol society that some members felt that they could no

---

Church would be much the better for our people.' John Pawson to Charles Atmore, MS letter, 30 March 1786 (MCA: PLP 82.2.7).

[100] Ibid.

[101] Baker, *John Wesley and the Church of England*, 265.

[102] Henry Durbin to CW, MS letter, 4 November 1784 (MCA: Letters chiefly to the Wesleys, vol. ii).

[103] JW to Thomas Coke, Francis Asbury, and 'Our Brethren in America', MS copy letter, 10 September 1784 (MCA: DDCW 9/3).

longer receive the Sacrament from John Wesley's hands.[104] It is apparent from this letter and other unpublished correspondence between Charles and the Anglican-Methodists Henry Durbin and William Pine that the ordinations were part of a complex tale of rivalry and struggle over the Methodist future. This is not an episode that portrays either party in a favourable light, which is perhaps one reason why the letters have remained largely unpublished.

In his draft response, written in shorthand on the back of Durbin's letter,[105] Charles attributes his brother's action to 'extreme old age' and to his being outmanoeuvred by the ambitious Thomas Coke. John had apparently broken a promise to Charles that he would not separate from the Church without his brother's consent. He also makes the interesting statement that John's treatment of Pine, and Durbin is now 'fully explained' and this allusion provides an opportunity to look deeper at the prevailing tension.

On 23 September 1784, the Bristol printer William Pine had written to Charles Wesley with an update of events connected with a bitter dispute between Thomas Coke and John Wesley on the one hand, and Durbin and Pine on the other.[106] The roots of the controversy went back to the previous summer of 1783 when Durbin, Pine, and their fellow trustees at the New Room refused to change the terms of the chapel deed allowing John, and after him the Conference, the right of appointing preachers to serve at the chapel.[107] This refusal stemmed from the trustees' view that by controlling access to the pulpit, they were safeguarding the New Room 'for the use of the Methodist Church, in connexion with the Church of England'.[108] Charles Wesley did not play a public role in the affair but was kept informed of developments by his Bristol friends. His opinion can be found in an annotation on his personal copy of the trustees' minutes refusing to change the deed—'Durbin and Bristol Stewards refusing to betray their trust'.[109]

---

[104] Henry Durbin to CW, MS letter, 4 November 1784 (MCA: Letters chiefly to the Wesleys, vol. ii).

[105] Ibid.

[106] William Pine to CW, MS letter, 23 September 1784 (MCA: Letters chiefly to the Wesleys, vol. ii).

[107] Vickers, *Thomas Coke*, 59.

[108] Bristol New Room Chapel Trustees, MS minutes of a trustees' meeting, 29 July 1783 (MCA: Letters chiefly to the Wesleys, vol. ii).

[109] Ibid.

The controversy lasted for over a year and became very personal indeed. Coke denounced his opponents from the pulpit referring to them as 'wolves in sheep's clothing' and, rather implausibly, as a 'savage ruffian band'.[110] Several accusations were levelled specifically against Durbin, including telling lies and '*insidiously* endeavouring to undermine *us*, by making Mr *Charles Wesley* one of your party, etc'.[111] Coke based this second allegation on the grounds that Charles had known nothing of the affair until Durbin spoke to him in London. Pine's response on Durbin's behalf was equally caustic, referring to his opponents as '*busy-bodies*, who are ever meddling in other men's matters; and make it their business to cringe and fawn, and traduce their brethren, in order to raise themselves on the ruins of the reputations of others'.[112]

The little that has been said concerning this unsavoury dispute has concentrated on the role of Thomas Coke.[113] The extent of John Wesley's personal involvement has remained undisclosed, yet it is clear that he himself was ruthless in his dealings with the trustees. In a letter of 15 October 1784 to Charles, Durbin related that because of Coke's accusations he had been judged:

not a proper person to be in the society, till my character was cleared up, which your brother has not *the right proper to do ... so I am put on trial ...* he [John Wesley] said I had not been in the society for some time, as I had not met a class, but he forgot, that about three years ago he declared ... that any serious person *might have a ticket and meet* in the society without meeting a class and I have always had a ticket ... *indeed your* brother's letter has much stunned me ... it has taught *me to call no man rabbi*.[114]

By the time that Durbin wrote again to Charles on 5 January 1785,[115] his resentment had intensified. His treatment at the hands of John Wesley, which by now included an unspecified slander, was much talked about within Bristol Methodism and, if Durbin is to be believed, nowhere approved of. Even after making due allowance for

---

[110] William Pine to CW, MS letter, 23 September 1784 (MCA: Letters chiefly to the Wesleys, vol. ii).
[111] Ibid.   [112] Ibid.
[113] For example, Vickers, *Thomas Coke*, 59–60.
[114] Henry Durbin to CW, MS letter, 15 October 1784 (MCA: Letters chiefly to the Wesleys, vol. ii).
[115] Henry Durbin to CW, MS letter, 5 January 1785 (MCA: Letters chiefly to the Wesleys, vol. ii).

Durbin's bias, it appears that the Methodist patriarch was in some measure pursuing a grudge against the rebel trustees. One of Durbin's colleagues, Joseph Flower met Wesley at New Passage near Bristol in September 1784 with some personal items for the evangelist's use. He waited until the late afternoon but was refused a lift back to Bristol in Wesley's carriage when it finally arrived. If other transport had not fortuitously passed by, Flower would have had an eleven-mile walk back to the city.[116]

Such vivid insights into the reality of life with the Wesleys are minor in themselves, but they accumulate to give a picture, which is sometimes at odds with the popular image of John Wesley as a saintly patriarch. Charles's brother possessed charm and charisma but he was also dictatorial and could be vindictive when crossed. These traits appear to have formed part of the family character—Samuel Wesley senior was notoriously unforgiving and dogmatic, while Charles's own volatility is well known. The Methodist leader had many positive qualities that have rightly received considerable attention, but there was a darker side to his personality. Durbin was certainly of the opinion that John was trying to frighten him into silence in advance of the ordinations and saw significance in the timing of the attacks against him.[117]

Corroboration concerning John Wesley's sharply honed political instinct comes from a man on the other side of the Anglican–Methodist divide, namely John Pawson, who wrote this critical assessment of Wesley's character just after the old man died in 1791:

In a great variety of affairs... he acted as a politician, and one could not help seeking something that looked artful and designing and there was a manifest want of that simplicity, sincerity and uprightness, which are so amiable both in the sight of God and man... his best friends always looked upon it as a very great and blameable weakness in him.[118]

It is against this background that Charles Wesley's comment concerning his brother's treatment of Durbin and Pine should be viewed.

---

[116] Henry Durbin to CW, MS letter, 5 January 1785 (MCA: Letters chiefly to the Wesleys, vol. ii).

[117] Henry Durbin to CW, MS letter, 4 November 1784 (MCA: Letters chiefly to the Wesleys, vol. ii).

[118] Entwisle, MS account of the life of John Pawson, 40.

Charles was stunned by news of the ordinations, although he does not appear to have made a public response.[119] Published records documenting his reactions to this issue are lacking, which raises an important point concerning nineteenth-century attitudes towards the primary material. No letter written between the Wesley brothers is extant for nearly two years between May 1783 and April 1785,[120] and while it is true that letters between them had declined in number since the 1750s, one would have expected some written communication during this crucial period.[121] The possibility should be considered that controversial material was destroyed by the Wesley family or by representatives of the Methodist Church. One should recall in this context the well-known incident of John Pawson burning large quantities of John Wesley's papers in 1797 at the back of City Road Chapel.[122] Such destruction was not always the product of intent to protect reputations,[123] but for certain proof of Methodism's propensity to tamper with the record, one should turn to Whitehead's life of John Wesley. The first edition of 1793–6 contains the following contentious statement:

The year 1784 brings us to the grand climacterical year of Methodism... if we regard the changes which now took place in the form of its *original* constitution. Not that these changes destroyed at once the *original* constitution of *Methodism*; this would have been too great a shock; but the seeds of its corruption and final dissolution, were this year solemnly planted, and have since been carefully watered and nursed by a powerful party among the preachers.[124]

A second edition was published in 1806, two years after Whitehead died but containing his revisions. In this work the passage quoted above was changed to omit any disparaging reference to preachers or

---

[119] 'Like Brer Rabbit, however, Charles lay low and said nothing.' Baker, *John Wesley and the Church of England*, 273.

[120] Ibid. 275.

[121] It is known from references in other letters that Charles and John did indeed correspond at this time concerning the ordinations, although the letters in question have not survived.

[122] Stevenson, *City Road Chapel*, 135–6.

[123] Pawson apparently considered any documents that did not centre on the study of divinity to be worthy only of destruction. Stevenson, *City Road Chapel*, 135.

[124] Whitehead, *John Wesley*, ii. 404

the corruption of Methodism's constitution.[125] Fortunately, a document has survived that illustrates the very process whereby Whitehead was pressured into making this change. In June 1798 John Pawson wrote the following to the preacher Henry Moore:

> I have read Dr Whitehead's Life of Mr Wesley...I have marked every part of it which I think wrong...There are some things in it misrepresented, I know, but he was led wrong by Mr Charles Wesley's papers. These chiefly are: Mr McNabb's affair; the preaching in the New Chapel when it was first built; the Sacrament, Ordination, and the Conference Deed. But if the Conference is willing, he [Whitehead] would be glad they print a new edition...He would read the book over with a few of the preachers who are acquainted with those things and leave out what is judged wrong, and alter what is misrepresented.[126]

Such evidence shows conclusively that in the post-Wesley period there was a largely successful and deliberate attempt to write the history of early Methodism from a specific viewpoint, namely that which was most sympathetic to separatist preachers, while at the same time downplaying the existence of Methodism's bitter in-fighting.

Charles Wesley may have been lying low, but he was certainly not idle. In the months after the ordinations, he was in constant communication with his Bristol allies and consulting Lord Chief Justice Mansfield regarding the legal position. He also wrote verse attacking his brother which was circulated in Bristol,[127] to which he must have consented. Charles's replies to Durbin and Pine survive in shorthand on the back of their letters and reveal the extent of his anger and the lengths to which he was prepared to go, or at least to contemplate going. On 3 December 1784, Durbin sent to Charles a

---

[125] Whitehead, *The Life of the Rev. John Wesley, M.A. some time Fellow of Lincoln College, Oxford. Collected from his private papers and printed works; and written at the request of his executors. To which is prefixed, some account of his ancestors and relations; with the life of the Rev. Charles Wesley, A.M. collected from his private journal and never before published. The whole forming a History of Methodism, in which the principles and economy of the Methodists are unfolded copied chiefly from a London edition, published by John Whitehead, M.D. To which is subjoined, an appendix, containing characteristics of the Rev. Messrs. John and Charles Wesley, as given by several learned contemporaries*, 2 vols. new and revised edn. (Dublin: printed by John Jones, 1805–6), ii. 383–4.

[126] Wesley Swift, 'Headingley Papers IV: Two Letters from John Pawson to Henry Moore', *Proceedings of the Wesley Historical Society*, 29 (1953–4), 135.

[127] Baker, *John Wesley and the Church of England*, 273.

document that Durbin himself had written but signed 'a dissenter'. This applauded John Wesley for finally acknowledging 'that bishops and presbyters are the same order, and consequently have the same right to ordain... so he is convinced of his error, in what he has wrote in defence of the Church of England ordination... we hope that Mr John Wesley will continue firm... and he may bring many thousands over to us dissenters'.[128] In his covering note, Durbin suggested that Charles give this to a friend to insert in the London press, which was something that Charles himself had mentioned as an option.[129] This deliberate attempt to damage John Wesley's credibility was the tactic that one might have expected from anti-Methodists, yet it was proposed by influential men within Wesley's own movement who had good reason to expect that Charles would endorse their action. In his shorthand response on the back of Durbin's letter, Charles drew back: 'I thought I owed it to my brother to talk over the affair in plain[?] calm love. My letter was not lost. He disclaims any design of further [ordinations?]... You see then [this] is not the time for his friends to argue with him. I shall screen him all I can and stop slings... Your letter I lay by for the present.'

Charles may have hesitated at conniving in this specific public attack, but it was not long before he did cross the line. In 1785, *Strictures on the substance of a sermon preached at Baltimore at the ordination of the Rev. Francis Asbury... by Thomas Coke* was published in London. Its anonymous author described himself as a 'Methodist of the Church of England' and its contents constituted a sharp attack on Coke and by implication, John Wesley. In their listings of Anti-Methodist publications,[130] Green and Field identified the author as Charles Wesley based on a comment in a letter from the preacher Charles Boone to Samuel Bardsley:[131] 'I suppose you have heard of Mr C. Wesley's Strictures on Dr Coke's ordination sermon and

---

[128] Henry Durbin to CW, MS letter, 3 December 1784 (MCA: Letters chiefly to the Wesleys, vol. ii).

[129] 'as you say, a friend may put something in the papers'. Ibid.

[130] Richard Green, *Anti-Methodist Publications issued during the Eighteenth Century* (London: C. H. Kelly, 1902), 139; Clive Field, 'Anti-Methodist Publications of the Eighteenth Century: A Revised Bibliography', *Bulletin of the John Rylands University Library of Manchester*, 73:2 (Summer 1991), 237.

[131] See MS annotation to that effect in an unknown hand in the MCA copy of Green's work.

his further reactions against a separation from the Church.'[132] John Wesley's thoughts on this matter have not been recorded, although if his preachers had known the identity of the anonymous 'Methodist of the Church of England', it is inconceivable that he did not.

There are many gaps in the historical coverage of the ordinations and their background. Durbin's 'Letter by a Dissenter' has never been referred to despite its illustration of the bitterness that the ordinations caused, and what may be termed the persecution of the Bristol trustees has never been discussed in detail, at least with regard to the role of John Wesley. The Church Methodists were convinced that ordinations would in time be extended to the British work[133] and in this they were proved correct. At the Conference of 1785, Wesley ordained three preachers for Scotland on the grounds that the Anglican Church was not the Established Church in that country and ordinations did not therefore constitute separation;[134] others followed in 1786 and 1787 for Scotland, British North America, and the West Indies.[135] Finally in 1788, shortly after Charles Wesley died, his brother ordained Alexander Mather for the work in England. The events of 1784 had clearly paved the way for the establishment of a separate ministry in Britain as well as overseas.

On 14 August 1785, Charles wrote to John begging him to desist from further ordinations until God had made his will known.[136] John published his response in the *Arminian Magazine*,[137] but without naming his brother as the recipient—it is tempting to speculate that he may have been prompted to go into print by the fact that Charles had recently published his own attack on Thomas Coke. In this reply, John defended his right to ordain, but reiterated his determination not to break with the Church. He also displayed a stinging irritation with his correspondent: 'If you will go hand in hand with me, do. But do not hinder me, if you will not help. Perhaps if you had kept close to

---

[132] Charles Boone to Samuel Bardsley, MS letter, 3 November 1784 (MCA: PLP 10.27.3).

[133] Henry Durbin to CW, MS letter, 4 November 1784 (MCA: Letters chiefly to the Wesleys, vol. ii).

[134] Baker, *John Wesley and the Church of England*, 276–9.   [135] Ibid. 279.

[136] Ibid. 276–7.

[137] John Wesley, 'On the Church: in a Letter to the Rev. [Charles Wesley]', *The Arminian Magazine for the Year 1786, consisting chiefly of extracts and original treatises on universal redemption*, 9 (January 1786), 50–1.

me, I might have done better. However, with or without help I creep on.' Charles replied on 8 September 1785 pleading with his brother to see that Coke had already separated and was intent on founding a 'new episcopal Church of his own'.[138] Losing all patience, John replied that as there could be no agreement between them, the matter might as well rest.[139]

The reaction within the societies to this sequence of events has never been touched on in detail and it is to this that attention is now turned. Chapel trustees such as Durbin and Pine were fiercely opposed to separation and events from later in the 1790s indicate that the majority of their colleagues would have agreed with them. The trustees were, however, only a small minority within the movement and their views may not have been representative. Unfortunately, the written opinions of ordinary Methodists concerning the ordinations are virtually non-existent and instances of general society reaction are also few in number, but sufficient evidence does exist to allow certain theories to be aired.

The Bristol Methodists were apparently against the ordinations, although this view is based on Durbin's testimony which may be unreliable.[140] There was also a separation in 1785 at Plymouth Dock led by the itinerant William Moore. Writing in 1829, Adam Clarke stated that Moore and over one hundred people had left the Methodists to establish their own congregation.[141] The separatists accounted for slightly less than half the membership in the Plymouth circuit;[142] the rest remained loyal and Clarke, who was sent to repair the damage, was able to report that 'we had a great revival of religion that year'. Moore's justification for leaving the Connexion touches directly on an important aspect of the Anglican-Methodist question. He claimed to be responding to concern that people could not receive

---

[138] Quoted by Baker, *John Wesley and the Church of England*, 277.
[139] Ibid. 278.
[140] 'hundreds in Bristol know of the apology and ordination, and are much *concerned at* it'. Henry Durbin to CW, MS letter, 25 November 1784 (MCA: Letters chiefly to the Wesleys, vol. ii).
[141] Adam Clarke, 'Original Letter of Dr Adam Clarke', *Proceedings of the Wesley Historical Society*, 18 (1931–2), 22.
[142] Based on the membership figure of 222 given for the Plymouth society in 1784. *Conference Minutes*, i. 171.

the Sacraments from the itinerants—'the instruments of their Conversion', and that rather than receive them from others, they would rather leave both the Methodists and the Church of England.[143] This grievance may have applied to some of the Plymouth Methodists, but not necessarily to all, and when one looks at the local circumstances, other explanations do suggest themselves.

Plymouth Dock came into being in 1691 with the construction of a naval dockyard two miles from Plymouth,[144] and by the end of the eighteenth century the Dock had a population of over 23,000, 7,000 more than Plymouth itself.[145] The opportunities for Anglican worship in the two towns were very poor; until 1823, there were just two churches to serve a combined population that had reached 55,000 by 1820,[146] and neither of the churches was situated at the Dock. It is hardly surprising that local Methodists felt starved of the Sacraments and as many of them would have only recently immigrated in search of employment, they would have had no sentimental attachment to the local parish church. Plymouth Dock appears therefore to represent a good example of Methodism filling a vacuum left by Anglican failure to respond to demographic change. In such cases, a strong argument can be made that many people were, initially at least, separatists of convenience rather than conviction.

Clarke's letter of 1829 raises other interesting points about Methodism in the early days of his itinerancy, which commenced in 1782. He had apparently 'found many people in most places... very weary of not having the... Lord's Supper administered in our own chapels',[147] but it was not until 1788 that he began to view this as evidence of a wish to separate from the Church of England. In that year, he was surprised to discover that many people in Bristol were indifferent when he tried to distribute printed copies of a sermon in favour of remaining within the Church, and this 'among the people that were considered the purest Methodists in England'. He went on to state the startling opinion that 'it was not our *Societies* who held the

[143] Clarke, 'Original Letter of Dr Adam Clarke', 24–5.
[144] Richard Worth, *History of Plymouth from the earliest period to the present time*, 2nd edn. revised and augmented (Plymouth: W. Brenden & Sons, 1873), 83–4.
[145] Ibid.   [146] Ibid. 159.
[147] Clarke, 'Original Letter of Dr Adam Clarke', 22.

High Church opinions—but the *preachers*'.[148] It is clear from the rest of the letter that Clarke, despite his own pro-Anglican sympathies, reached the conclusion that by the end of Wesley's life, the majority of British Methodists supported separation and that the preachers were simply responding to popular demand.

If Clarke is correct, one would expect a definite call to leave the Church by the majority within a large number of the societies during the 1780s, but there does not appear to have been any such widespread agitation. The Plymouth Dock separatists wanted the Sacraments but that may have stemmed from nothing other than an inability to celebrate in a parish church. As for the Bristol society in 1788, their indifference to yet another development in a long running saga may have been precisely that, indifference rather than dissatisfaction. After all, Clarke himself, for all his later conviction, did not equate a call for administration of the Sacraments with a wish to leave the Church until at least 1788.[149] The most perceptive comment concerning the relationship with the Church of England was voiced by John Wesley that same year when he spoke in Conference against Coke's formal proposal that Methodism part company with the Anglicans: '[Coke] *skips like a flea; I creep like a louse. He would tear all from top to bottom*—I will not *tear* but *unstitch*.'[150] Wesley knew through experience and instinct, the pace at which to proceed with regard to silent opinion within the movement. In this context, it must again be emphasized that Methodism was not just the societies, the trustees, the preachers, or even the Wesleys, but also encompassed the many thousands who attended worship, but did not seek formal membership and would never have countenanced a definitive break with the Church.

The events of 1784 were a watershed, as John Wesley steered the societies onto a course that resulted in Methodist independence in the United States and de facto separation in Britain. With regard to the ordinations, the catalyst was North America, but it could be argued that Wesley would have ordained in any case, if not necessarily at that time. For nearly fifty years he had laboured tirelessly to build a 'Connexion' and he had not allowed loyalty to denomination, marriage, or family tradition to stand in his way. For a man with such a sense

[148] Ibid. 23.   [149] Ibid. 22–3.   [150] Ibid. 25–6.

of destiny and matching determination, it was inconceivable that this monument to God's glory would die with him.

Charles on the other hand remained true to Methodism's original aim of breathing new life into the national Church. In the early years he was as radical as his brother and until the end of his life, continued to acquiesce in breaches of church order, such as leading Methodist worship in the hours of Anglican services. Such contradictions paint a picture of a man who, in true Wesley fashion, was prepared to stand on a point of principle, but there were innovations that Charles Wesley refused to contemplate, ordination being a prime example, and his was not a lone voice. Without the benefit of hindsight, there was little reason to believe that he was incorrect in his fears for the future. The foundations for the eclipse of his brand of Methodism, which was in truth the original vision behind the Revival, were laid in 1784: it was not the preachers, Anglican prejudice or the wishes of the societies, but John Wesley's will that was the decisive factor in this transition from revival movement to denomination.

The ordinations did not, however, represent the end of the Church-Methodist story. In the United States the break with the past was clean and decisive—separation would have certainly occurred without John Wesley's intervention, and the ordinations can even be seen as his last desperate attempt to retain some influence over Francis Asbury and the upstart Americans, but in Britain another generation was to pass before the separation controversy was finally laid to rest; even then the legacy of Charles Wesley's struggle did not completely fade away.

10

Charles Wesley—His Final Years and Legacy

The four years between 1784 and Charles Wesley's death can appear anticlimactic. With his brother firmly fixed on a policy of ordinations, Charles was excluded from any significant participation in the decision-making process. He had not occupied a central place in John's counsels for many years and after the events of 1784 this isolation was made complete. Charles remained a figure of local importance in London and Bristol, but his influence on a national level had receded. The first generation of Methodists was passing away, men and women who had known Charles during the heroic years of his itinerancy; his hymns were sung in every chapel but younger worshippers would have known little of their author. It is noticeable when reading the correspondence of lay Methodists during the period 1770–90 that while John is mentioned on a regular basis, there is little reference to his brother outside of his circle of friends and sympathizers. This slide into relative obscurity was exacerbated by the fact that Charles published very little with the exception of his hymns, many of which were in any case issued under the brothers' joint names. By contrast, John Wesley travelled ceaselessly and by the time of his death in March 1791, was a legend to Methodist and non-Methodist alike.[1] John also produced a never-ending stream of publications on subjects as diverse as medicine and French grammar; these helped to keep his name in the public eye and have provided a readily available source of research material ever since.

---

[1] One non-Methodist obituary described Wesley as 'one of the most extraordinary characters this or any age ever produced'. Anonymous, 'Obituary of John Wesley', *Gentleman's Magazine*, 69 (1791), 284.

Charles's disappearance from public view and the lack of information concerning his ministry was a godsend to his opponents. As we have seen, within a few years of his death, deliberate efforts were made to rewrite aspects of Methodist history and his contribution was specifically identified as an area of concern. This chapter will examine the state of Charles's reputation and relations with others as his life came to a close and will also look beyond 1788 to the survival of the Anglican-Methodist ethos that he personified.

RELATIONS BETWEEN THE BROTHERS

It is a commonly held opinion that the Wesley brothers ultimately agreed to disagree concerning the Methodist relationship with the Church of England. Charles stated as much himself in his letters: in April 1787, he told his brother: 'Let us agree to differ, I leave America and Scotland to your latest thoughts and recognitions.'[2] Such evidence has been used to paint a picture of men who were able to resolve their differences just in time for the final curtain. Gill summed up the general scholarly opinion as follows: 'Although John's action almost broke his brother's heart, the latter never carried out his threat to dissolve the partnership, and remained at his side until the end... There was no further bitterness.'[3] There is some truth in this interpretation, as the Wesleys, for all that they bitterly—and often publicly—disagreed, never made a complete break on a personal level, although they came perilously close on more than one occasion.

Charles probably spoke for both men when he wrote to John on 8 September 1785: 'I thank you for your intention to remain my friend; herein my heart is as your heart; whom God hath joined let not man put asunder. We have taken each other for better or worse, till death do us—part? No; but unite eternally. Therefore in the love which never faileth, I am your affectionate friend and brother.'[4] In the weeks before Charles's death in March 1788, John's concern was unmistakable. He wrote to his brother in February urging him to go

---

[2] Quoted by Tyerman, *John Wesley*, iii. 523. [3] Gill, *Charles Wesley*, 200.
[4] Quoted by Tyerman, *John Wesley*, iii. 447.

out every day and not to worry about financial expense, as he would want for nothing while John was alive.⁵ He wrote also to Charles's children with suggestions as to how their father's decline could be reversed.⁶

However, there is evidence to indicate that there was coldness in the fraternal relationship until the very end and even afterwards. Even as he was writing to John in September 1785 that those 'whom God hath joined let not man put asunder',⁷ Charles must have been preparing for the press his anonymous attack on Thomas Coke and his brother, as this was published towards the end of the same year.⁸ This could hardly be described as an olive branch. Charles never tempered his attitude to separation or its advocates: at the conclusion of the Bristol Conference in 1786 he preached from one of his favourite texts 'I will bring the third part through the fire', and in July 1787 he gave a highly inflammatory address to the London society concerning the ordinations: 'I told you forty years ago that from among yourselves grievous wolves would arise who would rend and tear the flock. You now see my words are fulfilled. These self-created Bishops and self-made priests are the very men; but I charge you all in the presence of God never receive the Sacrament of any of them...'⁹ One might argue that John Pawson, who is our source for the speech, was exaggerating, but there would have been little reason to do so in the context of a private letter, and certainly the sentiments and aggressive style are what people had come to expect from Charles Wesley when his passions were aflame. Pawson made the valid point that Charles was urging the people not to receive the Sacraments from John Wesley himself 'for who but he is the self-created Bishop?'¹⁰ In fairness, Charles was probably referring to Thomas Coke but the description could equally be applied to his brother.

Much has been made of the episode where John collapsed in tears in Bolton chapel when one of Charles's hymns was announced just after his death.¹¹ This has been seen as proof that their relationship

---

⁵ Gill, *Charles Wesley*, 222.   ⁶ Ibid. 223.
⁷ Quoted by Tyerman, *John Wesley*, iii. 447.
⁸ [Charles Wesley], *Strictures on the substance of a sermon*.
⁹ John Pawson to [Charles Atmore], MS letter, 8 August 1787 (MCA: PLP 82.8.1).
¹⁰ Ibid.
¹¹ Gill, *Charles Wesley*, 225; Brailsford, *A Tale of Two Brothers*, 281.

had survived the tensions of the preceding forty years. An equally valid interpretation is that John wept because they had not been close and that was a source of deep hurt now that reconciliation on this side of the grave was impossible. If one accepts that the personal bond between the Wesleys was severely weakened at the end of their lives, this would explain Charles's surprisingly short obituary in the printed minutes of the 1788 Conference. With regard to his brother's ministry, all that John had to say was 'his least praise, was his talent for poetry'.[12] This was scant acknowledgement for a man whom he had once regarded as his most valuable colleague and closest friend.

Even after his death, Charles retained the ability to irritate his older brother. His refusal to be buried at City Road Chapel because the ground was unconsecrated annoyed John so much that on 14 May 1788, just weeks after the funeral, he wrote a letter that was subsequently published in the *Arminian Magazine*.[13] This condemned the consecration of churches and churchyards as a 'mere relic of Romish superstition' and he concluded with the following dismissive observation: 'I wonder that any sensible Protestant should think it right to countenance it: much more that any reasonable man should plead for the necessity of it! Surely it is high time now that we should be guided, not by custom, but by Scripture and Reason.'[14] As was customary when the Wesleys attacked one another in print, no names were mentioned, but as Charles's refusal to be interred at City Road was common knowledge among the preachers,[15] John's pointed rebuttal would not have gone unnoticed.

Part of the problem was that the Wesleys were too much alike. Both were exceptionally strong characters raised in a family that attached great importance to fighting for one's principles. Once Charles became aware of the fact that he had been too much under John's influence, the stage was set for an intermittent clash of wills that lasted for decades. Neither was willing to abandon his viewpoint and they became equally disillusioned with each other. The extent of this is easier to document with Charles as he wore his heart very much

---

[12] *Conference Minutes*, i. 201.

[13] John Wesley, 'Thoughts on the Consecration of Churches and Burial Grounds', *Arminian Magazine*, 11 (1788), 541–3.

[14] Ibid. 543.

[15] John Pawson to [Charles Atmore], MS letter, 28 April 1788 (MCA: PLP 82.4.4).

on his sleeve, but John was equally stubborn, and even at the end of Charles's life seems to have expected his younger brother to fall into line with his instructions. It would, of course, be too much to say that their differences were solely the product of sibling conflict, but it had a part to play.

PUBLIC AND PRIVATE REACTIONS TO CHARLES WESLEY'S DEATH

The Methodist response to Charles Wesley's demise was mixed, running the gamut of reaction from grief through indifference to satisfaction at his removal. Within the London and Bristol societies, there was considerable dismay. On 6 April 1788 the prominent itinerant Samuel Bradburn preached Charles's funeral sermon at the premier chapels of West Street and City Road;[16] the services were well attended and there were displays of emotion.[17] News of Charles's death reached Bristol on 31 March, and the itinerant John Valton, who owed a part in his own conversion to Charles's ministry, reported the reaction in his diary:

Just before preaching, word was brought me that that man of God Mr Charles Wesley was dead. I mentioned this awful circumstance to the society. Tears and cries took place through the [New] Room, and had I not given out a hymn, I do not know what would have been the consequence. One woman continued in fits for some time.[18]

Charles's personal ministry had clearly made a considerable impression on the lives of people in his vicinity. According to Pawson, funeral sermons were also preached in Hull, Newcastle, and Sheffield, and chapels in London, Bristol, and Sheffield were put in mourning.[19] However, one must question whether people outside London and Bristol could have felt much grief for a man who was a stranger to

---

[16] Samuel Bradburn, MS Memoranda book 1, 6 April 1788 (MCA: Diaries collection).
[17] Telford, *Charles Wesley*, 291–2.
[18] John Valton, MS diary, 31 March 1788 (MCA: Diaries collection).
[19] John Pawson to [Charles Atmore], MS letter, 28 April 1788 (MCA: PLP 82.4.4).

them. Charles had abandoned the itinerancy more than thirty years before his death and would have been nothing more than a name to the majority of British Methodists. An examination of diaries from the period indicates that lay people and preachers outside Bristol and London tended not to remark on Charles's passing:[20] one exception is John Pawson whose comments will be discussed later. It is true that Methodist diaries were often vehicles for spiritual self-examination rather than comment on current affairs, but one might have expected some reference to the death of one of the early leaders of the Connexion and the brother of John Wesley. An absence of a personal name in primary sources is difficult to interpret, but the most likely explanation in this case is that outside his localized ministry, the death of Charles Wesley represented a ripple rather than a splash in Methodist affairs.

A further indication of the depressed state of Charles's public profile can be seen in the non-Methodist reporting of his passing. John Wesley's obituary in the *Gentleman's Magazine* in 1791 extended to three pages;[21] Charles warranted three lines in the 1788 issue[22] despite being referred to as the co-founder of the Methodist movement. The obituary of a Northumberland fisherman appears on the same page—his death merited nine lines although his only claim to fame was a minor role in the 1715 Jacobite rebellion and, what was probably of more interest to the readership, that he had married at the age of eighty-two and fathered three children. It is obvious that Charles's death was of little public interest and then only as the 'brother of the celebrated Mr John W'.[23]

Some of the preachers were pleased to see the back of Charles Wesley. John Pawson made his dislike of the dying man abundantly clear in a letter written to Charles Atmore: '[Thomas Coke] says that Charles Wesley breaks fast. I cannot say that I am sorry for it, as I really think he [will] not do much good in this world whatever may

---

[20] The following manuscripts diaries were consulted; John Goodfellow of Ditcheat, R. Bennet Dugdale of Dublin and the itinerant preacher Zachariah Yewdall (MCA: Diaries collection).

[21] Anonymous, 'Obituary of John Wesley', *Gentleman's Magazine*, 69 (1791), 282–4.

[22] Anonymous, 'Obituary of Charles Wesley', *Gentleman's Magazine*, 63 (1788), 368.

[23] Ibid.

Charles—Final Years and Legacy 219

become of him in the next.'[24] Pawson returned to the subject with grim relish in his manuscript narrative for the year 1788:

> This year also Mr Charles Wesley died. It was said that he died in peace. However that might be God knows, but he died as he had lived for many years full of High Church bigotry, and left no good testimony behind him that I could hear of. I have known so much of his conduct for some years past, that I cannot conceive how he could be saved without deep repentance... O that all bitter zeal and High Church bigotry may die with him, and be buried in his grave for ever, amen.[25]

John Pawson was at the extreme end of the separatist party and it is unlikely that his colleagues among the body of itinerants would have approved of his venom. However, it is important to note that he went on to serve two terms as President of Conference, and played a leading role in Methodist affairs in the crucial decades immediately before and after John Wesley's death. His friend and sympathizer Atmore also served as President, and wrote the popular *Methodist Memorial*,[26] which remains an important source for the lives of the early preachers. Such men helped to influence the evolution of the nineteenth-century image of early Methodism, and given their views of Charles Wesley, it is surprising that they left him with any reputation at all.

THE CONTINUING CHURCH-METHODIST STRUGGLE

The fact that Charles Wesley was a largely forgotten figure by the time of his death does not mean that his views died with him. Jackson described Charles's allies as 'croakers and busy-bodies',[27] implying that they were few in number and represented more of an irritant

---

[24] John Pawson to [Charles Atmore], MS letter, 17 March 1788 (MCA: PLP 82.4.3).
[25] Entwisle, MS account of the life of John Pawson, 36.
[26] Charles Atmore, *The Methodist Memorial; being an impartial sketch of the lives and characters of the preachers, who have departed this life since the commencement of the work of God, among the people called Methodists, late in Connection with the Rev. John Wesley, deceased. Drawn from the most authentic sources and disposed in alphabetical order. Introduced with a brief account of the state of religion from the earliest age and a concise History of Methodism. To which is added, a chronological list of the preachers who are now engaged in the same Work* (Bristol: Richard Edwards, 1801).
[27] Jackson, *Charles Wesley*, ii. 137.

than an influence, but the reality was very different. The pro-Church party comprised not only the wealthiest and most influential laymen in the Connexion but many ordinary Methodists who felt an equal if not greater loyalty to the Church of England than to the societies. Class constraints and educational limitations ensured that such people were not as vocal as Durbin or Horton, but their collective influence was significant and long-lasting. It is to this survival of Charles Wesley's Anglican-Methodist vision that our attention is now turned.

The 1790s were a decade of great turbulence within Methodist affairs. John Wesley's death in April 1791 exposed disagreements between his successors on a range of matters from the question of episcopacy to that of lay representation in Conference. One of the central issues remained the link with the Church of England. By his ordinations and Deed of Declaration, John made legal separation possible, but he stubbornly maintained to the very end of his life that Methodism remained an integral part of the Church. This particular bone of contention was left to his successors to deal with.

The Anglican–Methodist question was addressed for the first time by a post-Wesley Conference in 1792 when it was decreed that 'The Lord's Supper shall not be administered by any person among our societies...for the ensuing year, on any consideration whatsoever, except in London.'[28] The delegates also ruled that worship at the time of Anglican church-hours should not be introduced in any new place without the consent of Conference. The strong feelings that this issue provoked are not reflected in the bare record of decisions in the printed Conference minutes, but John Pawson commented upon the mood of the meeting in a letter written to the pro-Anglican preacher Joseph Benson: 'I am at present exceeding sorrowful...The reason is, what I heard and saw [at] the last Conference...such disorder, such confusion, such burning anger, such storms of passion...The people tell me that they have heard that we had a very peaceable Conference. I really do not know what to say to them.'[29]

Opinion was so divided on the Sacramental issue that recourse was made to drawing lots to determine policy for the following year and

---

[28] *Conference Minutes*, i. 260. London was an exception because of the presence of Anglican clergymen who were working within the Methodist society and were allowed to administer Communion by virtue of their orders.

[29] John Pawson to Joseph Benson, MS letter, 1 September 1792 (MCA: PLP 82.8.6).

Pawson acknowledged that many itinerants were either undecided on the question of separation or were opposed. In a letter written before Conference gathered, he revealed that even Thomas Coke had swung towards a pro-Anglican viewpoint[30] and went on to say that the separatists would certainly be out-voted at the forthcoming assembly.

These violent and seemingly contradictory swings in opinion require explanation. Just seven years before, Pawson had been convinced that the majority of preachers and laymen were in favour of turning their backs on the Anglican Church,[31] yet by 1792 this had apparently changed. Part of the explanation lies in the fact that there was a perceptible shift to a conservative position in response to John Wesley's death. Now that the preachers were in the driving-seat, they were unsure of the future and until such time as their confidence increased, they displayed a natural reluctance to deviate from the Wesleyan legacy, which point was specifically stated by the Conference of 1791.[32] Also, the secular political situation had changed dramatically in the preceding three years. The terrors that accompanied the French Revolution resulted in suspicion of non-Establishment elements within British society. At a time when fear of civil war and sectarian conflict surfaced again in the public mind and was reflected in government policy, it benefited the Methodists to be associated with the Church of England. Formal separation from the ecclesiastical arm of the State no longer seemed a good idea to men such as Thomas Coke who declared in a letter to Joseph Benson:

I see a separation from the Established Church, whether gradual or immediate, pregnant with all the evils you mention. It would probably drive away from us and from God thousands of our People. We should lose our grand field of action. When once the members of the Established Church had embraced a confirmed idea that we were a *proper Dissenting* body, they would pass by the doors of our *meeting houses*... More than this we should soon

---

[30] 'Not that he cares a straw for the Church, but he thinks that if we separate from it, then our usefulness would be at an end, as the Church people would not come to hear us.' John Pawson to Charles Atmore, MS letter, 15 June 1792 (MCA: PLP 82.8.5).
[31] Entwisle, MS account of the life of John Pawson, 32.
[32] 'We engage to follow strictly the plan which Mr Wesley left us at his death.' *Conference Minutes,* i. 246.

imbibe the Political Spirit of the Dissenters; nor should I be much surprised, if in a few years some of our people, warmest in politics, and coolest in religion, would toast...*a bloody summer and a headless King*.[33]

Coke even ventured to criticize John Wesley's policy of ordinations, describing it as a 'great imprudence and will be very prejudicial, unless—(what shall I say?)—God intended by suffering us to run into error, to bring about a sifting time'.[34]

With the supporters of separation on the defensive, Church Methodists were quick to make a stand for what was now seen as traditional Wesleyanism and a gesture of support for King and Country. In Newcastle in early 1792, there were angry protests when the preacher Joseph Cownley administered the Sacraments.[35] In response, the powerful Newcastle loyalists decided that the trust deed to the Orphan House chapel should be examined to ensure that the society would continue to be run in accordance with Wesley's 'old plan'. They resolved that vacant trustee positions would only be filled 'with such persons as strictly adhered to Mr Wesley's principles, and by a new deed...to preserve the House to the purposes for which it was originally intended'.[36] The Newcastle separatists were not completely cowed by this dramatic change in the political and religious climate. In May 1792, Charles Atmore and Joseph Cownley ordained three preachers in the town, although Atmore himself entertained doubts as to the 'strict propriety' of such a step. Writing after the Manchester preachers followed the Newcastle example, Atmore admitted that 'these proceedings injured the cause they were intended to promote. They produced general alarm both among the preachers and the people.'[37] Such was the furore that the 1792 Conference decreed that no further ordinations were to take place without Conference consent on pain of expulsion.[38]

The primary sources reveal that British Methodism during the early 1790s was riddled with fear and uncertainty. The Sacramental issue and other matters directly related to the Church of England

[33] Thomas Coke to Joseph Benson, MS letter, 15 July 1791 (MCA: PLP 28/7/22).
[34] Ibid.
[35] William Stamp, *The Orphan House of Wesley with Notices of Early Methodism in Newcastle-Upon-Tyne and its Vicinity* (London: John Mason, 1863), 164–78.
[36] Quoted by Stamp, ibid. 167.
[37] Ibid. 169. [38] *Conference Minutes*, i. 259–60.

would in themselves have been sufficient cause for worry, and to these were added concerns connected with the worsening international situation. These strands were drawn together by Sarah Crosby in a letter of January 1794 to Mary Fletcher:

> This should indeed 'be a season of much *faith* and *prayer*' for it is an awful period of time... I trust, He will defend our *nation*: and bless our *King* and *Queen*... With regard to Church matters: *we do* as you have *observed*, for which many have blamed us; and said we were too *quiet*. As we, and many are *decidedly for the Old Plan*, which has not hitherto been interrupted at *Leeds*. But Mr Hanby has been giving the Sacraments at several Societies around it; at which many are grieved. Could it be as you observe, none need object, but we know it has caused divisions in every place, where they have tried it... W. Westerman made some stir about it at the first, and a few persons have left the Society.[39]

It is interesting to note that Fletcher and Crosby were Anglican loyalists and yet were radical in important aspects of their ecclesiology, most notably in the fact that they were among the earliest Methodist female preachers. This is one more illustration of the ambiguity and contradiction that was an intrinsic part of Wesley's movement and, more subtly, of the denomination in which Methodism was born.

Conference during the 1790s was a battleground. It is unnecessary to provide a detailed account of the controversies, but a glance at what happened behind the scenes at one Conference, that of 1794, is illuminating. A memoranda book of Charles Atmore records that a delegation of trustees from London and Bristol presented an address from a general meeting of Church Methodists complaining that itinerants had tried to introduce innovations and that local de facto separation was the result in some circuits. The trustees made certain demands designed to pull the movement back into line with the position bequeathed by John Wesley. These included the immediate discontinuation of ordinations and use of such titles as Reverend, exclusive administration of the Sacraments by Anglican clergymen, and the decision that 'the temporal and spiritual affairs shall be

---

[39] Sarah Crosby to Mary Fletcher, MS letter, 24–9 January 1794 (MCA: MAM Fl 2.5A/10).

divided. The latter to be conducted by the preachers and the former by the trustees and people.'[40]

The result was a long and heated discussion among the preachers, who were of course the only voting members of the assembly, and the drawing up of a list of those specific places where the Lord's Supper could be administered, namely where 'the society has been unanimous for it, and would not have been contented without it'. A letter was drafted and sent to the societies essentially agreeing to many of the trustees' demands.[41] There is no reference in the printed minutes to the background behind the decisions or the acrimony that attended them.

The disputes of the 1790s resulted in a series of compromises culminating in the 'Plan of Pacification' hammered out at the 1795 Conference. This decreed that Communion, baptism, and burial of the dead would be administered in chapels only with the consent of the majority of trustees, stewards, and leaders. Communion would be administered according to Anglican rites and never on Sundays where it was available in the parish church.[42] The Plan of Pacification ended the major disputes over the separation question as it appears to have been regarded by the contending parties as a fair compromise. In any case, worry over this decades-old problem was swiftly replaced by more pressing concerns over the question of democracy within the Connexion.

RESULTS OF THE PLAN OF PACIFICATION

The Plan of Pacification has been regarded as marking the final defeat of Church Methodism.[43] There are grounds for this view as society after society petitioned Conference for the rights on offer,[44] accompanied by a stream of anti-separatists leaving the movement, including

[40] Charles Atmore, MS Memoranda book, 1776–1811 (MCA: Diaries collection).
[41] *Conference Minutes*, i. 299–300.   [42] Ibid. 322–3.
[43] Harrison, *The Separation of Methodism from the Church of England*, 56–7; Oliver Beckerlegge, 'The Church Methodists', *Proceedings of the Wesley Historical Society*, 34 (September 1963), 64; Thomas Percival Bunting, *The Life of Jabez Bunting* (London: Longman, Brown, Green, Longmans, & Roberts, 1859), i. 86–7.
[44] Harrison, *The Separation of Methodism*, 57.

such important laymen as William Hey of Leeds and Henry Durbin of Bristol. How many people left over this issue cannot be accurately determined but it seems to have been a problem throughout the country. Durbin's obituary in the *Methodist Magazine* remarks that he was joined by 'many other respectable persons, who had long been highly valued by us'.[45] In the Methodist heartland of west Yorkshire local Methodists left the society in protest over the Sacramental issue,[46] while in Newcastle three class leaders and twenty members withdrew after the disturbances of 1792;[47] and later in the decade there was a secession of Church Methodists in the Lancashire town of Oldham.[48] Taken nationally, it appears that the number of people who returned to the Church of England was quite significant.

The effects of this split were hidden by the phenomenal growth of Methodism during the first half of the nineteenth century. At the time of Wesley's death there were 72,476 members in the British Isles (including Ireland).[49] By 1800 this figure had reached 109,911[50] and by 1825 it was a quarter of a million.[51] Despite recurring financial problems and damaging secessions, Wesleyan Methodism by 1850 could legitimately claim to be the most important Protestant denomination in the British Isles after the Church of England. There were 323,000 Wesleyans in Britain in 1851, and when other Methodist denominations are included, membership of the Methodist family stood at well over half a million.[52]

CHARLES WESLEY AS THE SYMBOL OF A LOST CAUSE

Wesleyan prosperity as an independent body led to considerable triumphalism in works of Victorian denominational history. In 1878 Abel Stevens referred to the movement's 'prevalent and permanent

---

[45] John Pawson, 'A Short Account of Mr Henry Durbin', *Methodist Magazine*, 22 (1799), 488.
[46] Sarah Crosby to Mary Fletcher, MS letter, 24–9 January 1794 (MCA: MAM Fl. 2.5A.10).
[47] Stamp, *The Orphan House of Wesley*, 166.
[48] Smith, *Religion in Industrial Society*, 169–70.
[49] *Conference Minutes*, i. 244. [50] Ibid. ii. 53–4. [51] Ibid. vi. 42.
[52] Figures extracted from Conference Minutes and from Robert Currie, *Methodism Divided: A Study in the Sociology of Ecumenicalism* (London: Faber & Faber, 1968), 87.

success',[53] while Telford declared: 'if judgement is to be passed on the basis of results, John Wesley's policy is triumphantly vindicated'.[54] The impression given in such works is that by severing the Anglican link, the Methodist movement finally slipped its leash and fulfilled its true potential. This is reflected in the assessment of Charles Wesley's post-1756 contribution. Stevens adopted a pitying tone when he discussed Charles's reaction to the events of 1784: 'The poet was no legislator; he became pathetic in his remonstrances to his brother...He did soon after go to his grave in peace, except the alarms of his imaginary fears.'[55] George Smith in 1857 was equally dismissive:

> It is no serious dispraise of him [Charles Wesley] to say, that in one respect he was inferior to his brother John. Charles seemed either to cleave to the Established Church with more earnest tenacity, or not so fully to appreciate the vital importance of the work of God in the Methodist Societies as his brother. He certainly did on some important occasions allow his devotedness to the Church to warp his judgement...But, considering the magnitude of the work originated...it is evidently taking too limited a view of it, to suppose that there was no overruling Providence...Who now can say, that the retarding influence of Charles Wesley for a time was not thus rendered subservient to the constitution of the proper character of Methodism, as was the more enlarged and enlightened judgement of his elder brother?[56]

Smith's indictment may have been couched in the usual pious language of the period, but it was in its own way as damning as Pawson's violent denunciations of Charles Wesley's character and prospects for salvation.

The nineteenth-century view of Charles Wesley should be looked at in the context of what B. W. Young has termed the Victorian preoccupation with 'present-centred history'.[57] Stevens, Smith, and Telford were writing an interpretation of Methodism that was founded on the perceived reality of the Wesleyan Church of their own day rather than attempting a balanced assessment of events

---

[53] Stevens, *History of Methodism*, ii. 165.   [54] Telford, *Charles Wesley*, 283.
[55] Stevens, *History of Methodism*, ii. 165.
[56] George Smith, *History of Wesleyan Methodism*, 3 vols. (London: Longman, Brown, Green, Longmans, & Roberts, 1857–8), i. 582.
[57] B. W. Young, 'Knock-Kneed Giants: Victorian Representations of Eighteenth-Century Thought', in Jane Garnett and Colin Matthew (eds.), *Revival and Religion since 1700: Essays for John Walsh* (London: Hambledon, 1993), 92.

of a century previously. Young's summation of the effects of this brand of scholarship could have been written with the reporting of Charles Wesley in mind: 'history was inevitably distorted: heroes and villains were identified and religious and philosophical movements measured against the requirements of the times... the late twentieth-century scholar has to engage with the... [Victorians'] prejudices and blindspots'.[58]

THE SURVIVAL OF THE CHURCH METHODIST TRADITION

In dismissing Charles, historians also downplayed the role and influence of Church Methodism in general, and this applies not merely to the late eighteenth century but to its continuation. Not all Anglican Methodists left in the 1790s. John Horton, for example, remained true to Charles Wesley's vision until he died in 1802, while the Bristol merchant James Ireland maintained a neutral stance in the controversies and continued quietly to support both Anglican and Methodist causes.[59]

Many other Wesleyans continued to value the link with the Church for years after the Plan of Pacification. Typical of this group was the prominent laywoman Mrs Dobinson who pioneered the movement in Derby. When she died in 1803 after a long and useful ministry, Dobinson had a funeral sermon preached at the chapel but was interred at the parish church in keeping with her wish to 'be buried as an old Methodist'.[60] The businessman Harvey Walklate Mortimer was a leading light of the London society for many years and was regarded by John Wesley as a model lay official. As the treasurer of City Road Chapel, Mortimer fought a successful battle to preserve the link with the Church of England within that congregation until his death in 1826.[61] Nor was this duality confined to the older generation; Mary Tooth of Madeley served as a class leader for many years but was

---

[58] Ibid. [59] *Dictionary of Evangelical Biography*, ed. Lewis, i. 594.
[60] Anthony Seckerson, 'An Account of Mrs Dobinson', *Methodist Magazine*, 26 (1803), 557–66; Anonymous, 'Early Methodism in Derby', *Christian Miscellany* (December 1870).
[61] Stevenson, *City Road Chapel*, 153 and 554–5.

buried at the parish church in 1843,[62] while the prominent London bookseller William Baynes was regular in his attendance at both City Road Chapel and his parish church, where he served as churchwarden and assisted at Communion.[63]

At this indistinct boundary between the Church and the Methodist movement, people such as Mortimer and Mary Tooth acted as a link between the two traditions to the enrichment of both. In Bristol in 1796, local Methodists were regular in their attendance on the ministry of the Evangelical Anglicans William Tandey and Thomas Tregenna Biddulph and collaborated with Biddulph in the introduction of a series of evening lectures at St Werburgh's Church, much to the annoyance of the local preachers.[64]

The most perfect realization of the Church Methodist ideal occurred in the Shropshire town of Madeley, where the ministry of the chapel and the parish church were both subject to the oversight of the remarkable Mary Fletcher. Prior to her marriage to the Anglican Evangelical John Fletcher, Mary had been the first female preacher to be sanctioned by John Wesley. After her husband's death in 1785 she continued a personal ministry in her husband's former parish that ignored the gulf between Methodism and the Church. She built a chapel, one of the trustees of which was the Anglican incumbent, and also exercised the privilege of appointing the curate of the parish. After Mary's death in 1815, her companion Mary Tooth continued her legacy until the 1840s but with diminishing success.[65]

Several prominent nineteenth-century Anglican Evangelicals had Church-Methodist connections. Thomas Truebody Thomason, the pioneering missionary to India, was the stepson of Josiah Dornford, active in both Methodist and Anglican causes and a close friend of Mary Fletcher.[66] John Ryle, the first Anglican bishop of Liverpool, was the son and grandson of men who financed the building of Wesleyan chapels in Macclesfield and served as trustees, while at the same time

---

[62] Anonymous, 'Recent Deaths [Mary Tooth]', *Methodist Magazine*, 66 (1843), 1036–7.

[63] Stevenson, *City Road Chapel*, 422–3.

[64] Elizabeth Ritchie to Mary Fletcher, MS letter, 28 June 1796 (MCA: MAM Fl. 6.7.10).

[65] Fletcher-Tooth Archive (MCA: MAM Fl.).

[66] *Dictionary of Evangelical Biography*, ed. Lewis, ii. 1096; Fletcher-Tooth Archive (MCA: MAM Fl.)

remaining members of the Established Church.[67] At a less prominent level also there are examples of Victorian Anglican ministers who were proud to have Methodist antecedents. Two of the sons of Joseph Benson, President of Conference in 1798 and 1810, entered the Anglican priesthood with their father's blessing,[68] as did the son of Harvey Walklate Mortimer.[69] Perhaps more predictably, Charles Wesley's grandson was also a minister of the Church of England and finished his days as Subdean of the Chapel Royal and Chaplain-in-Ordinary to Queen Victoria—his grandfather, after whom he was named, would certainly have approved.

On a society level also, Church Methodism was a vital force for decades after the Wesleys died.[70] It remained the custom in several places such as Manchester, Macclesfield, and Bradford for Methodist congregations collectively to attend Sacramental worship at the parish church.[71] In 1821 the Vicar of Bridgerule in Devon wrote of the local Methodists that 'They all attend [the parish] Church as the House of God, and more regularly than those who have no such meeting.'[72] As late as 1870 a few chapels were still refusing to allow preachers to administer the Sacraments or permit worship during the hours of Anglican services.[73]

The strongest expression of pro-Anglican sentiment occurred in Ireland where in the three years from 1815 over 10,000 Wesleyans, constituting more than one-third of the national membership, left the parent Connexion rather than receive the Sacraments from Methodist

---

[67] Benjamin Smith, *Methodism in Macclesfield* (London: Wesleyan Conference Office, 1875), 74–6, 230–1, and 255; *Dictionary of Evangelical Biography*, ed. Lewis, ii. 967.

[68] *Dictionary of Evangelical Biography*, ed. Lewis, i. 84–5.

[69] Elizabeth Mortimer to Mary Fletcher, MS letter, 14 February 1806 (MCA: MAM Fl. 6.7.23).

[70] In 1788 at Cornelius Bayley's proprietary church of St James in Manchester, which was the largest Anglican congregation in the city, one-quarter of the seat holders were Methodists, contributing a total of 350 worshippers. E. A. Rose, 'Cornelius Bayley and the Manchester Methodists', *Proceedings of the Wesley Historical Society*, 34 (September 1964), 155–6.

[71] Ibid. 156.

[72] Quoted by Arthur Warne, *Church and Society in Eighteenth-Century Devon* (Newton Abbot: David & Charles, 1969), 109.

[73] Owen Chadwick, *The Victorian Church*, Part 1, 2nd edn., An Ecclesiastical History of England, 5 (London: Adam & Charles Black, 1970), 370–1.

preachers.[74] The rebels established the Primitive Wesleyan Methodist Connexion in 1818, which reached a membership peak of just under 16,000 in 1844, and remained a society within the Anglican Church until 1878 when it rejoined the parent Methodist body after Irish disestablishment. Special circumstances were of course applicable to Ireland, but it was still an unexpectedly vigorous reaction from a supposedly defeated Church-Methodist party a quarter of a century after John Wesley's death.

There is no doubt that with the passage of years, Methodism established itself more and more as a distinct denomination with aspirations that sometimes produced friction with the Anglicans, but there is equally little doubt that the attachment to the Church of England remained a feature of many societies and individuals for decades after the Wesleys died. This influence extended to aspects of the liturgy and practice of the new Church. The Wesleyans used an abbreviated form of the Anglican Book of Common Prayer until 1882[75] and ordination as a specific rite was not used between 1793 and 1836—itinerants were instead 'received' into Connexion.[76] This is not to say that Methodism was a pale imitation of the Church of England; whether Charles Wesley would have agreed or not, his personal ministry had helped to establish forms of worship and devotional practice that became cornerstones of a new denomination. Chapels and circuits were administered on very different lines from the parish system, while the Conference and its officials had no Anglican counterpart.

The Wesleyan Church, which was the original Methodist body, was the denomination that preserved the closest link with the Anglican past. Break-aways from the Wesleyans such as the Methodist New Connexion tended to be further removed from the Church of England. However, the Wesleyans were by a considerable margin the largest and most influential branch of British Methodism and the one with the greatest overseas outreach.

The Anglican contribution to the hybrid character of the Wesleyan body received scant acknowledgement from Methodist

---

[74] F. Jeffery, 'Church Methodists in Ireland', *Proceedings of the Wesley Historical Society*, 34 (December 1963), 73–5.
[75] *A Dictionary of Methodism*, ed. Vickers, 341.   [76] Ibid. 260.

commentators.[77] In part, this was a product of the concentration on the Church as a national body. The activities of policy-makers such as Jabez Bunting received significantly more attention than did analysis of individual societies or the survival of aspects of the movement's Anglican heritage, and this research gap was carried over into the twentieth century, so that there is still very little known about the views of ordinary Methodists at this crucial time. There was a wish in the denominational histories to promote the separate identity and astonishing vibrancy of this new Church and applaud the fact that John Wesley had laid the foundations with such consummate skill. To bring out the fact that many nineteenth-century Methodists actually chose to retain a link with what Tyerman referred to as 'a corrupted church'[78] was certainly not on the denominational agenda. There was in certain important quarters of the Methodist ministry a curiosity concerning what might have been achieved if separation had occurred in the middle of the eighteenth century. This is made clear in a passage from Stevens's discussion of the controversy of the 1750s:

> Had Methodism taken a more independent stand at this early period, when it had so many intolerable provocations... and the popular mind so little ground of sympathy with the clergy, it is the opinion of not a few wise men that it might before this time have largely superseded the Anglican hierarchy, and done much more than it has for the dissolution of the unscriptural connection of the Church and State.[79]

In these comments we are provided with a quite compelling reason why some important Methodists in the Victorian period resented Charles Wesley for his retarding influence on their denomination's glorious progress.

The distaste that some prominent Methodists felt for the Church of England was exacerbated by the emergence of the Tractarian movement in the 1830s. Anglican dalliance with Roman Catholicism was anathema to men such as Thomas Jackson who published a spirited defence of Methodism against the attacks of the Tractarian Edward

---

[77] For an exception to this tendency, see J. Robinson Gregory and Arthur Gregory, 'Wesleyan Methodism—The Middle Period', in George Eayrs, W. J. Townsend, and H. B. Workman (eds.), *A New History of Methodism*, 2 vols. (London: Hodder & Stoughton, 1909), i. 387–8.
[78] Tyerman, *John Wesley*, ii. 382.
[79] Stevens, *History of Methodism*, i. 313–14.

Pusey in 1842.[80] This forms another part of the background to the period when Jackson and other Wesleyans were writing works about the origins of Methodism that did not portray the Church of England or its Methodist champions in a positive light.

One of the important aspects of this question is the way that it illustrates the gulf that exists between the view from the Connexional centre, which is the one that receives the most attention, and what was actually happening in the circuits. It appears that the issues attendant on separation simply passed by many members of the societies. They occupied the minds of important ministers such as Benson, Bradburn, and Moore, but many people simply carried on worship in the way that best suited them. Mary Fletcher stated an important truth when she reassured Sarah Crosby in 1794 that 'none need object' to preachers administering the Sacraments.[81] For all the anti-Anglican sentiment apparent in the higher reaches of the Connexion, the Methodists never sought to prevent their members from attending the worship of the Church of England, nor did that Church formally expel them.[82] If a Methodist wanted to enjoy the Sacraments in both a Methodist and an Anglican setting, he or she was perfectly entitled to do so.

The intricacies of the Church-Methodist link were of little practical importance to people such as Mrs Dobinson of Derby or the Wesleyans of Bridgerule. They continued to attend both church and chapel and suffered no crisis of conscience. Many of them had been raised as Anglicans and seem to have viewed their continued association with the Established Church almost as a birthright. Rather than signalling the defeat of the Church-Methodist party, the Plan of Pacification allowed Methodism to remain an inclusive organization,

---

[80] Thomas Jackson, *A letter to the Rev. Edward B. Pusey, D.D: being a vindication of the tenets and character of the Wesleyan Methodists, against his misrepresentations and censures* (London: Wesleyan Conference Office, 1842).

[81] Sarah Crosby to Mary Fletcher, MS letter, 24–9 January 1794 (MCA: MAM Fl. 2.5A/10).

[82] 'The Methodists have never yet, as a body, renounced all connexion with the Establishment; they have never disowned her fundamental doctrines nor prohibited attendance on her services, nor made it binding upon their people to forsake *her* communion... Nor have they ever been excommunicated.' [George Osborn], *Modern Methodism, Wesleyan Methodism*, Wesleyan Tract for the Times, 5 (London: Wesleyan Conference Office, 1842), 10.

an important feature of the movement since the earliest days. Once it was realized that people did not have to make a choice, it ceased to be a controversial issue. Anglican Methodism did not disappear after 1795, but remained an integral part of the denominational make-up.

Charles Wesley was not the sad and isolated figure that has been portrayed by historians. Their dismissal of Charles and his allies as an embarrassing irrelevance was a necessary stage in their elevation of John Wesley to the highest place in the Methodist pantheon, despite the fact that he also refused to countenance formal separation. Charles's views would have struck a chord with many Methodists fifty years or more after he died and this Anglican-Methodist legacy made a permanent contribution to the unique identity and character of the Wesleyan Church.

Concluding Remarks

The primary aim of this book has been to present a new evaluation of aspects of the life and ministry of the Evangelist and hymn-writer Charles Wesley. Such an approach is long overdue, as it is certain that his reputation and place within church history have never received the attention that he deserves. It is a sad and surprising truth that the most detailed biography of Charles was written in 1841 and many of its conclusions have never been seriously challenged.

This state of affairs came about for a number of reasons and it is valuable to briefly summarize the position with regard to the evolution of Charles Wesley scholarship. Charles was a controversial figure, disliked and even hated by some of his contemporaries; John Pawson and Michael Fenwick are the most obvious examples and there would have been others who felt the same way. Even preachers who respected Charles Wesley were exasperated at his outspoken ways, as shown by this passage from a letter written to Charles by John Valton:

Was it likely to do good to the cause of God to tell a friend of mine, that Mr J. Wesley had a hard matter to keep us [the preachers] together, *pride had got such a* footing among us, and that as soon as your brother's head was laid, you *forsaw what would be the consequence?* Did you not speak stronger things in your sermon at the fast day? Dear Sir *what good can such unhappy* prophecies *do the preachers* or *the cause of God?* It will irritate the men of little grace, and *distress* the sincere preachers of the Word.[1]

Such negative undercurrents had an inevitable effect on the way that Methodist historians treated Charles Wesley, with particular regard to the controversies that plagued his post-itinerant ministry.

John Wesley himself may consciously have promoted the perception of his brother as a man who in his later years was out of step with Methodism. Their disagreements were reasonably well known and neither was averse to attacking the other in print, albeit anonymously. In addition to the examples already cited, it is intriguing to consider

---

[1] John Valton to CW, MS letter, 13 November 1779 (MCA: DDPr 2/55).

the following excerpt from a letter by Thomas Coke to John Wesley dated 15 December 1779:

> I was totally ignorant of your brother's spirit till very lately. He appeared to me to be a *proud man* but I am now satisfied that he is a man of *genuine humility*. I thought him an *enemy* to Methodism; but I now find him its *real friend*, as far as Methodism is a friend to the Church of England; and on your plan the Church of England never had so great a friend. I looked upon the [musical] concerts which he allows his sons to have in his own house, to be highly dishonourable to God; and himself to be criminal, by reason of his situation in the Church of Christ: but on mature consideration... I cannot now blame him.
>
> I laboured during part of these two last years with some who saw your brother in the same light as I did; and no doubt their prejudices served to heighten mine.[2]

This letter was published in the 1790 issue of the *Arminian Magazine*, which had a national circulation as the official periodical of the Methodist movement. John exercised close editorial oversight and it is inconceivable that the letter, which in this instance was printed with little attempt to disguise identities, was published without his approval. It is true that Coke was, on the surface at least, 'correcting' his former poor opinion of John's dead brother, but one effect of the document is to highlight the accusations levelled at Charles and expose the hostility felt towards him.

John Wesley was ruthless in his treatment of those he considered rivals or who had let him down in some way. Charles was under no illusions about this aspect of his brother's personality and indeed, in the early part of his ministry, joined enthusiastically with John in conflict with others. On 11 June 1755 at the height of the controversy over preachers administering the Sacraments, Charles confided to the Countess of Huntingdon his fear that his brother would treat him as a 'deserter'.[3] Five years later, Charles's refusal to travel to Norwich to deal with dissident preachers was partly based on his worry that John's 'fear and dissimulation will throw all the blame upon me and perhaps disown me'.[4] These suspicions appear justified from the

---

[2] [Thomas Coke,], 'From the Rev. Dr. C. to the Rev. J. Wesley', *Arminian Magazine*, 13 (1790), 50–1.
[3] Quoted by Baker, *John Wesley and the Church of England*, 168.
[4] CW to John Wesley, MS copy letter, 2 March 1760 (MCA: DDCW 7/57).

evidence represented by the publication of Thomas Coke's letter, as well as such curious incidents as the threadbare obituary inserted in the minutes of the 1788 Conference.[5]

In his early biography of John Wesley, John Hampson stated that the Methodist leader 'never doubted, that the plans he had formed, were the best that could be devised; so, when any of the preachers were of a different opinion, and refused to concur in his measures, he treated them as the mariners treated Jonah. He threw them overboard with the most perfect indifference.'[6] John could not eject his brother from the Methodist ship as this would have been too controversial, and in any case many people agreed with Charles's views, but that did not stop him from placing a discreet black mark against his brother's posthumous name and reputation. In so doing, he gave his own seal of approval to the negative perception of Charles's later ministry.

With the exception of his poetic works, twentieth-century scholars largely failed to meet the challenge represented by one of the most important leaders of the eighteenth-century Revival. The result is that more than two hundred years after Charles Wesley's death we are far from understanding in a balanced way his personality and ministry, with specific regard to his vision of the Methodist movement.

The question must be asked if this negative view of Charles Wesley is justified. With regard to his personality, there can be no doubt that he gave ammunition to his critics—Charles was a temperamental man, subject to outbursts of fury that verged at times on the irrational. Valton's impassioned letter is testimony to the fact that John Wesley's brother displayed minimal restraint when a principle was at stake. Charles's annotation on the letter consists simply of Valton's name, indicating that Charles was unconcerned with such minor details as declaring controversial views from the pulpit.[7] His sharp tongue and provocative opinions rendered him a difficult biographical subject and one might conclude that had it not been for the fact that he was one of the most prolific and talented of hymn-writers, Charles Wesley would have been consigned to the footnotes of Methodist history in much the same way as Benjamin Ingham and Vincent Perronet.

---

[5] *Conference Minutes*, i. 201.   [6] Hampson, *John Wesley*, iii. 199–200.
[7] John Valton to CW, MS letter, 13 November 1779 (MCA: DDPr 2/55).

The argument could be made that Charles does not warrant a more significant place in the annals of the movement. After all, he retired from the itinerancy in 1756 and if his personal standing at the time of his death is anything to go by, he was barely missed. One of the things that annoyed John during the last thirty years of his brother's life was the sheer negativity indulged in by his sibling. After 1756, Charles refused to play any further substantial role in the leadership, with the sole exception of opposing separation. John's letter to Charles written on 19 August 1785 summed up his frustration: 'if you will go hand in hand with me, do. But do not hinder me if you will not help. Perhaps if you had kept close to me, I might have done better.'[8] However, a strong case can be made for Charles's post-itinerant impact on Methodism being greater and more positive than previously supposed. This can be argued in two ways; first, his personal influence over his brother, and secondly, his championship of a considerable body of silent opinion within the movement.

At several crucial points, Charles's intervention appears to have proved decisive in preventing a formal division from the Anglicans. During the Sacramental dispute of 1754–5, John wavered on the brink of ordaining preachers, but was pulled back by Charles's fierce protestations and rallying of pro-Anglican support. In the years that followed, Charles used his privileged position to wage a bitter war against the separatists: even in the aftermath of the 1784 ordinations, he was able to exert sufficient pressure to swing John back to an avowedly pro-Anglican viewpoint. In a series of conversations towards the end of 1785, Charles dragged from his brother the statement that 'He has not separated from the Church of England—and has no thought of it.'[9] Charles expressed doubts at the time concerning the value of this assertion, but the fact remains that in the months that followed, other observers remarked on John's renewed loyalty to the Church of England.[10] The hope entertained by John Pawson

---

[8] John Wesley, 'On the Church: in a Letter to the Rev.—', *Arminian Magazine*, 9 (January 1786), 51.

[9] CW to Henry Durbin, MS copy letter, 10 November 1785 (MCA: Memoranda book, Charles Wesley box 5).

[10] 'I have heard from various quarters of Mr Wesley's [declaring] himself in very strong terms in favour of the Church.' John Pawson to [Charles Atmore], MS letter, 2 June 1786 (MCA: PLP 82.2.8).

and his friends that there would be formal separation from that 'old withered harlot' had once more been dashed.[11]

The brothers' special relationship was seriously frayed by the time the ordinations took place, but Charles remained one of the few men capable of shifting John from an entrenched position. After 1756, Charles played little part in the making of policy and he was deliberately excluded from involvement in certain issues, but he retained until the end of his life a foothold in John's deliberations, and he used this to maximum effect with regard to the all-important subject of separation. It was with good reason that John Pawson referred to Charles's death as the removal of 'the grand hindrance'.[12] This residual influence may have been one of the reasons why Charles was not given advance warning of the 1784 ordinations. John must have harboured some concern over the wisdom of his decision, but having made up his mind, did not wish to have his doubts exacerbated by his brother—he must also by this time have been thoroughly weary of Charles's habit of making impassioned interventions in both his ministry and his personal life.

One of the most powerful weapons in Charles's arsenal was his being able to speak on behalf of pro-Anglican sentiment within Methodism. Time and time again, he stressed to his brother the absolute necessity of appeasing this body of opinion. During the Norwich dispute of 1760 for example, he was careful to enlist the support of men like Christopher Hopper, John Nelson, and William Grimshaw, while during the battle for control of the pulpit of City Road Chapel in 1778–9, he was quick to point out that many subscribers to the chapel's building costs were Anglicans, not Methodists.[13] It was through this championship of Church Methodism that Charles made the most positive impact after his retirement from the itinerancy. This is a point of fundamental importance, as it runs counter to the view that Charles and his supporters were in the minority by the 1780s.[14] Instead, it is apparent from

---

[11] John Pawson to [Charles Atmore], MS letter, 13 February 1786 (MCA: PLP 82.2.6).

[12] John Pawson to [Charles Atmore], MS letter, 28 April 1788 (MCA: PLP 82.4.4).

[13] Baker, *Charles Wesley as Revealed*, 132.

[14] For example, Harrison, *The Separation of Methodists from the Church of England*, 12–13; Leslie Church, *More about the Early Methodist People*, 255–6; Rack, *Reasonable Enthusiast*, 525; Jackson, *Charles Wesley*, i. pp. vii–viii and ii. 377.

the primary sources that a substantial number of British Methodists, perhaps even the majority, would have been opposed to separation, or at least felt uncomfortable at the prospect. This is shown not only by the actions of chapel trustees, who were of course few in number, but by the strong attachment to the Church of England evidenced on a society level throughout the eighteenth century and for decades after 1800. Even if Church Methodism had been confined to wealthy trustees such as Horton and Pine, it would still have made a significant contribution by underwriting chapel building costs and the work among the poor. The fact that many other Methodists also felt attachment to the Church simply reinforces the point.

It is interesting to speculate what would have happened if John Wesley had separated in the 1750s, when he was hovering on the brink. In the event of such a division, prominent lay people would probably have chosen the Church of England if only for reasons of social status and avoidance of discrimination. As for the rank and file of the societies, many would have followed Wesley into Dissent, but a substantial if indeterminate number would have returned to the Anglican fold. This is shown by the fact that many people from all walks of life left the movement after 1791 despite the fact that they were never presented with a stark choice between Methodism and the Church. If separation had occurred during the 1750s, when the national membership was fewer than 25,000,[15] the damage would have been considerable. John Wesley himself acknowledged this; in a letter of 21 February 1786 referring to events of forty years previously, he made the point that 'if we had then left the Church, we should not have done a tenth of the good which we have done'.[16]

By 1791, after more than fifty years of struggle and steady growth, Methodism was strong enough to prosper as an independent denomination and, with a membership of 72,476, it could afford to lose people back to the Church of England. Infrastructure too had attained a level of sophistication that could accommodate continued expansion. This may not have been the case a generation previously—many of the four hundred preaching houses that were serving Methodist

---

[15] Membership figures were first published in the 1767 Minutes of Conference when the figure of 25,911 was recorded. *Conference Minutes*, i. 71.
[16] JW to Thomas Taylor, MS letter, 21 February 1786 (MCA: DDX 56).

societies by 1784 had been acquired only in relatively recent times, and it was Church Methodists who contributed disproportionately to building costs. Also, it was only in the generation after 1756 that Methodism spread to other areas of the English-speaking world. The movement may have enjoyed overseas success as a Dissenting Church, but given the disruption that separation would have caused within the parent body, it is just as likely that expansion would have received a severe check.

By staving off separation until Methodism was in a position to flourish independently of a link with the Anglicans, Charles Wesley, far from being a 'retarding influence',[17] helped to pave the way for prosperity in the century that followed. This is not something that he himself would have anticipated or welcomed, but he should receive credit for a vital contribution to the success and unique identity of what became the Wesleyan Methodist Church in Britain, and the Methodist Episcopal Church in the United States.

In any assessment of Charles Wesley's importance, one should also remember his ministry in the years before 1756 when he played a vital role in the establishment of a distinctive Wesleyan movement. His partnership with his brother was a major factor in Methodism's survival during those crucial years, and in some areas of their joint ministry such as preaching and pastoral supervision, Charles appears to have been the more effective of the two men.

This in-depth study of the life and ministry of Charles Wesley and the contribution made by Church Methodism has highlighted other significant points concerning the movement's early history. Charles's papers represent an exceptionally rich resource for the study of the Evangelical Revival in its wider aspects, complementing the better-known and infinitely better-used John Wesley archive. There are approximately eight hundred surviving letters by Charles,[18] several hundred in-letters, and a huge amount of supplementary material. By presenting a different view from within the Revival's leadership, this collection sheds new light on important events, one that can support radical departures from the existing paradigm. Yet the collection remains considerably underused.

---

[17] Smith, *History of Wesleyan Methodism*, i. 582.
[18] Information provided by Kenneth Newport of Liverpool Hope University.

Concluding Remarks 241

The neglect accorded to Charles is both a symptom and a result of a John Wesley-centred view of early Methodist history that has held sway for over two hundred years. Among other significant casualties of this preoccupation, one might give special mention to John Fletcher, who did much to establish a systematic Wesleyan theology and was regarded by his contemporaries, as nothing less than a Methodist saint.[19] There is no complete edition of Fletcher's works, and the personal papers compiled by Fletcher and his wife, the pioneering preacher Mary Bosanquet, have until recently been neglected despite the fact that they constitute the largest single collection in the British Methodist Archives. The detailed contributions made by George Whitefield and the Moravians have also been largely overlooked by Methodist scholarship.

It is not just the leaders who have been consigned to John Wesley's shadow: the ordinary people without whom there would have been no Methodism have never received the attention that they deserve.[20] Yet there is in archives in Britain and the United States a wealth of unexplored correspondence, diaries, sermons, and memoranda books written by Methodists from all social classes, providing an invaluable insight into the reality of the early movement and charting its peculiar evolution. By way of contrast, John Wesley studies are in a flourishing state with new publications added each year. This point is made not to question his significance, but rather to stress the fact that there is a need to study Methodist history from the perspective of others. Such work can shed new light on John Wesley himself, as well as highlight the contribution made by other people to one of the great success stories of the post-Reformation Church.

The view of Charles Wesley that one gleans from close examination of the primary texts is of a man who was possessed of extraordinary gifts. It is highly doubtful whether John Wesley would have achieved so much without his brother at his side. In addition to his preaching powers, literary prowess, and pastoral skills, Charles displayed a human touch that John lacked. This did not always surface in a positive fashion, but he was responsive to ordinary people in a way

---

[19] Patrick Streiff, *Reluctant Saint? A Theological Biography of Fletcher of Madeley*, trans. G. W. S. Knowles (Peterborough: Epworth, 2001), p. vii.

[20] 'Too little work has yet been done on the Methodists as distinct from Wesley.' Rack, *Reasonable Enthusiast*, 558.

that his brother was not. That Methodism survived and prospered is a testimony to the hard work and complementary abilities of both Wesley brothers. The Church that emerged from the years of bitter controversy was not simply the brilliant creation of one man, but a compromise born of the different visions of John and Charles Wesley, and of their followers.

Bibliography

ABELOVE, HENRY, *Evangelist of Desire: John Wesley and the Methodists* (Stanford: Stanford University Press, 1990).
ANONYMOUS, 'Obituary of Charles Wesley', *Gentleman's Magazine*, 63 (1788), 368.
—— 'Obituary of John Wesley', *Gentleman's Magazine*, 69 (1791), 282–4.
—— 'Recent Deaths [Mary Tooth]', *Methodist Magazine*, 66 (1843), 1036–7.
—— 'Early Methodism in Derby', *Christian Miscellany* (December 1870).
ATMORE, CHARLES, *The Methodist Memorial; being an impartial sketch of the lives and characters of the preachers, who have departed this life since the commencement of the work of God, among the people called Methodists, late in Connection with the Rev. John Wesley, deceased. Drawn from the most authentic sources and disposed in alphabetical order. Introduced with a brief account of the state of religion from the earliest age and a concise History of Methodism. To which is added, a chronological list of the preachers who are now engaged in the same Work* (Bristol: Richard Edwards, 1801).
AVIS, PAUL, *Anglicanism and the Christian Church: Theological Resources in Historical Perspective* (Minneapolis: Fortress, 1989).
BAKER, FRANK, *Charles Wesley as Revealed by his Letters* (London: Epworth, 1948).
—— *William Grimshaw (1708–1763)* (London: Epworth, 1963).
—— *John Wesley and the Church of England* (London: Epworth, 1970).
—— 'Poet in Love—The Courtship of Charles Wesley, 1747–49', *Methodist History*, 29:4 (July 1991), 235–47.
BANKS, MARION, 'Diary of a Birmingham Methodist', *Proceedings of the Wesley Historical Society*, 39 (February 1974), 97–103.
BEBBINGTON, DAVID, NOLL, MARK, and RAWLYK, GEORGE, eds., *Evangelicalism: Comparative Studies of Popular Protestantism in North America, the British Isles and Beyond, 1700–1990* (Oxford: Oxford University Press, 1994).
BECKERLEGGE, OLIVER, 'The Church Methodists', *Proceedings of the Wesley Historical Society*, 34 (September 1963), 63–5.
BENHAM, DANIEL, *Memoirs of James Hutton: comprising the annals of his life, and Connection with the United Brethren* (London: Hamilton, Adams, & Co., 1856).

BENSON, JOSEPH, 'Character and Death of John Horton', *Methodist Magazine*, 1:26 (1803), 211–15.
BENSON, LOUIS, *The English Hymn: Its Development and Use in Worship* (Philadelphia: The Presbyterian Board of Publication, 1915).
BERGER, TERESA, *Theology in Hymns? A Study of the Relationship of Doxology and Theology* (Nashville: Kingswood Books, 1989).
BOWMAN, WILLIAM, *The Imposture of Methodism Displayed in a letter to the inhabitants of Dewsbury, occasioned by the Rise of a certain Modern Sect of Enthusiasts among them call'd Methodists* (London: printed for Joseph Lord of Wakefield, 1740).
BOWMER, JOHN, *The Sacrament of the Lord's Supper in Early Methodism* (London: Dacre, 1951).
BRAILSFORD, MABEL, *A Tale of Two Brothers: John & Charles Wesley* (London: Rupert Hart-Davis, 1954).
BROWN-LAWSON, ALBERT, *John Wesley and the Anglican Evangelicals of the 18th Century* (Bishop Auckland: Pentland, 1994).
BULLER, JAMES, *A reply to the Rev. Mr Wesley's address to the clergy* (Bristol: printed by S. Farley, 1756).
BUNTING, THOMAS PERCIVAL, *The Life of Jabez Bunting*, 2 vols. (London: Longman, Brown, Green, Longmans, & Roberts, 1859).
CHADWICK, OWEN, *The Victorian Church*, Part 1, 2nd edn., An Ecclesiastical History of England, 5 (London: Adam & Charles Black, 1970).
CHALONER, W. H., 'Manchester in the latter half of the Eighteenth century', *Bulletin of the John Rylands Library*, 42 (1959–60), 40–60.
CHILCOTE, PAUL, *She Offered them Christ: The Legacy of Women Preachers in Early Methodism* (Nashville: Abingdon, 1993).
CHURCH, LESLIE, *The Early Methodist People* (London: Epworth, 1948).
—— *More about the Early Methodist People* (London: Epworth, 1949).
CHURCH, THOMAS, *Some farther remarks on the Rev. Mr John Wesley's last journal, together with a few considerations on his 'Farther Appeal', shewing the inconsistency of his conduct and sentiments with the constitutution and doctrine of the Church of England, and explaining the articles relating to justification; to which is annexed, a vindication of the 'Remarks', being a reply to Mr Wesley's answer, in a second letter to that gentleman* (London: printed and sold by M. Cooper, 1746).
CLARKE, ADAM, 'Original Letter of Dr Adam Clarke', *Proceedings of the Wesley Historical Society*, 18 (1931–2), 21–9.
[COKE, THOMAS], '[From the Rev. Dr. C. to the Rev. J. Wesley]', *The Arminian Magazine for the Year 1790, consisting chiefly of extracts and original treatises on universal redemption*, 13 (1790), 50–1.

Cook, Faith, *William Grimshaw of Haworth* (Edinburgh: Banner of Truth Trust, 1997).
Cornwall, Robert, *Visible and Apostolic: The Constitution of the Church in High Church Anglican and Non-Juror Thought* (Newark: University of Delaware Press, 1993).
Crookshank, Charles, *History of Methodism in Ireland*, 3 vols. (Belfast: R. S. Allen, 1885–8).
[Cruttenden, Robert], *The principles and preaching of the Methodists considered in a letter to the Reverend Mr***** (London: printed for James Buckland, 1753).
Currie, Robert, *Methodism Divided: A Study in the Sociology of Ecumenicalism* (London: Faber & Faber, 1968).
Dallimore, Arnold, *A Heart Set Free: The Life of Charles Wesley, Preeminent Hymn-Writer, Fearless Evangelist, Powerful Preacher* (Welwyn: Evangelical Press, 1988).
──── *George Whitefield; The Life and Times of the Great Evangelist of the 18th Century Revival*, 2 vols. (Edinburgh: Banner of Truth Trust 1970).
Dawson, Joanna, 'Methodism at the Grassroots within the Great Haworth Round', *Proceedings of the Wesley Historical Society*, Yorkshire Branch Occasional Paper, 3 (1978).
Dews, Colin, *A History of Methodism in Haworth from 1744: Comprised for the One Hundred and Fiftieth Anniversary of the Sunday School, 3 May 1981* (Keighley: Bronte Print, 1981).
Durston, Christopher, and Eales, Jacqueline, eds., *Culture of English Puritanism 1560–1700* (Houndmills: Palgrave Macmillan [1996]).
Eayrs, George, Townsend, W. J., and Workman, H. B., eds., *A New History of Methodism*, 2 vols. (London: Hodder & Stoughton, 1909).
Edwards, Maldwyn, *Family Circle: A Study of the Epworth Family Household in Relation to John and Charles Wesley* (London: Epworth, 1949).
Este, Thomas, *Methodism Display'd: A farce of one act, as it was intended to be perform'd at the Moot Hall in Newcastle, Nov. 4 1743. Alter'd and publish'd by Mr Este from a farce call'd 'Trick upon Trick; or, The vintner in the suds'* (Newcastle upon Tyne: printed for the publisher, 1743).
Field, Clive, 'Anti-Methodist Publications of the Eighteenth Century: A Revised Bibliography', *Bulletin of the John Rylands University Library of Manchester*, 73:2 (Summer 1991).
Fletcher, Nathaniel, *A Methodist dissected; or, A description of their errors* (York: printed by Caesar Ward, 1749).
Garnett, Jane, and Matthew, Colin, eds., *Revival and Religion since 1700: Essays for John Walsh* (London: Hambledon, 1993).

[GIBSON, EDMUND], *The Bishop of London's pastoral letter to the people of his diocese, especially those of the two great cities of London and Westminster, by way of caution against lukewarmness on one hand and enthusiasm on the other* (London: printed by S. Buckley, 1739).

[―――], *Observations upon the Conduct and Behaviour of a Certain Sect, usually distinguished by the name of Methodists* (London: ?printed by E. Owen, 1744).

GIBSON, WILLIAM, *Church, State and Society 1760–1850* (New York: St Martin's, 1994).

――― *The Church of England 1688–1832: Unity and Accord* (London: Routledge, 2001).

GILL, FREDERICK, *Charles Wesley the First Methodist* (London: Lutterworth, 1964).

GOODWIN, CHARLES, 'Vile or Reviled? The Causes of the Anti-Methodist Riots at Wednesbury between May, 1743 and April, 1744 in the Light of New England Revivalism', *Methodist History*, 35:1 (October 1996), 14–27.

GREEN, RICHARD, *Anti-Methodist Publications issued during the Eighteenth Century* (London: C. H. Kelly, 1902).

GREEN, VIVIAN, *The Young Mr Wesley: A Study of John Wesley and Oxford* (London: Epworth, 1963).

――― *John Wesley* (London: Thomas Nelson & Sons, 1964).

GREEN, VIVIAN, *Religion at Oxford and Cambridge: A History c.1160–c.1960* (London: SCM, 1964).

GREGORY, BENJAMIN, *Sidelights on the Conflicts of Methodism during the Second Quarter of the Nineteenth Century* (London: Cassell, 1898).

GREGORY, JEREMY, *Restoration, Reformation and Reform, 1660–1828: Archbishops of Canterbury and their Diocese* (Oxford: Clarendon, 2000).

GREGORY, J. ROBINSON, *A History of Methodism Chiefly for the Use of Students*, 2 vols. (London: C. H. Kelly, 1911).

HAAKONSSEN, KNUD, ed., *Rational Dissent in Eighteenth Century Britain* (Cambridge: Cambridge University Press, 1996).

HAMPSON, JOHN, *Memoirs of the late Rev. John Wesley, A.M. with a review of his Life and Writings, and a History of Methodism, from its commencement in 1729 to the present time*, 3 vols. (Sunderland: printed for the author by James Graham, 1791).

HARRISON, A. W., *The Separation of Methodism from the Church of England*, Wesley Historical Society Lecture, 11 (London: Epworth, 1945).

HAYDON, COLIN, TAYLOR, STEPHEN, and WALSH, JOHN, eds., *The Church of England c.1688–c.1833. From Toleration to Tractarianism* (Cambridge: Cambridge University Press, 1993).

Bibliography

HEITZENRATER, RICHARD, *Mirror and Memory: Reflections on Early Methodism* (Nashville: Kingswood Books, 1989).

—— *Wesley and the People Called Methodists* (Nashville: Abingdon, 1995).

HINDMARSH, BRUCE, *John Newton and the English Evangelical Tradition between the Conversions of Wesley and Wilberforce* (Oxford: Clarendon, 1996).

HOLLAND, BERNARD, *Baptism in Early Methodism* (London: Epworth, 1970).

HOLMES, GEOFFREY, and SZECHI, DANIEL, *The Age of Oligarchy 1722–83* (London: Longman, 1993).

[HORSLEY, SAMUEL], *An Apology for the Liturgy and Clergy of the Church of England: In answer to a pamphlet, entitled Hints etc. submitted to the serious attention of the clergy, nobility, newly associated: by a layman. In a letter to the author, by a clergyman* (London: printed for J. F. and C. Rivington, 1790).

INGHAM, BENJAMIN, *Diary of an Oxford Methodist Benjamin Ingham, 1733–1734*, ed. Richard Heitzenrater (Durham: Duke University Press, 1985).

JACKSON, THOMAS, *The Life of the Rev. Charles Wesley, M.A. sometime Student of Christ-Church Oxford: comprising a review of his poetry; sketches of the rise and progress of Methodism; with notices of contemporary events and characters*, 2 vols. (London: Wesleyan Methodist Conference Office, 1841).

—— *A letter to the Rev. Edward B. Pusey, D.D: being a vindication of the tenets and character of the Wesleyan Methodists, against his misrepresentations and censures* (London: Wesleyan Conference Office, 1842).

—— *The Lives of Early Methodist Preachers, chiefly written by themselves,* edited, with an introductory essay, 3 vols. (London: Wesleyan Conference Office, 1871; repr. as a retypeset from the original 6 vols. of the 4th edn., Stoke on Trent: Tentmaker Publications; Lewes: Berith Publications, 1998).

JACOB, W. M., *Lay People and Religion in the Early Eighteenth Century* (Cambridge: Cambridge University Press, 1996).

JEFFERY, F., 'Church Methodists in Ireland', *Proceedings of the Wesley Historical Society*, 34 (December 1963), 73–5.

JENNINGS, THEODORE, *Good News to the Poor: John Wesley's Evangelical Economics* (Nashville: Abingdon, 1990).

JOLLY, CYRIL, *The Spreading Flame: The Coming of Methodism to Norfolk 1751–1811* [Dereham]: Cyril Jolly, n.d).

JONES, DORA, *Charles Wesley: A Study* (London: Skeffington, 1919).

LANGFORD, PAUL, *Public Life and the Propertied Englishman 1689–1798* (Oxford: Clarendon, 1991).

—— *A Polite and Commercial People: England 1727–1783*, New Oxford History of England (Oxford: Oxford University Press 1992).

LAYCOCK, J. W., *Methodist Heroes in the Great Haworth Round 1734 to 1784* (Keighley: Wadsworth, 1909).

LEARY, WILLIAM, *My Ancestors were Methodists*, 2nd edn. (London: Society of Genealogists, 1990).

LEESE, ROGER, 'The Impact of Methodism on Black Country Society, 1742–1860' (Manchester University PhD thesis, 1972).

LLOYD, A. KINGSLEY, *The Labourers's Hire: The Payment and Deployment of the Early Methodist Preachers 1744–1811*, Wesley Historical Society Lecture, 34 (Bunbury: Wesley Historical Society, 1968).

LLOYD, GARETH, 'Charles Wesley, Junior: Prodigal Child, Unfulfilled Adult', *Proceedings of the Charles Wesley Society*, 5 (1998), 23–5.

—— 'A Cloud of Perfect Witnesses: John Wesley and the London Disturbances 1760–1763', *The Asbury Theological Journal* (Fall 2001/Spring 2002), 117–36.

MACDONALD, JAMES, *Memoirs of Joseph Benson* (London: sold by T. Blanshard, 1822).

MARTIN, J. HENRY, *John Wesley's London Chapel*, Wesley Historical Society Lecture, 12 (London: Epworth, 1946).

MASER, FREDERICK, *The Story of John Wesley's Sisters, or Seven Sisters in Search of Love* (Rutland: Academy Books, 1988).

—— 'Discovery', *Methodist History*, 38:1 (October 1999), 63–5.

MICHELL, CRICHTON T., *Charles Wesley: Man with the Dancing Heart* (Kansas City: Beacon Hill, 1994).

MOORE, HENRY, *The Life of the Rev. John Wesley*, 2 vols. (London: printed for John Kershaw 1824–5).

MYLES, WILLIAM, *A Short Chronological History of the Methodists* (Rochdale: J. Hartley, [1798]).

—— *A List of the Methodist Preachers who have laboured in Connexion with John Wesley* (Bristol: William Myles, 1801).

NEWPORT, KENNETH, and LLOYD, GARETH, 'George Bell and Early Methodist Enthusiasm: A New Manuscript Source from the Manchester Archives,' *Bulletin of the John Rylands University Library of Manchester*, 80:1 (Spring 1998), 89–101.

NEWTON, JOHN, *Susanna Wesley and the Puritan Tradition in Methodism*, 2nd edn. (London: Epworth, 2002).

[OSBORN, GEORGE], *Modern Methodism, Wesleyan Methodism*, Wesleyan Tract for the Times, 5 (London: Wesleyan Conference Office, 1842).

OVERTON, JOHN, *Life in the English Church 1660–1714* (London: Longman's, Green, 1885).

PAWSON, JOHN, 'A Short Account of Mr Henry Durbin,' *Methodist Magazine*, 1:22 (1799), 487–9.

PIBWORTH, NIGEL, *The Gospel Pedlar: The Story of John Berridge and the Eighteenth-Century Revival* (Welwyn: Evangelical Press, 1987).
PODMORE, COLIN, *The Moravian Church in England, 1728–1760* (Oxford: Clarendon, 1998).
RACK, HENRY, *Reasonable Enthusiast: John Wesley and the Rise of Methodism* (London: Epworth, 1989).
RATTENBURY, JOHN, *The Eucharistic Hymns of John and Charles Wesley* (London: Epworth, 1948).
Religion in Victorian Nottinghamshire: The Religious Census of 1851, ed. Michael Watts, 2 vols., Centre for Local History Record Series, 7, (Nottingham: University of Nottingham Department of Adult Education, 1988).
ROSE, E. A., 'Cornelius Bayley and the Manchester Methodists', *Proceedings of the Wesley Historical Society*, 34 (September 1964), 153–8.
RUPP, GORDON, *Religion in England 1688–1791*, Oxford History of the Christian Church (Oxford: Clarendon, 1986).
SECKERSON, ANTHONY, 'An Account of Mrs Dobinson,' *Methodist Magazine*, 26 (1803), 557–66.
SIMON, JOHN, *John Wesley: The Last Phase*, 2nd edn. (London: Epworth, 1962).
SMITH, BENJAMIN, *Methodism in Macclesfield* (London: Wesleyan Conference Office, 1875).
SMITH, GEORGE, *History of Wesleyan Methodism*, 3 vols. (London: Longman, Brown, Green, Longmans, & Roberts, 1857–8).
SMITH, LUKE, *A preservative against separation from the established Church of England, in two parts, dedicated to the archbishops, bishops and clergy of the Church of England* (London: printed for the author, 1745).
SMITH, MARK, *Religion in Industrial Society: Oldham and Saddleworth 1740–1865* (Oxford: Clarendon, 1994).
STAMP, WILLIAM, *The Orphan House of Wesley with Notices of Early Methodism in Newcastle-Upon-Tyne and its Vicinity* (London: John Mason, 1863).
[STEBBING, HENRY], *An earnest and affectionate address to the people called Methodists* (London: printed by J. Oliver, 1745).
STEVENS, ABEL, *History of the Religious Movement of the Eighteenth Century called Methodism*, new edn., 3 vols. (London: Wesleyan Methodist Book Room, 1878).
STEVENSON, GEORGE, *City Road Chapel, London, and its Associations, Historical, Biographical, and Memorial* (London: George J. Stevenson, 1872).
—— *Memorials of the Wesley Family: including biographical and historical sketches of all the members of the family for two hundred and fifty years* (London: S. W. Partridge [1876]).

STREIFF, PATRICK, *Reluctant Saint? A Theological Biography of Fletcher of Madeley*, trans. G. W. S. Knowles (Peterborough: Epworth, 2001).

SWIFT, WESLEY, 'Headingley Papers IV: Two Letters from John Pawson to Henry Moore', *Proceedings of the Wesley Historical Society*, 29 (1953–4), 131–5.

SWINDLEHURST, MARJORIE, *John Wesley and Wigan* (Wigan: Owl Books, 1991).

SYKES, NORMAN, *Church and State in England in the XVIII Century* (Cambridge: Cambridge University Press, 1934).

TAMKE, SUSAN, *Make a Joyful Noise unto the Lord: Hymns as a Reflection of Victorian Social Attitudes* (Athens, Ohio: Ohio University Press, 1978).

TELFORD, JOHN, *The Life of John Wesley* (London: Hodder & Stoughton, 1886).

—— *The Life of the Rev. Charles Wesley, M.A., sometime student of Christ Church, Oxford*, rev. and enlarged edn. (London: Wesleyan Methodist Book Room, 1900).

TUCKER, JOSIAH, *A Brief History of the Principles of Methodism, wherein the rise and progress, together with the causes of the several variations, divisions and present inconsistencies of this sect are attempted to be traced out and accounted for* (Oxford: printed for James Fletcher, 1742).

TYERMAN, LUKE, *The Life and Times of the Rev. Samuel Wesley, M.A.* (London: Simpkin, Marshall, 1866).

—— *Life and Times of the Rev. John Wesley, M.A., founder of the Methodists*, 3 vols. (London: Hodder & Stoughton, 1871–2).

VALENTINE, SIMON, *John Bennet and the Origins of Methodism and the Evangelical Revival in England*, Pietist and Wesleyan Studies, 9 (Lanham, Md.: Scarecrow, 1997).

VICKERS, JOHN, *Thomas Coke: Apostle of Methodism* (London: Epworth, 1969).

—— ed., *A Dictionary of Methodism in Britain and Ireland* (Peterborough: Epworth, 2000).

WARNE, ARTHUR, *Church and Society in Eighteenth-Century Devon* (Newton Abbot: David & Charles, 1969).

WATSON, RICHARD, *The English Hymn: A Critical and Historical Study* (Oxford: Clarendon, 1997).

WATTS, MICHAEL, *The Dissenters*, 2 vols. (Oxford: Clarendon, 1978–95).

—— *The Dissenters: The Expansion of Evangelical Nonconformity 1791–1859*, (Oxford: Clarendon, 1995), ii.

WESLEY, CHARLES, *Short Hymns on Select Passages of the Holy Scriptures*, 2 vols. (Bristol: printed by E. Farley, 1762).

[____] *Strictures on the substance of a sermon preached at Baltimore in the state of Maryland before the General Conference of the Methodist Episcopal Church, on the 27th of December 1784 at the ordination of the Rev. Francis Asbury to the office of superintendent by Thomas Coke, LL.D., superintendent of the said Church* (London: G. Herdsfield, 1785).

____ *Sermons by the late Rev. Charles Wesley, A.M. Student of Christ-Church, Oxford. With a memoir of the author by the editor* (London: Baldwin, Cradock, & Joy, 1816).

____ *The Journal of the Rev. Charles Wesley, M.A., sometime Student of Christ-Church, Oxford. To which are appended selections from his correspondence and poetry, with an introduction and occasional notes*, ed. Thomas Jackson, 2 vols. (London: Wesleyan Methodist Book Room, 1849).

____ *The Journal of Charles Wesley 1736–1739*, ed. John Telford (London: Robert Culley, 1910).

____ *Charles Wesley: A Reader*, ed. John Tyson (Oxford: Oxford University Press, 1989).

____ *The Sermons of Charles Wesley: A Critical Edition with Introduction and Notes*, ed. Kenneth Newport (Oxford: Oxford University Press, 2001).

WESLEY, JOHN, *A Collection of Psalms and Hymns* (Charles-Town: printed by Lewis Timothy, 1737).

____ *Rules etc of the United Societies* ([London], 1743).

____ *Modern Christianity Exemplified at Wednesbury and other adjacent places in Staffordshire* (Newcastle upon Tyne: printed by John Gooding, 1745).

____ *The Principles of a Methodist farther explained: occasioned by the Reverend Mr Church's second letter to Mr Wesley in a second letter to that gentleman* (London: printed by William Strahan, 1746).

____ *Reasons against a Separation from the Church of England* (London: printed by W. Strahan, 1758).

____ 'On the Church: in a Letter to the Rev. [Charles Wesley]', *The Arminian Magazine for the Year 1786, consisting chiefly of extracts and original treatises on universal redemption*, 9 (January 1786), 50–1.

____ 'Thoughts on the Consecration of Churches, and Burial Grounds', *Arminian Magazine*, 11 (1788), 541–3.

____ *John Wesley's Last Love*, ed. J. A. Leger (London: J. M. Dent & Sons, 1910).

____ *The Letters of the Rev. John Wesley, A.M. Sometime Fellow of Lincoln College, Oxford*, ed. John Telford, 8 vols. (London: Epworth, 1931).

WESLEY, JOHN, *John Wesley's First Hymn-Book: A Facsimile with Additional Material*, ed. Frank Baker and George Williams (London: Wesley Historical Society Publication 6, 1964).
―― *The Works of John Wesley*, i. *Sermons I*, ed. Albert Outler (Nashville: Abingdon, 1984).
―― *The Works of John Wesley*, iii. *Sermons III*, ed. Albert Outler (Nashville: Abingdon, 1986).
―― *The Works of John Wesley*, xviii. *Journals and Diaries I, 1735–1738*, ed. Richard Heitzenrater and W. Reginald Ward (Nashville: Abingdon, 1988).
―― *The Works of John Wesley*, xix. *Journals and Diaries II, 1738–1743*, ed. Richard Heitzenrater and W. Reginald Ward (Nashville: Abingdon, 1990).
―― *The Works of John Wesley*, xx. *Journals and Diaries III, 1743–1754*, ed. Richard Heitzenrater and W. Reginald Ward (Nashville: Abingdon, 1991).
―― *The Works of John Wesley*, xxi. *Journals and Diaries IV, 1755–1765*, ed. Richard Heitzenrater and W. Reginald Ward (Nashville: Abingdon, 1992).
―― *The Works of John Wesley*, xxiii. *Journals and Diaries V, 1776–1786*, ed. Richard Heitzenrater and W. Reginald Ward (Nashville: Abingdon, 1995).
―― *The Works of John Wesley*, xxv. *Letters I, 1721–1739*, ed. Frank Baker (Oxford: Clarendon, 1980).
―― *The Works of John Wesley*, xxvi. *Letters II, 1740–1755*, ed. Frank Baker (Oxford: Clarendon, 1982).
WESLEY, SUSANNA, *Susanna Wesley: The Complete Writings*, ed. Charles Wallace jun. (Oxford: Oxford University Press, 1997).
WESLEYAN METHODIST CHURCH, *Minutes of the Methodist Conferences from the first held in London by the late Rev. John Wesley, A.M. in the year 1744* (London: Methodist Conference Office, 1812), i.
―― *Minutes of the Methodist Conferences from the first held in London by the late Rev. John Wesley, A.M. in the year 1744* (London: Wesleyan Methodist Conference Office, 1813), ii.
―― *Minutes of the Methodist Conferences from the first held in London by the late Rev. John Wesley, A.M. in the year 1744* (London: John Mason of City Road, 1833), vi.
WHITEFIELD, GEORGE, *George Whitefield's Journals* (London: The Banner of Truth Trust, 1960).
WHITEHEAD, JOHN, *Some Account of the Life of the Rev. Charles Wesley, A.M. Late Student of Christ-Church Oxford, collected from his Private Journal* (London: printed by Stephen Couchman, 1793).
―― *The Life of the Rev. John Wesley, M.A. some time Fellow of Lincoln College, Oxford. Collected from his private papers and printed works; and written at the request of his executors. To which is prefixed, some account of his ancestors and relations; with the life of the Rev. Charles Wesley, A.M. collected from*

his private journal and never before published. *The whole forming a History of Methodism, in which the principles and economy of the Methodists are unfolded*, 2 vols. (London: printed by Stephen Couchman, 1793–6).

—— *The Life of the Rev. John Wesley, M.A. some time Fellow of Lincoln College, Oxford. Collected from his private papers and printed works; and written at the request of his executors. To which is prefixed, some account of his ancestors and relations; with the life of the Rev. Charles Wesley, A.M. collected from his private journal and never before published. The whole forming a History of Methodism, in which the principles and economy of the Methodists are unfolded copied chiefly from a London edition, published by John Whitehead, M.D. To which is subjoined, an appendix, containing characteristics of the Rev. Messrs. John and Charles Wesley, as given by several learned contemporaries*, 2 vols. new and rev. edn. (Dublin: printed by John Jones, 1805–6).

WORTH, RICHARD, *History of Plymouth from the earliest period to the present time*, 2nd edn. rev. and augmented (Plymouth: W. Brenden & Sons, 1873).

Index

Alleine, Joseph, 73
Alleine, Richard, 73
Annesley, Samuel, 11
Annesley, Susanna, 12; see also Wesley, Susanna
Archer, Isaac, 16
Asbury, Francis, 207, 212
Atlay, John, 200
Atmore, Charles, 199, 218–19, 222–3
Austen, Margaret, 34
Austin, John, 74

Bardsley, Samuel, 185, 207
Barlow, Thomas, 17
Barnard, Thomas, 83
Barrow, Hannah, 37
Batty, William, 58
Baxter, Richard, 26
Bell, George, 80–1
Bennet, Grace, 106; see also Murray, Grace
Bennet, John, 36, 98–101, 105–8, 115–17
Benson, Joseph, 193, 200, 220–1, 229
Berridge, John, 160
Biddulph, Thomas Tregenna, 228
Birch, Thomas, 16–17
Blackwell, Ebenezer, 107, 135–8, 142, 145, 150, 152, 157, 190, 192
Böhler, Peter, 45, 47–8
Boone, Charles, 207
Bradburn, Samuel, 217
Bray, John, 47, 49, 121
Bridgerule, 229
Briggs, William, 138
Bristol, 32, 34, 53–4, 66, 80, 144, 153, 179, 190, 201, 209–11, 215, 223
Bristol, New Room, 33, 50, 117, 132, 162, 202–4, 217
Bristol, St Werburgh's, 228
Bristol, Tabernacle, 145
Buchanan, Molly, 89
Buller, James, 79

Cennick, John, 54, 62, 112–13
Charles I, 10–11, 79
Charles II, 10–11, 18
Charterhouse school, 22–3
Church and State, 9–11, 13–20, 76, 79–81, 86, 157–8, 175, 185–6, 221–2; see also Church of England; Methodism (Wesleyan); Nonconformity
Church of England, 8–10, 15–20, 64–87, 140, 154–8, 175–8, 196, 210; Cambridge Platonism, 12, 15–16; Evangelicals (non-Methodist), 75, 158, 163, 192, 197, 201, 211, 228–9; High Church, 8–10, 13–15, 18–19, 23, 26, 65–71, 79, 82; hymns, 73–5; Latitudinarians, 9, 15–16, 79; Nonjurors, 10, 15–16, 26, 60, 76, 79, 85; opposition to Methodism, 35, 44, 51, 59–61, 76, 79–81, 85–7, 110, 114, 193–4; parish puritans, 16–18, 60, 85–6; Pietism, 18–19, 23, 26, 65–71, 79, 82; Tractarianism, 231–2; see also Church and State; holy club; Methodism (Calvinistic); Methodism (Wesleyan); Moravians; religious societies; Sacraments
Clarke, Adam, 178, 200, 209–11
Clayton, John, 26, 79
Coke, Thomas, 95, 189, 193–5, 197–9, 201–3, 207, 209, 211, 215, 218, 221–2, 235
Cownley, Joseph, 122, 148, 151, 154, 156, 222
Crosby, Sarah, 223, 232
Cudworth, William, 167–8

Darney, William, 61, 115–16, 118
Dartmouth, earl of; see Legge, William
Davis, Mark, 183–4, 186–7
Degge, Mary, 144

Index

Derby, 227
Devonport, 209–11
Dissent, *see* Nonconformity
Dobinson Mrs, 227
Doddridge, Phillip, 73
Dornford, Josiah, 228
Dover, 176
Durbin, Henry, 184, 201–4, 206–9, 225

Eastchurch, 174
Edwards, Jonathan, 43
Eggington, Edward, 59
Epworth, 2–20
Este, Thomas, 27

Fenwick, Michael, 117–18, 148–9
Fletcher, John, 111, 183, 193, 201, 228, 241
Fletcher, Mary, 223, 228, 232, 241
Flower, Joseph, 204
Folgham, John, 186, 192
French Prophets, 48–50

Gambold, John, 26, 28, 45
Garden, Alexander, 57
George II, 14, 131
Georgia, 29–31, 46–7, 51, 74, 92
Gilbert, Francis, 177
Gilbert, Nathaniel, 181
Gillespie, Robert, 117–18
Green, Thomas, 173–4
Greenwood, Paul, 164, 169, 172
Grimshaw, William, 111, 126, 166–7, 170–4, 183, 238
Gwynne, Marmaduke, 90, 145
Gwynne, Sarah, 89–92, 94–8, 102–3; *see also* Wesley, Sarah

Halfpenny, Elizabeth, 69
Hall, John, 17
Hall, Martha, 40, 139
Hampson, John, 6, 40–1, 130, 199, 236
Hanby, Thomas, 223
Hardwick, Thomas, 143
Harley, Brilliana, 12
Harley, Edward, 12
Harris, Howell, 43, 77, 179

Hastings, Selina, Countess of Huntingdon, 33, 59, 122–3, 125, 137, 144–5, 151, 235
Haworth, 169, 171–4
Hey, William, 184, 225
holy club, 25–7, 30, 43, 46, 50, 58, 65, 67, 121
Hopper, Christopher, 99, 148, 179, 238
Horneck, Anthony, 18
Horsley, Samuel, 174
Horton, John, 163, 184, 186–8, 192, 227
Huntingdon, Countess of, *see* Hastings, Selina
Hutton, James, 53, 90
hymns, 73–5, 88, 96, 121, 143, 159, 213, 215

Ingham, Benjamin, 26, 43, 45, 58
Ireland, 83–4, 229–30
Ireland, James, 227

Jaco, Peter, 189
James II, 10, 15
Johnson, John, 177–8, 193
Jones, Griffith, 43
Jones, John, 148, 169

Keach, Benjamin, 73
Keith, Jeanie, 99, 104
Kemp, Richard, 186, 192
Kingswood, 37, 69, 96, 142

Law, William, 16, 26
Leeds, 101, 103, 126–7, 129, 197, 223
Legge, William, earl of Dartmouth, 163
Leominster, 82–3
Lloyd, Samuel, 144, 163
London, 81, 124, 152, 162–3, 170, 181, 215
London, City Road, 175, 186, 188–92, 194, 205–6, 216–17, 227–8
London, Fetter Lane, 32, 45, 47–9, 77
London, Foundry, 33, 50, 96, 163, 184, 186
London, Spitalfields, 69, 165–6, 169
London, West Street, 124, 163, 217

Macclesfield, 228
Madeley, 228
Manchester, 130, 156, 222, 229
Mansfield, earl of, and Lord Chief Justice Mansfield; *see* Murray, William
Margate, 146
Marriott, Thomas, 153
Marriott, William, 163, 184
Mary II, 9–10
Mather, Alexander, 187–8, 208
Methodism (Calvinistic), 44–5, 54–8, 144–5, 167–8; *see also* Methodism (Wesleyan); Whitefield, George
Methodism (Wesleyan); birth of, 31–5; Church Methodism, 121, 144, 163–4, 170, 184–8, 192, 195, 201–4, 206–9, 212, 219–25, 227–33, 238–9; Conference, 36, 112–13, 120–2, 125–8, 130–1, 165–6, 178–80, 195–8, 215–16, 220–4; Deed of Declaration, 180, 193–6, 199, 206; denominational scholarship, 160, 166, 191, 205–6, 214, 219, 225–7, 231–3, 236, 240–1; female ministry, 82–3, 223, 228; Finance, 75, 95–6, 123, 138–42, 144, 149, 184–5, 188, 192; opposition to, 35, 44–5, 59–61, 79–81, 85–7, 114, 193–4; ordinations, 70, 125–6, 180, 196–202, 205–12, 215, 222–3, 230, 237–8; organisation and worship, 36–8, 44, 48, 66–85, 111, 175–6; preachers, 65, 76–83, 111–19, 122–33, 147–51, 155–7, 163–71, 177–9, 183–4, 187–92, 196–201, 205–6, 218–24; Sacraments, 67–70, 124–8, 164–9, 171–2, 175–7, 192, 210–11, 220–4, 229; separation from the Church of England, 70, 110, 120–33, 154–8, 163–82, 194–202, 206–12, 219–25, 237–40; *see also* Methodism (Calvinistic); Methodist New Connexion; Primitive Methodist Wesleyan Connexion; Wesleyan Methodist Church
Mitchell, Thomas, 164, 172
Moore, Henry, 206
Moore, William, 209
Moravians, 19, 36, 44–50, 58–9, 72, 74, 241
Morgan, William, 27, 30
Mortimer, Harvey Walklate, 227, 229
Murlin, John, 164–5, 169
Murray, Grace, 94, 98–103, 109; *see also* Bennet, Grace
Murray, William, earl of Mansfield and Lord Chief Justice, 196, 206

Nelson, John, 58, 127, 178
Newcastle, 100–1, 225
Newcastle, Orphan House, 98, 222
Newton, John, 75, 155
Newton, Samuel, 58
Nitschmann, David, 46
Nonconformity, 10–13, 58, 64, 73–5, 167, 171–2, 186, 207, 221; *see also* Puritanism and Quakers
North America, 43, 57, 164, 181; *see also* Georgia; United States
Norwich, 58, 114–15, 164–70, 177–9, 235
Norwich, Tabernacle, 167–8
Nottingham, 185

Olivers, Thomas, 187–8
Oxford Methodists, *see* holy club
Oxford University, 3, 24–30, 86, 136; *see also* holy club

Pawson, John, 153–4, 189–90, 194, 197, 200, 204–6, 215, 217–21, 237–8
Perrin, Sarah, 82–3, 117, 123, 155
Perronet, Charles, 116, 124, 127–8
Perronet, Edward, 90, 116, 127, 138
Perronet, Vincent, 92–3, 99, 104, 118, 122, 135
Pine, William, 202–4, 206, 209
Plymouth, 209–10
Plymouth Dock, 209–11
politics, *see* Church and State
preachers, *see* Methodism (Wesleyan)
Primitive Methodist Wesleyan Connexion, 230
Puritanism, 10–12, 16–18, 71–3, 79, 85; *see also* Church of England; Nonconformity
Pusey, Edward, 231–2

Index

Quakers, 83, 172

Ramsay, Mary, 51–2
Rankin, Thomas, 189
Reading, 124
religious societies, 18–19, 33, 36, 46–8, 61–2, 71–2, 85
Richardson, John, 189, 194
Rotherham, 129
Rowland, Daniel, 43
Ryle, John, 228

Sacraments, 9, 14, 16–19, 25, 50, 67–71, 121, 124–8, 130, 164–9, 171–2, 174–8, 192, 196, 210–11, 215, 229, 232
schools, *see* Charterhouse; Westminster
Scotland, 198, 208, 214
Sellon, Walter, 125–6, 201
Seward, William, 54–5
Shaw, John, 48
Shent, William, 104, 127
Skelton, Charles, 116, 122
South Petherton, 193–4
Stebbing, Henry, 80
Steele, Anne, 73
Stonehouse, George, 50
Sutcliffe, Joseph, 189, 191, 200–1

Tandey, William, 228
Tennant, Thomas, 69
Thomason, Thomas Truebody, 228
Tillotson, John, 16–17, 84
Tooth, Mary, 227–8
Toplady, Augustus, 75
Trathen, David, 118
Treswell, 176
Tucker, Joseph, 130, 156

United States, 180–1, 196–7, 199, 201, 207, 211–12, 214; *see also* Georgia; North America
universities, *see* Oxford

Valton, John, 217, 234
Vasey, Thomas, 197
Vazeille, Mary, 40, 98, 101, 108–9, 134–8
Vigor, Elizabeth, 92–3

Wake, William, 84–5
Walker, Samuel, 128, 163
Walsh, Thomas, 124, 128
Watson, James, 118, 200
Watts, Isaac, 73–4
Wednesbury, 59–60
Wells, Edmund, 117
Wesley, Bartholomew, 10–11
Wesley, Charles (1707–88); biographers, vi–x, 64, 88, 92–3, 147–8, 154, 161, 214, 219–20, 225–7, 234, 236; Church of England, 14, 20, 29, 64–87; conversion, 31, 47, 65, 103; courtship and marriage, 89–98, 102–3, 109, 132; death, 94, 160, 208, 213–19; family life, 141–6, 153, 159–62, 181; female ministry, 82–3; finance, 3, 24, 91–3, 95–6, 136–42, 149; Georgia, 25, 29–31, 46–7; health, 91, 123–4, 146, 159–60; High Church influence over, 1, 9, 13–15, 18, 20, 23, 26, 65–70, 82, 116; holy club, 25–7, 43, 65, 67; hymns, vi, 21, 74–5, 88, 96, 143, 159, 213, 215; itinerant ministry, 32–5, 37, 66, 86, 89, 96, 113–14, 117, 119, 129–31, 145–6, 152, 156, 158–63, 173, 180, 213, 218; Moravian influence over, 46–50; obituary, 216, 218, 236; ordinations, 125, 180, 196–7, 201–2, 205–9, 212, 215, 238; Oxford University, 24–31, 66, 85–6, 160; personality, 1, 3, 15, 23–4, 30–1, 35, 38, 44, 49, 55–7, 62–3, 89–90, 100–9, 119, 132–4, 138, 143, 146–7, 152–3, 160–1, 178–9, 212, 236; preaching ministry of, 31–5, 50, 52, 54–5, 69, 76–9, 81–3, 86, 121, 127, 129, 150, 160, 215, 234; relationship with George Whitefield, 50–7, 107–8, 144–5; relationship with John Wesley, 15, 21–2, 27–42, 64, 88–9, 91–110, 117–18, 122–41, 144–7, 150–1, 160–1, 165–6, 207–9, 214–17, 234–8; relationship with other Methodists, 33–4, 64, 106–7, 111–19, 122–9, 143–4, 147–54, 163,

Wesley, Charles (*cont.*)
170, 188–91, 194–5, 206–8, 217–19, 234–5; separation from the Church of England, 64, 70, 88, 95, 120–33, 165–6, 169–70, 174–5, 178–80, 182, 187–8, 192, 196–7, 201–2, 206–9, 211–12, 215, 237–40; upbringing, 2, 5–8, 13, 19–20, 22–3, 30, 40; *see also* Church of England; Methodism (Wesleyan)

Wesley, Charles (1794–1859), 229

Wesley, Emily, 4–5

Wesley, John (1636–70), 10–11

Wesley, John (1703–91); conversion, 31, 47, 103; courtship and marriage, 93–4, 97–103, 108–9, 132, 134–6; death, 204, 220; finance, 3, 94–6, 136–42; Georgia, 25, 29–31, 46–7, 74; High Church influence over, 13, 15, 18, 20, 26, 66–71, 116; holy club, 25–7, 121; hymns, 74, 121; Moravian influence over, 46–50, 72, 74; ordinations, 125, 180, 196–201, 205–9, 211, 213, 222, 237–8; Oxford University, 24–31, 66, 85–6, 136, 160; personality, 3, 15, 30–1, 38–42, 44, 56–8, 62–3, 98, 102–4, 120, 141–3, 146–7, 153–4, 160, 166, 187–8, 203–4, 211–12, 216–17, 235–6; relationship with Charles Wesley 15, 21–2, 27–42, 64, 88–9, 91–110, 117–18, 122–41, 144–7, 150–1, 160–1, 165–6, 207–9, 214–17, 234–8; relationship with George Whitefield, 50–4, 56–7; relationship with other Methodists, 112–19, 151, 153–4, 168, 201–4; relationship with the social elite, 143–4, 184–5, 188, 202–4; separation from the Church of England, 70, 95, 120–1, 124–33, 158, 165–7, 174–5, 179–82, 188, 196–9, 209, 211–12, 215, 220, 239; upbringing, 5–8, 13, 22–3, 40; *see also* Church of England; Methodism (Wesleyan)

Wesley, Mary, *see* Vazeille, Mary

Wesley, Martha, *see* Hall, Martha

Wesley, Martha Maria, 138

Wesley, Samuel (1662–1735), 2–5, 8–16, 19, 22–3, 30, 66–7, 74, 81, 84, 204

Wesley, Samuel (1690–1739), 9, 20, 22–3, 27–9, 79, 81, 120–1, 147

Wesley, Sarah (1726–1822), 21, 136–41, 143–7, 153, 159; *see also* Gwynne, Sarah

Wesley, Sarah (1759–1826), 160

Wesley, Susanna, 2, 5–15, 22, 29–30, 32, 67, 78, 85, 120; *see also* Annesley, Susanna

Wesleyan Methodist Church, 164, 176, 192, 220–33

West Indies, 164, 208

Westminster school, 8, 22–3, 28, 30

Wheatley, James, 114–15, 117–18, 167

Whitefield, George, 26, 32, 34, 37, 43, 45, 50–8, 61, 86, 98, 101, 107–8, 144, 151, 157, 173, 241; *see also* Methodism (Calvinistic)

William III, 9–10

Zinzendorf, Nicholas Ludwig von, 45–6